www.worldbank.org/safefoodimperative

DID YOU KNOW?

UNSAFE FOOD REDUCES HUMAN CAPITAL

Foodborne illnesses cost low- and middle-income economies about US$110 billion in lost productivity and medical costs in 2016.

FOOD CAN BE MADE SAFER ALL ALONG THE FOOD CHAIN

Simple investments and changes in the way food is handled from farm to fork can avoid millions of dollars in losses and save millions of people from hardship.

UNSAFE FOOD THREATENS YOUNG CHILDREN THE MOST

Children under age 5 are only 9% of the world's population, but they suffer almost 40% of foodborne diseases and 30% of deaths related to unsafe food.

Learn more about the impact of foodborne illnesses and solutions for safer food in **The Safe Food Imperative: Accelerating Progress in Low- and Middle-Income Countries, World Bank, 2019.**

www.worldbank.org/safefoodimperative

SMALL CHANGES CAN MAKE A BIG DIFFERENCE IN THE SAFETY OF OUR FOOD

CARROTS VS. **STICKS**

Authorities should promote compliance with food safety rules rather than focusing only on inspection and sanctions.

TIN ROOF VS. **LEAKY TARP**

Low-cost infrastructure upgrades can reduce food's exposure to environmental hazards and improve conditions for vendors.

CARCASS IN OPEN AIR VS. **MEAT IN AN ICEBOX**

Simple equipment can help keep meat at a safe temperature during transport.

WORLD BANK GROUP

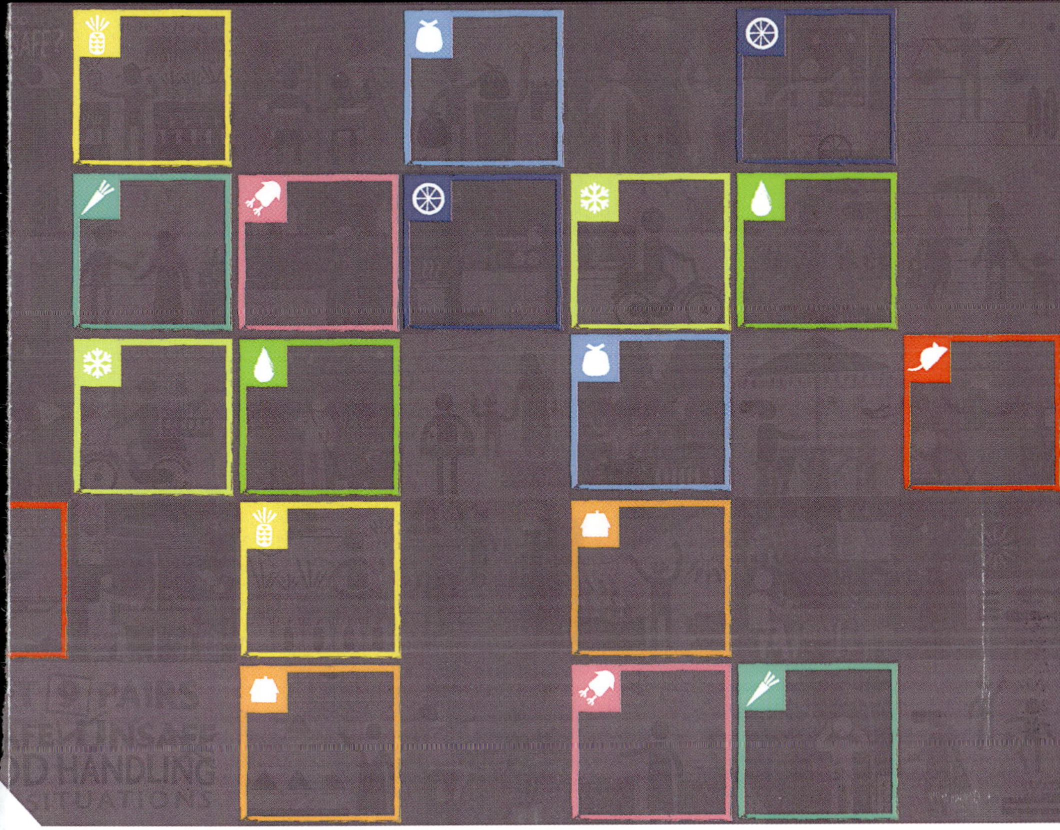

PRODUCE SOLD IN STALL VS. **ON THE GROUND**

Food should be kept at least 15 cm off the ground. Avoiding direct sunlight also prevents loss of food quality and nutrition.

CLEAN WATER VS. **STANDING POOLS**

Keeping market areas clean and mopped reduces environmental contamination as well as disease vectors and pests.

MODERN FOOD CART VS. **IMPROVISED FOOD STALL**

Modernizing food carts creates a cleaner and safer environment for street food.

CHICKEN AND PRODUCE VS. **CHICKEN ALONE**

Meat sales should be done separately from fresh produce sales to avoid cross contamination.

TRASH CANS VS. **OPEN BURNING OF WASTE**

Proper disposal of waste avoids attracting bacteria-spreading vermin and flies.

CLEAN VS. **UNCLEAN FOOD RESTAURANT**

Adopting and enforcing hygiene standards in restaurants has a direct impact on the safety of food.

SPOT 9 PAIRS OF SAFE UNSAFE FOOD HANDLING SITUATIONS

WORLD BANK GROUP

THE SAFE FOOD IMPERATIVE

AGRICULTURE AND FOOD SERIES

A strong food and agriculture system is fundamental to economic growth, poverty reduction, environmental sustainability, and human health. The Agriculture and Food Series is intended to prompt public discussion and inform policies that will deliver higher incomes, reduce hunger, improve sustainability, and generate better health and nutrition from the food we grow and eat. It expands on the former Agriculture and Rural Development series by considering issues from farm to fork, in both rural and urban settings. Titles in this series undergo internal and external review under the management of the World Bank's Agriculture and Food Global Practice.

Titles in this series

The Safe Food Imperative: Accelerating Progress in Low- and Middle-Income Countries (2019)

The Land Governance Assessment Framework: Identifying and Monitoring Good Practice in the Land Sector (2011)

Rising Global Interest in Farmland: Can It Yield Sustainable and Equitable Benefits? (2011)

Gender and Governance in Rural Services: Insights from India, Ghana, and Ethiopia (2010)

Bioenergy Development: Issues and Impacts for Poverty and Natural Resource Management (2009)

Building Competitiveness in Africa's Agriculture: A Guide to Value Chain Concepts and Applications (2009)

Agribusiness and Innovation Systems in Africa (2009)

Agricultural Land Redistribution: Toward Greater Consensus (2009)

Organization and Performance of Cotton Sectors in Africa: Learning from Reform Experience (2009)

The Sunken Billions: The Economic Justification for Fisheries Reform (2009)

Gender in Agriculture Sourcebook (2008)

Sustainable Land Management Sourcebook (2008)

Forests Sourcebook: Practical Guidance for Sustaining Forests in Development Cooperation (2008)

Changing the Face of the Waters: The Promise and Challenge of Sustainable Aquaculture (2007)

Reforming Agricultural Trade for Developing Countries, Volume 2: Quantifying the Impact of Multilateral Trade Reform (2006)

Reforming Agricultural Trade for Developing Countries, Volume 1: Key Issues for a Pro-Development Outcome of the Doha Round (2006)

Enhancing Agricultural Innovation: How to Go Beyond the Strengthening of Research Systems (2006)

Sustainable Land Management: Challenges, Opportunities, and Trade-Offs (2006)

Shaping the Future of Water for Agriculture: A Sourcebook for Investment in Agricultural Water Management (2005)

Agriculture Investment Sourcebook (2005)

Sustaining Forests: A Development Strategy (2004)

THE SAFE FOOD IMPERATIVE

ACCELERATING PROGRESS IN LOW- AND MIDDLE-INCOME COUNTRIES

Steven Jaffee, Spencer Henson, Laurian Unnevehr, Delia Grace, and Emilie Cassou

WORLD BANK GROUP

1 2 3 4 21 20 19 18

ISBN (paper): 978-1-4648-1345-0
ISBN (electronic): 978-1-4648-1346-7
DOI: 10.1596/978-1-4648-1345-0

Cover Illustration: ©JESS3. Used with the permission of JESS3. Further permission required for reuse.

Cover design: Critical Stages, LLC

Library of Congress Cataloging-in-Publication Data has been requested

CONTENTS

Boxes

Figures

Tables

FOREWORD

Every day around the globe, families and friends eat to provide themselves with essential energy and nutrients to lead healthy and productive lives, as well as for pleasure and comfort. Yet every day, on average, unsafe food makes close to two million people sick, keeping them from school and work, and sometimes dramatically degrading or curtailing their lives. Worst of all, foodborne illness disproportionately strikes populations that can least afford to be sick. Low- and middle-income countries in South Asia, Southeast Asia, and Sub-Saharan Africa account for 41 percent of the global population but are afflicted with 53 percent of all foodborne illness, and 75 percent of related deaths.

Whether the consequences of unsafe food are measured in suffering, disability, and loss of life, or foregone income and wages, these personal and social costs are unnecessarily high. According to estimates from the World Health Organization, foodborne disease made some 600 million people sick and caused 420,000 premature deaths in 2010. Translated into economic terms using 2016 income data, illness, disability, and premature deaths induced by unsafe food lead to productivity losses of about US$95 billion a year in low- and middle-income countries. Unsafe food undermines food and nutritional security, human development, the broader food economy, and international trade.

The Safe Food Imperative argues that much of the burden of unsafe food can be avoided through practical and often low-cost behavior and infrastructure changes at different points along food value chains, including in traditional food production and distribution channels. In many countries, concerted action on domestic food safety has been sporadic and reactive, coming in the wake of major outbreaks of foodborne disease or food adulteration scandals. Yet what is needed are sustained investments in prevention, including ones that build countries' core competencies to manage food safety risks, and motivate and empower many different actors, from farm to fork, to act responsibly and with consumer health in mind.

Drawing on experiences across the globe, the report highlights examples of effective food safety management. It calls for a higher prioritization of food safety, along with more investment in the development of coherent national food safety management systems in low- and middle-income countries. Governments do not and cannot have the sole responsibility for ensuring safe food—it is a shared responsibility. Public agencies, farmers, food businesses, and consumers all have constructive roles to play.

Apart from more and smarter public investment in food safety, there is also a critical need for new regulatory approaches that place more emphasis on facilitating compliance and engaging consumers. Countries as diverse as Chile, India, Kenya, Ukraine, Uruguay, and Vietnam have demonstrated that better health and commercial outcomes are possible with the joint involvement of public agencies, businesses, and consumers in food safety.

Individuals across income levels, age groups, and regions all need safe food, but food safety is also a national necessity. Countries need safe food to develop their human capital—to fuel a healthy, educated, and resilient workforce and to feed a vibrant economy. More and better investments in food safety are needed for countries to unleash their full potential to grow their economy inclusively and sustainably.

Annette Dixon
Vice President, Human Development, World Bank

Laura Tuck
Vice President, Sustainable Development, World Bank

ACKNOWLEDGMENTS

The report team was led by Steven Jaffee of the World Bank and involved a core team of Spencer Henson (University of Guelph), Delia Grace (International Livestock Research Institute), Laurian Unnevehr (University of Illinois at Urbana-Champaign), and consultants Emilie Cassou, Mateo Ambrosio, and Anissa Collishaw. Important contributions were provided by Arie Havelaar (University of Florida), Clare Narrod (Joint Institute for Food Safety and Applied Nutrition, University of Maryland), and Vivian Hoffman (International Food Policy Research Institute); independent consultants Donald Macrae, Shashi Sareen, and Jairo Romero; and World Bank Group staff Franck Cesar Jean Berthe, Sarah Ockman, and Kateryna Onul.

The report was made possible by generous funding from the U.S. Food and Drug Administration. The team thanks the administration, particularly Mary Lou Valdez and Kristin Wedding, for their support and technical guidance. The report benefited enormously from collaboration with several other institutions; this included sharing restricted data and reports, without which important analysis in this report would not have been possible. Special recognition is given to the support provided by the World Health Organization and members of its Foodborne Disease Burden Epidemiology Reference Group, and the World Organisation for Animal Health. Special thanks go to Amy Cawthorne, Brecht Devleesschauwer, Minh Li, and Francois Caya. The team also thanks the secretariat team at GLOBALG.A.P., Robert Ahern at the Inter-American Institute for Cooperation on Agriculture, the CGIAR Research Program on Agriculture for Nutrition and Health, and Melvin Spreij and Marlynne Hopper of the Standards and Trade Development Facility for generously sharing information and perspectives.

The team thanks Nathan Belete and the Global Food Safety Partnership through Lystra Antoine for their guidance, and it recognizes the contributions made by peer reviewers Sudhir Shetty, Selma Rasavac, John McDermott, Melvin Spreij, Paul Mayers, Chris Delgado, Ziauddin Hyder, and Julie Caswell to improve the quality of this report and its outputs.

ABOUT THE LEAD AUTHORS

Steven Jaffee is a lead agricultural economist with the World Bank's Agriculture Global Practice. His research, policy, and investment project work over 26 years at the World Bank has spanned many themes, including food security, food safety, agricultural risk management, agricultural policy, value chain development, and trade and standards compliance. He has field experience in Africa and Southeast Asia. He has co-led major regional research projects on rice and food security, agricultural pollution, agri-food system transformation, and agri-environmental measures in export industries. He has a BA from the University of Pennsylvania and a DPhil in agricultural economics from Oxford University.

Spencer Henson is a professor in the Department of Food, Agricultural, and Resource Economics and director of the Guelph Institute of Development Studies at the University of Guelph, Canada. He is recognized internationally for his research on the economics of food safety, food quality, and nutrition in industrial and low- and middle-income countries. He has authored more than 90 peer-reviewed journal articles and edited three books. His research has involved fieldwork in over 60 countries for international organizations, public and private sector institutions, and civil society organizations.

Laurian Unnevehr is a professor emerita of agricultural and consumer economics at the University of Illinois at Urbana-Champaign. She has worked at the U.S. Department of Agriculture's Economic Research Service, the International Food Policy Research Institute, and the International Rice Research Institute.

She has published extensively on the economics of food safety and other food policy issues, including the economics of hazard analysis and critical control points, food safety in international trade, new technology in food marketing, and the role of food demand in shaping food value chains. The Agricultural & Applied Economics Association made her a fellow in 2009 in recognition of her contribution to the economics of food policy and demand. She has a PhD from the Food Research Institute, Stanford University, and a BA in economics from the University of California at Davis.

Delia Grace is an epidemiologist and veterinarian with more than 20 years of experience in developing countries. She leads research on zoonoses and food-borne disease at the Nairobi-based International Livestock Research Institute. Her research includes food safety, emerging diseases, gender studies, and animal welfare. Her career has spanned the private sector, field-level community development, aid management, and research. She has worked in Asia and Africa, and authored or coauthored more than 100 peer-reviewed publications, as well as training courses, films, articles, and blogs. She has worked at several universities, including University College Dublin, Edinburgh University, the Free University of Berlin, and Cornell University.

Emilie Cassou is a sustainable food systems specialist working with both the Agriculture and the Environment and Natural Resources Global Practices at the World Bank. She has coauthored, managed, and contributed to various studies, multistakeholder processes, and projects on agri-environmental and climate policy, food system performance, and behavioral change in the context of dietary transition. She has degrees from Brown University, Sciences Po, the Friedman School of Nutrition Science and Policy at Tufts University, and Columbia University's School of International and Public Affairs.

ABOUT THE CONTRIBUTORS

Mateo Ambrosio is a development specialist with over 20 years of experience in the analysis, design, and implementation of public policies and projects in agriculture and rural development. He has worked in Latin America, Africa, and Asia for multilateral and bilateral development organizations. He has a BA in economics and business management from universities in Spain and Germany and a European PhD in rural development and geography from the University of Cordoba and the University of Antwerp's Institute of Development Policy.

Franck Cesar Jean Berthe is a senior livestock specialist at the World Bank's Agriculture Global Practice. A One Health practitioner, he works across the agriculture, environment, and public health sectors on health issues at the human-animal-environment interfaces. He is vice president of the World Organisation for Animal Health's Biological Standards Commission. Before joining the World Bank, he headed the Animal and Plant Health Unit at the European Food Safety Authority. He has a DVM, a PhD in molecular taxonomy and epidemiology, and a Pasteur Institute diploma in bacteriology.

Anissa Collishaw is an applied economist whose main interest is the nexus of food value chains, agriculture, nutrition, and strategies to reduce undernutrition. She has an MS in food, agriculture, and resource economics from the University of Guelph. Her research primarily focuses on food safety and willingness-to-pay for nutritious food products in Canadian and international contexts.

Arie Hendrik Havelaar is a preeminent professor in the Animal Sciences Department of the Institute for Sustainable Food Systems and the Emerging Pathogens Institute at the University of Florida. His research focuses on the epidemiology, risk assessment, and prevention of foodborne and zoonotic diseases. He is chair of the Foodborne Disease Burden Epidemiology Reference Group and leads the Animal Disease Management and Food Safety Area at the USAID-funded Feed the Future Innovation Lab for Livestock Systems. He is a member of the external advisory boards of the College of Public Health and Health Professions at the University of Florida and the New Zealand Food Safety Research Consortium.

Vivian Hoffmann is a research fellow at the International Food Policy Research Institute. Her research focuses on how markets and institutions in developing countries affect public health outcomes. She has conducted several studies investigating the role of markets in aflatoxin control in settings where regulatory enforcement capacity is limited. She led the first randomized controlled trial testing the impact of aflatoxin on child growth. Her other areas of work have included the targeting of subsidies for preventive health technologies. Before joining the institute in 2013, she was an assistant professor at the University of Maryland and received a PhD in agricultural economics from Cornell University. She is associate editor of the *American Journal of Agricultural Economics*.

Donald Macrae, a former civil servant in the United Kingdom reaching director-general level, has built an international practice in advising on how to make regulatory systems work. Since 2007, he has worked in some 30 countries for private sector and international organizations, including the United Nations, World Bank Group, USAID, the Food and Agriculture Organization (FAO) of the United Nations, the Organisation for Economic Co-operation and Development, and the U.K. Department for International Development. His focus is on the implementation of regulatory systems, including those for food safety.

Clare Narrod is director of the Risk Analysis Program at the Joint Institute for Food Safety and Applied Nutrition and leads the institute's monitoring and evaluation for capacity building. Before joining the institute, she worked at the International Food Policy Research Institute, the U.S. Department of Agriculture, and the FAO. From 1998 to 2000, she was an American Association for the Advancement of Science Risk Analysis fellow at the Department of Agriculture. She has a PhD in energy management and environmental policy, and an MA in international development and appropriate technology from the University of Pennsylvania. She has field and teaching experience in Africa, Asia, and Latin America.

Jairo Romero is a food engineer with 29 years of experience in food safety management and international trade. His focus is on strengthening national food control systems in accordance with international best practices and guidelines. He is a Food Safety Preventive Controls Alliance lead instructor on preventive controls for human foods. He is the author of many publications and has been a presenter at over 100 international workshops and meetings. He has worked throughout the Americas, Europe, and Asia. He is a fellow of the International Academy of Food Science and Technology, and is a past president of the Colombian Association of Food Science and Technology and the Latin America and the Caribbean Association of Food Science and Technology.

Shashi Sareen has over 30 years of experience in food safety, quality, and nutrition in the public and private sectors and with international organizations. From 2010 to 2016, she worked as a senior food safety and nutrition officer in the FAO's Asia Pacific Regional Office, providing support to countries on food safety and quality policies and legislation, food control coordination mechanisms, and inspection and certification systems. Before that, she worked for the Government of India in various capacities, including director and chief executive, at the Export Inspection Council of India, the Bureau of Indian Standards, and the Agricultural Produce Export Development Authority. She has also worked in the retail private sector. She has MAs in food and nutrition, and human resource and organizational development.

EXECUTIVE SUMMARY

THE FOOD SAFETY CONTEXT

Food safety is linked in direct and indirect ways to achieving many of the Sustainable Development Goals, especially those on ending hunger and poverty, and promoting good health and well-being. Food and nutritional security are realized only when the essential elements of a healthy diet are safe to eat, and when consumers recognize this. The safety of food is vital for the growth and transformation of agriculture, which are needed to feed a growing and more prosperous world population, for the modernization of national food systems, and for a country's efficient integration into regional and international markets.

The safety of food is the result of the actions or inactions of many stakeholders operating under diverse environmental, infrastructure, and socio-political conditions. These stakeholders include farmers, food handlers and distributors, food manufacturers, food service operators, consumers, regulators, scientists, educators, and the media. Their behavior can be shaped by their awareness of food safety hazards; their technical, financial, and other capabilities to apply effective mitigating practices; and prevailing rules, incentives, and other motivators.

Food safety outcomes can be strongly influenced by policies, investments, and other interventions. These alter the awareness, capabilities, and practices of stakeholders, from farm to fork. Well-functioning markets can provide incentives for farmers and food business operators to supply products that match the safety characteristics consumers demand. Even so, there are many circumstances stemming from problems of information and costs where pure market signals fail and additional measures are needed. Problems of information include the actual attributes of food products, and the location and origins of food safety hazards.

For many developing countries, food safety has, until recently, received very little policy attention and only modest investment in capabilities to manage risks. Two main groups of factors contributed to this. The first group includes the weak empirical base for the country-level incidence of foodborne hazards and disease, the economic costs of unsafe food, and the efficacy of food safety interventions. The second group includes institutional factors: the fragmentation of food value chains and public institutional mandates, and the absence of effective consumer representation in most developing countries.

Because of scarce data and thematic leadership, food safety tends to appear on national radar screens only during crises. A typical crisis would be a major outbreak of foodborne disease (FBD) causing death, scandals involving deliberate food adulteration, trade bans, or widespread consignment rejections because of noncompliance with standards. In developing countries, these episodes have tended to spur reactive and defensive damage control, resulting in a flurry of regulatory actions or investments. When these are taken in crisis management mode, they often differ in target, content, approach, and lasting efficacy from when food safety measures are developed and adopted in a more deliberative, evidence-based, forward-looking, and consultative manner.

Years of inadequate policy attention and underinvestment have stunted the development of coherent national food safety management systems in many low- and middle-income countries (LMICs). Most of these countries have weak food safety systems in terms of scientific evidence, necessary infrastructure, trained human resources, food safety culture, and enforceable regulations. Governance of national food safety systems in LMICs—whereby stakeholder roles and accountabilities are well defined and understood—is also weak. While many LMICs have islands of strong food safety management capacity, these support only segments of the agri-food system and consumers (often the wealthiest). An especially weak area is the infrastructure and services needed to mitigate the food safety risks faced by the poor. Their FBD burden is often invisible and voiceless.

The dominant discourse on food safety in LMICs has focused on trade, but this needs to change. Complying with food safety regulations and the standards of international trade partners has been a prime objective of investments in food safety by LMIC governments and bilateral and multilateral donors. Trade-related compliance challenges have been highly visible to policy makers, and stakeholders have taken effective action. That said, most LMICs would benefit from widening or redirecting their food safety focus. Changing demographics and dietary patterns are creating new commercial opportunities in domestic food markets, but these are also increasing the exposure of LMIC populations to food safety hazards. Although statistically invisible, the domestic economic costs of unsafe food are significant and growing in many LMICs.

In recent years, various major international initiatives have given increased attention and resources to mitigate risks from unsafe food in LMICs. Examples include the work of the World Health Organization's Foodborne Disease Burden Epidemiology Reference Group (FERG), CGIAR's food safety research under its Agriculture for Nutrition and Health program, the Global Food Safety Partnership's country and regional initiatives, the Partnership for Aflatoxin Control in Africa, the World Bank Group's expanded investment lending and advisory services, and the African Union's initiative on food safety; the continued technical support provided to countries by the Food and Agriculture Organization, World Health Organization, and the Standards and Trade Development Facility; support by the U.K.'s Department for International Development, the U.S. Agency for International Development, and the Bill & Melinda Gates Foundation for research on FBDs and their control in developing countries; and various regional initiatives.

THE PUBLIC HEALTH BURDEN AND ECONOMIC COSTS OF UNSAFE FOOD

Research is shedding new light on the global burden of FBD. Until recently, data on the incidence of FBD and its associated costs were limited to high-income countries and regions, including the United States, Canada, and parts of Europe. To address this gap, FERG has been working on global estimates of the incidence of FBD since 2006. This work covers 31 of the most important foodborne hazards in 14 regions. The estimates are expressed in terms of disability-adjusted life years (DALYs) associated with ill-health and premature death.

For 2010, the base year, the global burden of FBD is estimated at 600 million illnesses and 420,000 premature deaths. This aggregates to the equivalent of 33 million DALYs (Havelaar et al. 2015). For comparison, the estimated 2015 global burden of tuberculosis was 40 million DALYs, and 66 million for malaria. These FBD estimates are considered to be highly conservative. For example, the incidence of illness associated with chemical hazards was substantially underestimated in FERG's earlier work because of data limitations, as will be confirmed by updated estimates to be published in late 2018.

The global burden of FBD is unequally distributed. Asia and Sub-Saharan Africa have the highest incidence of FBD, as well as the highest rate of deaths due to FBDs and the greatest loss of DALYs. LMICs in South Asia, Southeast Asia, and Sub-Saharan Africa, which make up 41 percent of the global population, are estimated to account for 53 percent of all foodborne illnesses, 75 percent of FBD-related deaths, and 72 percent of FBD-related DALYs. A disproportionate share of the burden falls on children under the age of five, who account for 9 percent of the global population but 38 percent of all cases of illness and 40 percent of the DALYs. An estimated 30 percent of premature deaths due to FBD are in children under the age of five. Geographically, children are most likely to die from FBD in Sub-Saharan Africa, followed by South Asia. Epidemiological studies show that the people most vulnerable to foodborne disease are the young, old, malnourished, poor, pregnant, and those who are immuno-compromised.

The economic costs of unsafe food take multiple forms and have both short- and long-term dimensions. Valuing these costs is challenging because of data and methodological limitations. Examples of these costs include the public health costs and loss of productivity associated with FBD, disruptions to food markets when outbreaks of illness occur as consumers avoid implicated foods or shift to alternatives that are perceived to be safer, impediments to agri-food exports due to real or expected food safety problems, and the costs of complying with food safety regulations and standards in foreign markets. More indirect and harder-to-measure costs include the costs of prevention and those associated with wary consumers shifting from high-nutrient fresh produce to processed foods. For most LMICs, reliable estimates of these costs and how they are distributed within society are lacking.

This report estimates the cost of FBD on the basis of "productivity losses," as measured by gross national income per capita and associated with disability or premature death captured in DALYs. The report uses FERG's DALYs by country or subregion for 2010 and the gross national income per capita estimates for 2016 from the World Bank's World Development Indicators Database. The total productivity loss associated with FBD in LMICs is estimated at US$95.2 billion a year. Of this, upper-middle-income countries account for US$50.8 billion, or 53 percent of the total. Lower-middle-income countries account for US$40.6 billion (43 percent), and low-income countries for US$3.8 billion (4 percent). By region, LMICs in Asia account for US$63.1 billion, and those in Sub-Saharan Africa for US$16.7 billion. The cost of treating foodborne illnesses should be added to this. These are estimated at US$15 billion a year in LMICs. Even without factoring in the hard-to-measure costs of domestic food market disruptions and consumer product avoidance, the domestic costs of unsafe food would aggregate to at least US$110 billion among LMICs.

Food safety performance and compliance costs affect the agri-food trade in LMICs, but the size of these costs is much smaller than the impacts on domestic public health and market development. Effectively competing in the international agri-food trade may entail considerable compliance costs for the public and private sectors, particularly to meet food safety requirements in high-income markets. Factors affecting the level of these costs include firm and industry size, the gap between preexisting food safety management capacity and the capacity required for compliance, and levels of collective action among exporting firms. The evidence suggests that the fixed costs of meeting stricter food safety requirements in export markets tend to favor established and larger exporters. In 2016, LMIC agri-food exports totaled US$475 billion. This report estimates that the value of LMIC food trade—which is either detained by food safety regulatory authorities, not initiated due to standard compliance concerns, or adversely impacted by very high compliance costs—totals some US$5 billion–US$7 billion per year, equivalent to between one-fifteenth and one-twentieth of the estimated domestic costs of unsafe food.

The burden of unsafe food generally evolves in a systematic manner, in line with processes of economic development; this can be called the food safety life cycle. The economic costs of unsafe food, in both absolute and relative terms, vary across countries according to their level of economic development. This variation is linked to the complex interplay of a wide range of economic, demographic, dietary, and environmental health factors. These affect the incidence and potential exposure of populations to food safety hazards, the strength of incentives for actors in agri-food value chains to prevent or manage these hazards, and the costs of food safety missteps. All LMICs are experiencing changes in diets, food sourcing and preparation patterns, and in the structures and governance arrangements in food value chains. But where they are positioned in this process of food system transformation varies considerably.

The food safety life cycle across countries and over time reflects evolving food safety challenges, and the degree of mismatch with food safety management capacity in the public and private sectors. The level of food safety management capacity reflects the market-based and political incentives for public and private sector actors to make required investments. While low-income countries certainly face a significant burden of food-related illness, diets in these *traditional* food markets tend still to be dominated by starchy staples, and policy attention is focused on the availability and affordability of these foods and on other public health issues (for example, malaria, HIV/AIDS, and waterborne diseases). Food safety concerns generally become more important in *transitioning* lower-middle-income countries that are experiencing rapid demographic and dietary change, giving rise to dynamic and visible food safety hazards, which typically overwhelm latent food safety management capacities. And because of greater access to media, improving wealth and a variety of psychological mechanisms, consumers become ever more concerned about food safety. The gap between need and capacity begins to close as countries advance through and beyond upper-middle-income status, as a result of which the relative economic burden of FBD subsides in the *modernizing* stage of the food safety life cycle. At more advanced levels of economic development—that is, countries at the *postmodern* stage—attention needs to switch to the management of periodic lapses in food safety, where the associated economic costs can still be considerable. This is also needed to respond to emerging hazards and changing consumer perceptions of food safety.

THE STATUS OF FOOD SAFETY MANAGEMENT

No representative and comprehensive benchmarking program exists for food safety management capacities in LMICs. This contrasts with the situation in Organisation for Economic Co-operation and Development countries, where several detailed comparative assessments of food safety performance have been carried out. For many LMICs, detailed assessments have been completed of the status of public food control systems; for example, the World Organisation for

Animal Health's framework for the performance of veterinary services. Yet the findings are generally not conducive to quantification—and thus, comparison—and many of these studies are not in the public domain. Various other studies and databases offer partial indications, while those providing greater breadth tend to reflect actions on paper (the presence of a law or agency, for example) more than institutional performance or functionality in practice. Food safety metrics and targets are generally not covered in development planning and monitoring initiatives.

A review of often non-publicly disclosed assessments points to common shortcomings in the national food safety systems of LMICs. These include:

- The absence of a comprehensive national food safety policy, translating into a lack of prioritization of investments;
- A focus on hazard rather than risk, often leading to the misallocation of resources;
- The presence of many regulations and standards, yet a lack of clarity on the extent to which these are voluntary or mandatory;
- The fragmentation of institutional responsibilities, especially for market surveillance and inspecting food production, processing, and handling facilities
- Fragmented systems for laboratory testing that do not function as a system and fail to reveal comprehensive inferences on the causes of FBD;
- The lack of effective food safety engagement with consumers, whether in relation to education, risk communication, and other matters;
- The failure to empower and incentivize the private sector to deliver food safety; and
- The lack of consistent and transparent border measures to address growing food imports.

Data and information gathered for this report are consistent with this picture of underdeveloped food safety management systems, especially in the public sector. For example, animal source foods account for a high proportion of FBD in many LMICs, yet underlying capacities to manage food safety hazards from animal sources are generally weak. This is especially true for functions that are considered critical public goods. Among the 34 Sub-Saharan African countries for which assessment data are available, only four are deemed to have adequate capacity for identifying and tracing animals and animal products, and only a similar number can adequately inspect abattoirs. Capacities for quarantine and border security are somewhat better, yet these are deemed adequate in only 21 percent of the 34 countries. Among the 35 lower-middle-income countries worldwide assessed by the World Organisation for Animal Health, only 6 percent were found to have adequate capacities for animal product identification and traceability, and 11–17 percent were deemed to have adequate capacities for inspecting abattoirs or meat distribution facilities, had effective regulations for veterinary drugs, or were able to ensure the quality of laboratory testing of animal products. The situation is different among upper-middle-income countries, where 30–45 percent of 29 rated countries had adequate capacities in these areas.

For the private sector, the situation is more varied in low- and lower-middle-income countries and, again, substantially more advanced in countries in later stages of economic development. What can be seen here are lead firms (major food manufacturers and supermarkets) requiring their suppliers to adopt good agricultural or manufacturing practices. However, in domestic markets, these do not affect most of the population because informal distribution channels and traditional community markets continue to play a predominant role, at least in Africa and Asia.

Within the private sector, more stringent primary production standards are being applied over a broader area. For example, the LMIC coverage area for certified GLOBALG.A.P. fruit and vegetable production, most of which is destined for export, increased from 700,000 hectares in 2010 to 1.87 million hectares in 2017, yet most of this expansion occurred in upper-middle-income countries. In 2017, these countries accounted for 80 percent of the total (versus 18 percent for lower-middle-income countries and 2 percent for low-income countries). Upgrades are also being made at the level of food manufacturing. In January 2018, some 118,000 food companies from outside the United States were registered with the U.S. Food and Drug Administration. Of these, 59 percent were from high-income countries. Of the over 48,000 LMIC-registered companies, 72 percent were from upper-middle-income countries, while 2 percent were from low-income ones.

The widest gaps between needed and actual food safety management capacity are in lower-middle-income countries. Especially the larger of these countries are important food safety "hot spots," where the exposure of populations to hazards is increasing, consumer food safety confidence is waning, and neither decentralized food safety regulatory capacity nor the governance arrangements of the formal private sector food industry are able to match the emerging challenges. These countries need comprehensive measures to curb what is likely to be a substantially higher health and economic burden of FBD in the coming years. Setting aside upper-middle-income China, the world's lower-middle-income countries accounted for 70 percent of the estimated human capital productivity loss from FBD of all developing countries in 2016.

The growing attention to domestic food safety has probably had little positive impact on the poor. The consumption of unsafe food by low-income populations stems from a combination of factors, including low access to potable water, the cohabitation of humans and animals, high exposure to environmental contaminants, the suboptimal use of inputs and other practices of semisubsistence farmers, poor rural infrastructure, poor hygienic conditions in urban community markets, and the widespread presence of food safety hazards in street food. A particularly high investment deficit relates to the physical condition of traditional community markets and small shops, where most poor people shop for fresh produce. Some market-based standards initiatives may be having the unintended consequence of securing safe produce for targeted distribution channels, but leaving the more contaminated, test-failing produce for the markets of lower-income consumers.

For many countries, capacities to manage food safety risks for exports appear to be considerably stronger than capacities to protect domestic consumers. Trade-related compliance with food safety regulations and standards has undoubtedly been the catalyst for the significant upgrading of food safety management capacity in many low- and middle-income countries, especially the latter. Thus, efforts to meet some of the toughest regulations and standards in high-income countries have driven many early and sustained upgrades in laws, control systems, and systems of private value chain governance for food safety. Unfortunately, evidence of substantive spillovers between trade-related capacity development and domestic systems is limited. And as noted earlier, many LMICs are not applying risk-based approaches to managing food imports. Inconsistent or burdensome border measures do not ensure safer food, but preventive and science-based measures can.

Compliance costs are not a big burden for leading LMIC exporters. Data on LMIC agri-food exports and on border rejections in high-income countries suggest that, while compliance with food safety regulations and standards does indeed involve costs, these are often little more than a "bump in the road" for the established export sectors and their lead firms in major exporting LMIC countries. Developing country exporters have been meeting the challenges of higher food safety standards in high-income markets for over two decades. Indeed, compliance with food safety regulations and standards might serve to accentuate the established competitive advantage of these countries, industries, and firms, reflecting their preferential access to support services and reliable logistics. In 2016, two-thirds of LMIC exports of food-safety-sensitive high-value foods came from 10 countries, nine of which were also the top exporters at the beginning of this century.

Compliance costs can be a burden for smaller LMICs. It is in these countries, and their less established and smaller sectors and firms, where the costs of compliance with food safety regulations and standards is more challenging. These costs can potentially be a make or break trade issue. Economies of scale in food safety management arise from high initial fixed investments in upgraded facilities and when new procedures and systems for value chain coordination and governance are established. Yet, the challenges of compliance typically accompany and can magnify wider weaknesses in competitiveness. Food safety is rarely the whole or a very large part of the story.

Emerging new trends in global agri-food trade will strongly affect the discourse on food safety and trade, and will have strategic implications for LMICs. High-income countries remain important buyers and sellers of high-value foods, yet their shares in both are declining. High-value food imports by LMICs have been growing at double-digit rates since 2000 and were just below US$150 billion in 2016. For low-income countries, two-thirds of their high-value food exports and imports involve trade with other developing countries.

For lower-middle-income countries, imports from and exports to other developing countries are growing at a fast pace. Trade among developing countries will account for most future growth in high-value food trade because of higher income elasticities and demand for dietary diversity, especially in middle-income countries.

Exporting to other developing countries poses challenges that differ from those in high-income markets. For high-income countries, standards are generally stringent, yet these are typically clear and consistently applied, though there are of course exceptions. In contrast to these markets, cross-border or longer distance South-South trade is often characterized by a lack of transparency in rules and procedures, limited use of science-based evidence in applying technical barriers to trade and sanitary and phytosanitary measures, high border transaction costs, and rapidly changing consumer demands for quality and safety (APEC Business Advisory Council 2016). Exporter country compliance often seems to be as much a political as a technical matter. This brings considerable uncertainties, especially for small and medium enterprises lacking the connections or resources to negotiate or maneuver through the necessary steps to gain and maintain market access. In many LMICs, informal or illegal cross-border trade is very common and is perhaps equivalent to formal legal trade in size, and animals and food products following this route lack any structured sanitary inspection.

THE WAY FORWARD

A significant share of food safety problems and associated costs can be avoidable if a concerted set of preventive measures are put in place. While various indicators support the notion of a food safety life cycle that tracks economic development, the typical rapid upward trajectory of public health costs and trade disruptions is not inevitable. Indeed, a significant share of food safety problems and associated costs is avoidable. Food safety issues and challenges evolve not only with the level of economic development and food system transformation, but also in relation to measures that are taken to ensure that food safety management capacity keeps up with emerging hazards. It is noteworthy that some countries do considerably better than others in terms of the burden of FBD, despite having similar constraints. With a proactive strategy and a proper prioritization of problems and measures, countries can avoid losses from the burden of FBD amounting to hundreds of millions of dollars a year (and these losses can run up to several billion dollars for larger countries). In doing so, countries can minimize disruptions to markets and livelihoods that come from periodic food safety scares and prevent these episodes from dominating consumer perceptions about the underlying quality and safety of local foods (and the integrity of the food governance arrangements in place).

While the safety of food is a "public good," governments do not and cannot have the primary responsibility for safe food. Rather, food safety needs to become a *shared responsibility*. Operationalizing this concept effectively is a significant challenge in many LMICs. Governments need to play effective vision-setting and convening roles; provide reliable information to other stakeholders; and effectively deploy a wide set of policy instruments, both carrots and sticks, to involve, incentivize, and leverage the actions of farmers, food business operators, and consumers. While practitioners once emphasized effective "official food control" systems, the most critical roles for government are now recognized to be facilitative ones that induce investments and behavior changes by actors that share with government the goal of and responsibility for safer food.

This inclusive concept of food safety management may require a paradigm shift in how emerging countries approach food safety regulation. The traditional model centers on enforcement through inspections of food facilities and product testing, and systems of legal and financial penalties for infractions. This strict authoritative model is seemingly appealing to the public, media, and therefore political decision makers, yet it is not altogether an effective model and it can be highly misplaced in contexts in which smallholder farmers, micro and small enterprises, and informal food channels predominate, and both surveillance and inspectorate capacities are limited. A shared management model implies a move from a regulator-regulated relationship toward efforts by governments to better incentivize and facilitate safe production, processing, and distribution of food. The role of regulation then becomes one in which the absolute minimum food safety standard is applied, thereby leaving food business operators with some degree of flexibility in how they attain that standard, and for government to offer information and other resources and support to motivate and assist compliance. Thus, the results of regulation are measured in terms of compliant enterprises and food safety outcomes rather than the number of fines or business closures.

Governments of LMICs not only need to invest more in food safety but also to invest more smartly. This means investing with a clear purpose and tracking the impacts of interventions; investing in the foundational knowledge, human resources, and infrastructure for food safety systems; balancing attention to hardware and software; realizing synergies among investments and in the pursuit of goals (One Health initiatives); ensuring the sustainability of investments and outcomes; and using public investment to leverage private investment.

Not all investments that can reduce the burden of FBD are ones typically regarded as "food safety" investments. Critical investments may be ones that address environmental health issues, such as those that increase access to potable water and improve sanitation or lessen environmental contaminants in soil, water, and air. Measures like these reduce the propensity for cross contamination in food supply chains. Also important are investments in public health systems, including those that improve the quality of and access to medical treatment, which can reduce morbidity and mortality related to FBD. Indeed, many countries with high estimated DALYs for FBD are also the ones where rates of access to potable water, improved sanitation, and local health services are relatively low.

A CALL TO ACTION

This report offers two sets of recommendations to national governments. The first is for more effective policy frameworks to govern food safety; the second is for better implementation. The first set of recommendations emphasizes the adoption of both systemic and inclusive concepts of food safety management, shifting the focus from hazards to risks, addressing risks from farm to fork, changing from a reactive to a proactive orientation on food safety, and adopting a consistent approach to prioritized decision making. To improve implementation, this report offers guidance for reforming food safety regulatory practices, investing more smartly in essential public goods, institutionalizing a structured approach to food safety risk management, and leveraging consumer concerns over food safety.

This report makes tailored recommendations for different stakeholders, and general priorities are highlighted for countries at different stages of the food safety life cycle. The recommendations for different stakeholders are summarized in box ES.1 and are discussed more fully in the report. Table ES.1 highlights priorities for countries at different stages of the food safety life cycle. These emphasize core principles and reflect the study team's perspective on what is most important and feasible for countries at different levels of economic development and food system modernization. More specific priorities and action plans will need to be determined and created by stakeholders at country or regional levels.

BOX ES.1 Recommendations for Stakeholders in the Food Safety Life Cycle

For ministries of finance or other coordinating economic ministries in low- and middle-income countries (LMICs):

- Calibrate public expenditures for food safety to the economic costs of unsafe food and the benefits of investing in its prevention and management.
- Emphasize forward-looking preventive measures to minimize future costs (avoidable losses) for, among other things, public health and market development.
- Balance public expenditures and investment between "hardware" (laboratories, market places) and "software" (management systems, human capital, awareness-raising for behavioral change).
- Ensure that proposals for significant public investments or programs are justified using cost-benefit or cost-effectiveness analysis, and that alternative approaches, including regulatory measures and facilitating private investment, have been considered.
- Use public investment and programs to leverage and incentivize private investment and other activities to build food safety capacity and improve outcomes.
- Strategically focus resource allocations by linking them to coherent, system-wide strategies for food safety investment and management.

(Continued)

BOX ES.1 Recommendations for Stakeholders in the Food Safety Life Cycle *(Continued)*

For lead food safety agencies or other coordinating bodies in LMICs:

- Develop a unified food safety strategy that defines priorities and responsibilities, guides the coordination of measures by government and private entities, and establishes funding needs.
- Using a structured approach, define evidence-based priorities using risk analysis and regularly update them to make more strategic use of resources.
- Redefine institutional roles to be less about finding and penalizing noncompliance and more about facilitating compliance by providing information, advice, incentives, and interventions to motivate and leverage investments and actions by value chain actors.
- Provide consumers with the tools to become partners in food safety through their own actions and through incentivizing and motivating food suppliers.
- Incorporate the science of behavior change by redesigning training programs, information campaigns, and other interventions.

For technical ministries—agriculture, health, trade, environment—in LMICs:

- Change key performance indicators to be less about noncompliant outcomes (infringements, value of fines collected, number of businesses closed) and more about food safety outcomes (magnitude of food safety risks, incidence of foodborne disease, standards-compliant trade).
- Take measures to minimize hazard entry into the food supply from farms, especially measures that offer co-benefits for public health and environmental protection.
- Direct attention to small and informal actors in the food system, with an emphasis on awareness-raising, adopting safer food handling practices, and improving physical operating conditions (that is, access to clean water and waste management facilities).
- Develop technical standards that help to correct the asymmetry of information that divides buyers and sellers of food from farm to fork.
- Remove policy, regulatory, or other barriers to private investments and services for food safety.
- Apply risk-based approaches to govern food trade, together with improved trade facilitation capabilities.

For chambers of commerce and food industry associations in LMICs:

- Participate in national processes for food safety policy development and prioritization.
- Play active advocacy roles by ensuring that small-actor constraints are factored into policy making and advocating for the least burdensome means and realistic time frames for regulatory compliance.
- Organize collective action to build food operator awareness; facilitate the adoption of good agricultural, manufacturing, and industry code practices; and strengthen food quality and the safety management of industry leaders, small and medium enterprises, and organized primary producers.

(Continued)

BOX ES.1 Recommendations for Stakeholders in the Food Safety Life Cycle *(Continued)*

- Support programs to improve food and pathogen traceability and transparency by establishing industry- wide norms and standards for record-keeping and sharing information along the value chain.

For research institutes and academia:

- Build capacity in the basic disciplines to address food hazards and use this capacity to conduct research on the epidemiology of foodborne disease, carry out risk assessments, and evaluate feasible alternatives for risk management.
- Develop, adapt, and pilot food safety technologies and approaches in partnership with industry and civil society organizations; evaluate the efficacy and cost-effectiveness of these technologies and approaches.
- Develop and contribute to professional training and accreditation programs for food safety professionals to create a cadre of trained personnel for industry and the public sector.

For bilateral development and trade partners:

- Strengthen incentives for preventive actions by LMIC trading partners by instituting more streamlined trade consignment inspection protocols, and act through memorandums of understanding and twinning arrangements to achieve mutual recognition of sanitary and phytosanitary management systems.
- Give increased priority to food safety interventions focused on promoting domestic public health in LMICs to make a significant contribution to achieving the Sustainable Development Goals.
- Improve the quality of bilateral food safety capacity support programs by applying more rigorous economic analysis and monitoring and evaluation, placing greater emphasis on capacity sustainability, and taking advantage of potential synergies, such as One Health initiatives.
- Promote low-cost, high-impact investments in food safety management capacity through the experimentation, demonstration, and facilitation of technology transfer and practice adoption.

For multilateral organizations and partnerships:

- Develop and apply a "food safety commitment index" as a global or regional benchmarking tool to monitor the level of commitment that LMIC governments are making to food safety, and to motivate them to take additional measures to improve underlying capacities and performance.
- Promote active experience sharing among LMICs, and document and promote good practices in food safety management upgrading policies and programs.
- Promote the application of formal processes of prioritization as part of the development of national strategies for enhancing food safety management capacity.
- Promote multidisciplinary research to better inform strategies, policies, and programs.

TABLE ES.1 Priorities for Countries at Different Stages of the Food Safety Life Cycle

Priority area	Traditional	Transitioning	Modernizing
Policy, strategy, and regulation	Integrate food safety concerns in national food and nutritional security strategies to mobilize attention. Establish a basic legislative framework for food safety (roles and responsibilities, legal authority). Update regulations for the use and marketing of agricultural chemicals and veterinary drugs.	Integrate food safety concerns into national strategies for agricultural transformation and trade diversification to mobilize attention. Align sanitary and phytosanitary standards with the potential for trade in relevant commodities. Develop a national multisector food safety strategy that sets priorities, addresses institutional strengthening and coordination, and lays out approaches for private sector collaboration and consumer engagement. In line with available enforcement and compliance capacity, strengthen the legal framework and align it with the Codex Alimentarius. Participate in regional harmonization efforts.	Integrate food safety concerns in national strategies for managing public health costs. Strengthen regulatory convergence with trading partners and international standards. Negotiate equivalence agreements to facilitate trade with important partners. Conduct cost-benefit analyses of proposed regulatory measures and incorporate regulatory impact assessments into policy making.
Risk assessment	Undertake qualitative assessments and quantitative risk ranking, where feasible, to identify the most significant risks to public health. Incorporate information from other health reporting systems. Pay particular attention to issues associated with neglected zoonoses and staple foods. Undertake value chain assessments to determine the locus and nature of risks in relation to food-safety-sensitive exports. Develop basic laboratory testing capacities while using regional and international labs for specialized or low-volume testing.	Set up programs for monitoring food consumption and purchasing patterns, and for estimating total dietary exposure to hazards. Develop a foodborne disease (FBD) surveillance and reporting system. Pay particular attention to microbial hazards, and hazards-related adulteration and use of agricultural inputs. Establish programs to monitor food safety hazards of public health concern and supplement them with studies to generate additional surveillance data to prioritize risks. Invest and facilitate investment in more extensive and professional quality assurance laboratory testing capacities	Draw up a national research plan to address food safety, with input from industry. Set goals of continuous reduction in FBD (as reported by surveillance system). Pay particular attention to emerging FBD and novel technologies. Apply mechanisms for the systematic collection, evaluation, and use of FBD surveillance data. Ensure that laboratory systems are internationally accredited, effectively networked, and financially sustainable.

(Continued)

TABLE ES.1 Priorities for Countries at Different Stages of the Food Safety Life Cycle (*Continued*)

Priority area	Traditional	Transitioning	Modernizing
Risk management	Ensure that synergies between water and sanitation upgrade initiatives and community-level food hygiene programs. Improve basic hygiene conditions in markets by investing in infrastructure, especially targeting markets where poor populations buy high-nutrient and perishable foods. Improve access to basic health services to minimize serious complications from FBD. Support community-based and peer-to-peer mechanisms for improving food safety in smallholder agriculture and the informal food sector linked with development initiatives. Establish border controls with a focus on likely high-risk products. Target important single-source hazards for feasible control measures. Undertake public-private initiatives to develop compliance with external requirements for sectors with significant export growth potential.	Develop a registry of food businesses in the formal sector and undertake risk profiling. Implement programs for the hygiene grading of food premises. Professionalize food inspectors and implement risk-based inspection plans. Introduce local good agricultural and animal husbandry practice programs targeting specific commodities in emerging formal sectors. Leverage consumer awareness and demand for safer food. Invest in (through public-private partnerships, if possible) improved food market infrastructure for perishable foods. Mainstream the adoption of good agricultural and animal husbandry practices through technical and market support programs, and ensure multisector synergies (through One Health, for example). Introduce procedures for investigating and responding to food safety incidents and emergencies, and for early warning systems. Strengthen border controls on a risk basis, and ensure that controls follow good trade facilitation practices. Develop an early warning system and contingency plan for food emergencies.	Build attitudes and incentives to mix robust enforcement and constructive compliance support for businesses. Incentivize the adoption of food safety management systems by small and medium enterprises (SMEs) and internationally benchmarked standards by larger enterprises. Remediate important environmental hazards. Strengthen fully documented national food recall and traceability systems. Strengthen decentralized capacities for regulatory oversight and advice. Use emerging information, biological, and other technologies in regulatory delivery and supply chain management. Ensure that border controls for food imports are consistent and effective. Ensure that procedures for recalls and food emergencies are well established.
Information, education, and communication	Educate consumers on basic food hygiene and avoidance of specific hazards. Develop targeted training for SMEs, informal food retailers, and street food vendors. Raise awareness of synergies and trade-offs between food safety, nutrition, and equity; and food safety and Sustainable Development Goals.	Implement national food safety awareness programs, targeting all stakeholders and age groups. Work with industry and universities to develop training and advanced education programs in food safety management. Develop and implement various elements of a risk communications program, including guidelines for different stakeholders and use of electronic platforms.	Establish a mechanism to systematically monitor public perceptions to inform food safety communications and education programs. Develop communication strategies to correct public misperceptions. Use behavioral science principles and empirical testing methodologies to design programs that influence consumer and food handler behavior. Support private efforts to label and certify products to promote consumer trust and reduce information asymmetry.

Source: World Bank.

REFERENCES

APEC Business Advisory Council. 2016. *Non-Tariff Barriers in Agriculture and Food Trade in APEC: Business Perspectives on Impacts and Solutions*. Los Angeles: University of Southern California.

Havelaar, A., M. D. Kirk, P. R. Torgerson, H. J. Gibb, T. Hald, R. J. Lake, N. Praet, et al. 2015. "World Health Organization Global Estimates and Regional Comparisons of the Burden of Foodborne Disease in 2010." *PLOS Medicine* 12 (2).

ABBREVIATIONS

ASEAN	Association of Southeast Asian Nations
COMESA	Common Market for Eastern and Southern Africa
DALY	disability-adjusted life year
EU	European Union
FBD	foodborne disease
FDA	Food and Drug Administration
FERG	Foodborne Disease Burden Epidemiology Reference Group
GAP	good agricultural practice
GNI	gross national income
HACCP	hazard analysis and critical control points
IFC	International Finance Corporation
LMIC	low- and middle-income country
PVS	performance of veterinary services
SDG	Sustainable Development Goal
SPS	sanitary and phytosanitary
WTP	willingness to pay

Introduction

THE FOOD SAFETY CONTEXT

Food safety hazards are increasingly being recognized as a major public health problem worldwide, which has significant and wide-ranging socioeconomic consequences for human welfare and economic performance. For industrial countries, a considerable body of research now exists on the nature and magnitude of these consequences; the economics of food safety regulations; and the efficacy of various approaches to strengthen food safety awareness, behavior, and management capacity. For developing countries, hard evidence in these areas is more limited and less accessible to policy makers, especially those who are not experts in this field. Because of this, the economic case for public investment in food safety systems is generally less well understood in low- and middle-income countries.

Many developing countries lack rigorous and comprehensive data on the level and nature of foodborne hazards and the prevalence of associated foodborne illnesses, though this situation is by no means uniform. In developing countries, most cases of foodborne illness are sporadic rather than occurring as part of a substantive outbreak, making them inconspicuous.[1] The 2015 publication of the long-awaited World Health Organization–sponsored report on the global burden of foodborne disease was a major advance. Yet, the findings

[1] This is not limited to developing countries. The U.S. Centers for Disease Control and Prevention estimate that 48 million cases of foodborne disease occur annually in the United States. Yet, only around 30,000 cases a year are reported as outbreaks.

were only for regions rather than countries, making the report something of a challenge for nonspecialists to understand and draw policy implications from.

Country data are frequently missing or unreliable on the incidence and level of food safety hazards, the occurrence of foodborne illness, and the financial costs to farmers and enterprises from market disruptions because of unsafe food. Food safety hazards and practices within informal food marketing channels are not assessed on a regular basis, despite the great importance of these channels for the food supply to the poor and often to the whole population. And the economic impacts of foodborne hazards are often complex, involving multiplier and feedback effects that can be difficult to identify—and even more difficult to quantify. Somewhat better proxy indicators are available to gauge the impact of food safety hazards on the export performances of developing countries, although this is also a challenging area to accurately quantify.

Thus, while many policy makers and other stakeholders in developing countries recognize that there are gaps and shortcomings in food safety systems, less well understood are the socioeconomic impacts of these weaknesses and, importantly, the size of the benefits from remedial or forward-looking investments or other measures to influence incentives and behavior.

And the playing field is changing. This includes significant demographic and economic changes that are resulting in major shifts in dietary and food purchasing patterns, and a fundamental and rapid process of restructuring domestic agri-food systems. Along with these forces are significant changes in the magnitude and types of hazards associated with the food of developing countries. Different countries are currently at different stages in the processes of dietary and food system structural transformation.

The limited evidence base on the costs of food safety lapses and on the benefits of preventive measures has contributed to underinvestment in food safety management systems in many developing countries. And the growing complexity of food safety hazards in many urbanizing middle-income countries is straining or outpacing food safety management capacity. This includes regulatory control systems, enterprise and value chain management systems, and associated infrastructure and human resources. In developing countries, investments in food safety are often reactive and defensive, occurring after a serious food safety outbreak or the imposition of a trade ban. Experience has shown that reactive investments turn out to be to be very expensive, not only financially but also in the cost to the reputation of the affected industry and the disruptive impacts on value chain actors. Yet, fragmented structures for food safety governance are common, and these tend to inhibit the development and application of forward-looking, preventive approaches to food safety risk management.

AIMS AND AUDIENCES

Developing countries face a multitude of competing demands for limited investment funds. The economic case for more significant and sustained investment in food safety systems needs strengthening. To do this, empirical evidence will need to be compiled on the impacts of foodborne hazards for public health, trade, and domestic market development among countries at different levels of economic development. This will also require additional evidence of the economic benefits of improvements in food safety and how these are distributed. Based on this evidence, recommendations can be made for food safety system investments and other public policy initiatives that lead to safer practices from farm to fork.

This report aims to increase the awareness of policy makers of the socioeconomic impacts of foodborne hazards in low- and middle-income countries, provide a rationale for greater policy attention and public resources to strengthen food safety capacities and incentives, and provide guidance on how to go about doing this. The report is primarily aimed at policy makers and policy analysts in low- and middle-income countries, both those associated with technical ministries (especially, agriculture, health, and trade) and those involved with economic and development planning and budgetary and fiscal management. The analysis and strategic perspectives offered in this report will also be relevant to development practitioners and partners seeking to devote greater attention to food safety matters in their support for public health, trade, and agricultural and food system transformation in low- and middle-income countries.

STUDY METHODS

The work on this report involved data analysis, literature reviews and synthesis, case studies, and some use of crowdsourcing techniques to gather material that has not been documented or put in the public domain. The report benefited enormously from collaboration with several other institutions; this included sharing restricted data and reports, without which important analyses for this report would not have been possible.

The report aims to advance the strategic prioritization of investments and other public policy initiatives related to food safety in developing countries. It does this by (1) positioning food safety challenges within the context of the broader Sustainable Development Goals; (2) combining insights from food safety specialists and various social science disciplines; (3) integrating evidence across different types of food safety hazards, product lines, and domestic and international markets; (4) contrasting the food safety challenges and experiences of countries at different levels of economic development; and (5) making these findings accessible to nonspecialists.

STRUCTURE OF THE REPORT

The report has four main sections. The first examines why safe food fundamentally matters for economic development. The second looks at the evidence on the costs of unsafe food in developing countries. The third section discusses the status of food safety management in these countries, and the fourth analyzes the strategic, policy, and institutional issues and options for strengthening food safety management systems. The report closes by offering recommendations for different stakeholders and proposes priorities for countries at different stages of economic development.

CHAPTER ONE

Why Safe Food Matters to Economic Development

INTRODUCTION

Unsafe food contains microbiological, chemical, or physical hazards that can make people sick, causing acute or chronic illness that in extreme cases lead to death or permanent disability. Unsafe food reduces the bioavailability of nutrients, particularly for vulnerable consumers, and is associated with malnutrition. The presence of food safety hazards can lead to food losses and reduce availability for food-insecure populations. For these reasons, food safety is seen as an integral part of food and nutritional security. Food safety hazards that have been addressed by public policies include microbial pathogens (for example, *Salmonella* spp.); zoonotic diseases (for example, highly pathogenic avian influenza); parasites (for example, intestinal worms); adulterants (for example, melamine); naturally occurring toxins (for example, aflatoxin); antibiotic drug residues; pesticide residues; and heavy metals (for example, cadmium).

Food safety hazards are not only a public health issue for low- and middle-income countries (LMICs) but they also affect the growth and modernization of domestic food markets and income and employment opportunities in food production, processing, and distribution. This is especially true where increases in income and urbanization—and the transformation of diets, among other factors—are generating increased demand for safe food (Ortega et al. 2012; Lagerkvist et al. 2013). Furthermore, the quality and safety of food is often a strong attraction—or, conversely, a deterrent—for domestic and international tourism (Croes and Rivera 2015).

Food safety is an increasingly important determinant of the trade performance of many LMICs, especially those competing in markets for high-value foods, including fresh fruit and vegetables, fish and fishery products, meat, spices, and nuts. To the extent that the enhancement of agri-food exports contributes to sustainable economic development and poverty reduction, investments in food safety can have significant positive development impacts. Thus, countries, and their agri-food sectors and firms, that have a limited capacity to manage food safety might find themselves excluded from lucrative export markets or face periodic yet costly rejections of product consignments and uncertainty about sustained market access.

In economic terms, costs associated with unsafe food are potentially high in both the short and long terms—and are manifested most directly in the public health costs and loss of labor productivity from foodborne disease (FBD). Food safety failures can also impose costs on producers, food manufacturers and distributors, and consumers. For example, concerns over food safety may force consumers to pay higher prices for "safe" food or lead them to avoid foods considered "unsafe," with possibly negative nutritional consequences. Affected businesses might incur costs in recalling products or face a loss of market access or brand reputation. Entire industries might see a contraction in consumer demand or a loss of access to lucrative export markets. Evidence on the public health and commercial costs of unsafe food is presented in chapter 2.

FOOD SAFETY AND THE SUSTAINABLE DEVELOPMENT GOALS

Of paramount importance for LMICs is the impact of unsafe food and investments in food safety management capacity on efforts to reduce poverty. Food safety intersects with poverty in two critical ways: the poor as consumers of food and as agents in agri-food value chains. A growing body of literature identifies the extent of food safety hazards in informal food markets, which are the predominant source of food for the poor, especially in urban areas (Grace et al. 2008; Feglo and Sakyi 2012; Jarquin et al. 2015). Food safety can affect the livelihoods of poor people employed in agri-food value chains as, for example, small-scale farmers, operators of micro and small food processing and distribution enterprises, and employees in commercial food enterprises. Thus, even a single food safety event can undercut livelihoods and push people into poverty—or back into poverty—if it causes consumers to shift purchasing and consumption patterns. Attempts to improve food safety by banning street food vendors can have negative consequences for livelihoods and nutrition. But there can be significant positive impacts on poverty if investments to increase the capacity to manage food safety enhances agri-food markets in a way that is inclusive of the poor.

Improving food safety and building the capacity to do this will play an important role in achieving the Sustainable Development Goals (SDGs). Indeed, food

BOX 1.1 Food Safety and the Sustainable Development Goals

Food safety will be vital for achieving many of the Sustainable Development Goals (SDGs), and particularly the following:

- *SDG 1: End poverty.* Foodborne disease (FBD) is a major cause of ill-health among the poor and is associated with a range of costs affecting them, including lost workdays, out-of-pocket expenses, and reduced value of livestock and other assets.
- *SDG 2: End hunger.* FBD has multiple complex interactions with nutrition. For example, toxins may directly lead to malnutrition, some of the most nutritious foods are the most implicated in FBD, and concerns over food safety may lead consumers to shift consumption away from nutritious foods.
- *SDG 3: Good health and well-being.* The health burden of FBD is comparable to that of malaria, HIV/AIDS, and tuberculosis, and the people most vulnerable to FBD are infants, pregnant women, the elderly, and those with compromised immunity.
- *SDG 5: Gender equality.* Women are the gatekeepers of household food safety, play important roles in traditional food chains, and often derive their livelihood in agri-food value chains.
- *SDG 6: Clean water and sanitation.* Lack of clean water increases the risk of food being unsafe, injudicious use of chemicals in food production can pollute water sources, and infectious FBDs can be transmitted via water.
- *SDG 8: Decent work and economic growth.* Inclusive food markets provide livelihoods and are a way out of poverty for many poor people.
- *SDG 11: Sustainable cities and communities.* Hundreds of millions of poor people work in urban agriculture and food-related services, and vibrant traditional food markets and street food make important contributions to culture, tourism, and livable cities.

safety will be integral or highly significant to achieving several SDGs, especially SDGs 1, 2, and 3, while also contributing to achieving several other goals (box 1.1).[1]

UNDERSTANDING THE SOCIOECONOMIC IMPACTS OF UNSAFE FOOD

To best understand the socioeconomic impact of enhancements in food safety management systems, it is important to adopt a food system perspective. Food systems encompass the entire range of activities and actors in the production, processing, marketing, consumption, and disposal of food, including the inputs needed and outputs generated at each stage. Food systems also encompass the

[1] FBD was not given explicit attention in the formulation of the SDGs. This may reflect the poor evidence base at the time, since the first global assessment of the burden of FBD was not published until after 2015. This may also reflect the low awareness of the importance of food safety among public health professionals and, especially, development practitioners. Considerable advances in some areas of public health, including declines in the incidence of malaria and tuberculosis, mean that the relative importance of food safety has increased, along with its growing share of the global infectious disease burden.

institutions that define the social, economic, political, physical, and technological environment in which these activities take place. A food system perspective recognizes the physical transformation and movement of food, and the rules and other institutions that organize and govern this system through the incentives for actors at various stages of the agri-food chain to behave in particular ways. The safety of food products can therefore be seen as an outcome of food systems, which, in turn, reflects the capabilities and incentives for actors within the system to adopt practices that enhance or maintain the safety of the end product.

The attention on food safety often focuses on specific agri-food value chains and the institutional context in which they operate—and this, in turn, reflects the wider social, economic, physical, and technological environment. Two critical factors influence the performance of value chains in terms of food safety. The first includes the capabilities of actors within value chains, both individually and collectively, to undertake the functions needed to manage food safety, and public and private sector actors outside value chains that provide necessary regulatory services and support functions. And the second factor includes the incentives for actors within and around value chains, again individually and collectively, to undertake the practices needed to ensure the safety of the end product. These incentives reflect the market demand of consumers and the regulatory actions of governments (which, themselves, may be influenced by multiple factors). A considerable body of theoretical and empirical evidence shows

BOX 1.2 Market Failures Associated with Food Safety

A well-functioning market provides incentives for food business operators to supply products that embody the characteristics of safety that consumers demand, both because these operators derive greater profit from doing so and because their reputation is essential for repeat sales. Under certain conditions, however, markets may fail to provide the safety that consumers demand or that is socially desirable.

For example, consumers may be unable to judge the safety of a food product at the point of purchase or before consumption. The safety of food is often imperceptible to the senses, and those consuming it may lack access to information on how food was handled before reaching them. This problem becomes more pronounced as supply chains become more impersonal. And in the event of food poisoning, consumers often have no way of identifying the source of contamination. This problem is called information asymmetry.

Because safety can increase costs for food business operators, this lack of information may reduce their incentive to incur those costs. Operators that have more information on the safety of the products they supply may be able to gain a strategic advantage over consumers or their competitors, leading to inappropriate price signals or false product differentiation on the basis of safety.

This situation is compounded by the safety and quality characteristics associated with food being typically complex, and significant transaction costs can be imposed on consumers searching for products that meet their particular demands

(Continued)

BOX 1.2 Market Failures Associated with Food Safety *(Continued)*

and in assessing the actual characteristics of these products. These transaction costs can impede market development.

Unsafe food not only imposes costs on the person eating it (for example, lost income for time away from work) but also imposes broader costs on society through the health care system. Normally, consumers do not take these costs—which economists call externalities—into account when choosing the food they buy, and so they tend to demand a lower level of food safety than society would prefer. Externalities, however, can also be positive. These are benefits that accrue to other parts of society beyond consumers themselves; for example, the protection of the environment when consumers buy safe food that is also environmentally friendly.

Governments can use food safety standards to try to tackle market failures to achieve levels of safety that are socially desirable and to reduce the costs of unsafe food. In extreme cases, this can take the form of product bans. More generally, food safety standards specify the ways in which food products are produced and their characteristics (for example, ingredients and storage conditions). Here, governments may specify the safety characteristics of the end product, but leave food business operators to choose the most appropriate way in which to grow or manufacture their products. In some cases, governments may also specify the information that must be disclosed to consumers and the format for this information.

This market-failure perspective presents public standards as instruments that correct inefficiencies in markets for food safety. But even a cursory observation of the prevailing environment for food safety standards provides examples of public standards that have been implemented in the absence of "market failure" or some other action that may have been able to correct the failure at lower cost.

The political economy perspective on food safety standards acknowledges that public authorities are influenced by the interest groups their actions affect—whether businesses, consumers, or taxpayers—and that the standards they implement will reflect, at least in part, the power of these actors. It is widely recognized that private interests can "capture" regulatory processes and steer them in directions to their economic advantage. In these cases, public standards can aggravate market failures and have considerable distributive impact.

Private standards are implemented by businesses and other entities, individually or collectively, and these standards evolve for different reasons. They are often devised to enhance economic efficiency by facilitating communication between buyers and sellers or by ensuring the compatibility of product components or products that are consumed jointly. Private standards can also be the basis of the competitive strategies of food business operators to communicate with consumers and enhance their reputations.

Market signals are sufficient to induce the development of private standards; the role of the government is to ensure that these standards do not constitute or conceal anticompetitive practices.

that the incentives in markets, when markets are left to their own devices, tend to be weak (box 1.2).

A focus on agri-food value chains also recognizes the distinct pathways through which food safety hazards occur and the pathways to better public health, economic, and social outcomes. Figure 1.1 shows that there are often

FIGURE 1.1 Public Health, Economic, and Social Outcomes of Unsafe Food

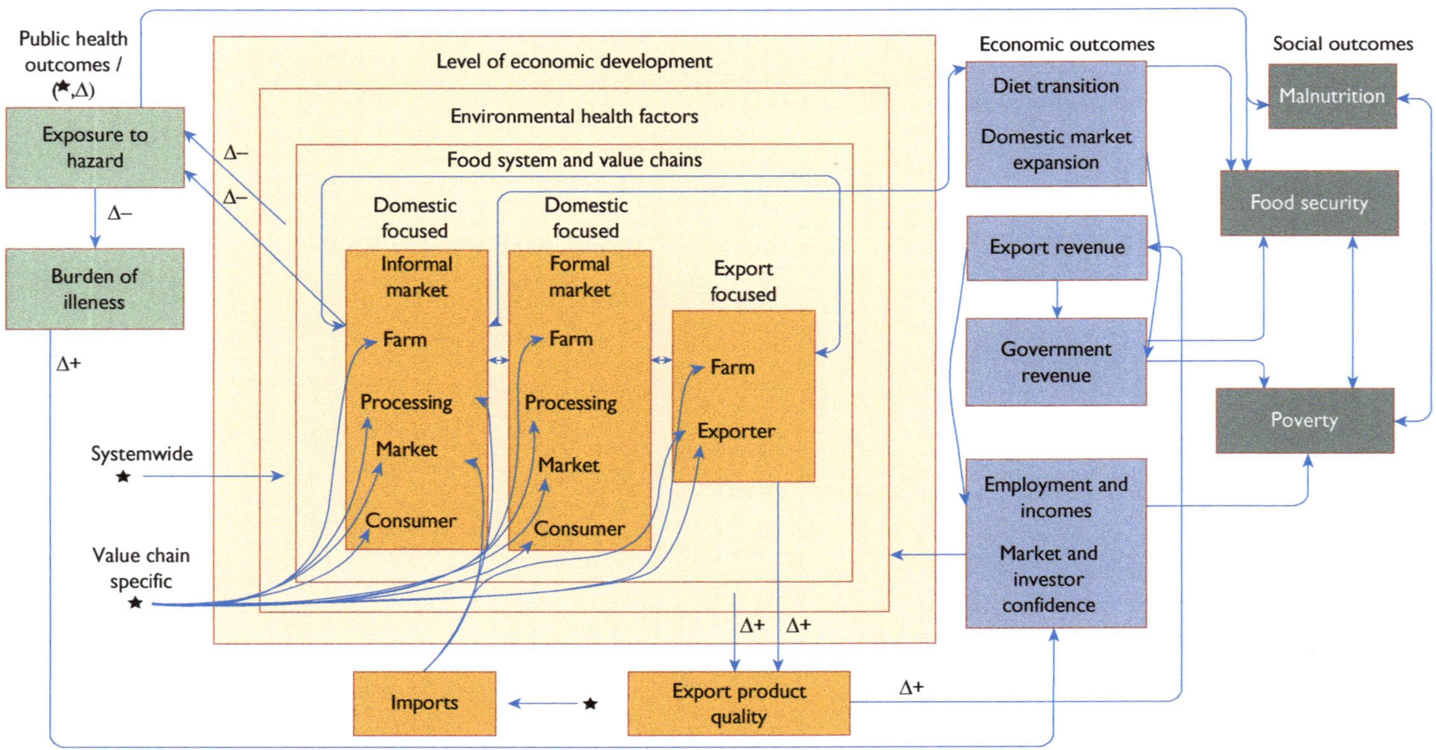

Source: World Bank.

distinctive value chains, both the informal and formal, focused on servicing domestic consumers or export markets. Agricultural raw materials and food can also be imported to service both the domestic market and export-oriented businesses. These value chains operate in a broader food system that also includes physical infrastructure and other institutions. This broader system is also influenced by a country's wider environmental health in terms of water and air quality. A country's level of economic development is a key determinant of the structure of agri-food chains, the relative importance of informal and formal distribution channels, and the state of the environment.

A distinction can be made between agri-food value chains focused on exports and those directed at consumers in domestic markets, reflecting two different pathways through which the economic and social outcomes of FBD occur. The first is the impacts on domestic consumers through exposure to food safety hazards that bring about FBD. This has economic consequences through costs associated with morbidity and premature mortality in terms of pain and suffering, and loss of income and productivity. The second pathway is the impacts on the performance of businesses operating in agri-food value chains, whether directed at domestic or export markets.

Importantly, the economic and social outcomes of FBD are seen at the micro level (for example, on individual consumers and businesses) and in the overall economy (for example, through economic growth, employment, and trade performance). These economic and social outcomes can also differ (for example, between poorer and richer consumers, and small and large businesses), resulting in considerable distributional consequences.

FBD can arise from environmental health conditions; for example, inadequate sanitation that leads to cross contamination in food handling. Many FBDs can also arise at multiple points in agri-food value chains, thereby increasing the level of contamination (table 1.1). FBDs can also be spread through the comingling of food products, especially when food markets expand and food is distributed over long distances. Importantly, agri-food chains exist and respond to a dynamic environment (for example, in the foods eaten by rich and poor alike, and the expected trajectory of diets in the future) (box 1.3).

For export-oriented value chains, food safety affects trade performance through compliance with public and private standards. Impacts on domestic food safety only occur to the extent that export-oriented value chains also supply local markets or there are capacity spillovers to value chains directed at local markets. Thus, poor product quality in these value chains may hurt exports, with consequences for business performance, employment, farm incomes, and government revenues.

The exposure of domestic consumers to food safety hazards reflects the food safety management capacity of agri-food value chains and the wider food system in which they operate. Informal value chains are typified by the preponderance of micro and small enterprises, a high rate of attrition of enterprises, weak regulatory oversight, and weak links between actors both vertically and horizontally within the chain. Conversely, value chains directed at formal food

TABLE 1.1 Food Safety Hazards on the Farm-to-Fork Pathway

Stage of pathway	Source of contamination	Examples of hazards
Production	Soil	Sewage effluents; animal manure; soil-associated microbial pathogens (*Listeria* spp., *Clostridium* spp.); heavy metals; industrial chemicals
	Freshwater	Microbial contaminants, parasite eggs, heavy metals, industrial chemicals
	Salt water	Marine toxins Bacteria: *Vibrio* spp.
	Fertilizer and soil amendments	Pellet manure and fish emulsion can contain biological hazards, inorganic fertilizers may contain hazardous chemicals, and biosolids may contain heavy metals
	Agricultural chemicals	Pesticides, fungicides, herbicides, rodenticides, antimicrobials, illegal growth promoters, disinfectants; fertilizers
	Fodder and roughage	Dioxins, mycotoxins, microbial pathogens (*Listeria*, *Neospora*, *Clostridium botulinum*, *Salmonella* spp.)
	Animal feeds	Microbes, mycotoxins, metals, processing aids, antinutrients, veterinary drugs, persistent organic pollutants, plant toxicants (alkaloids)
	Agricultural workers	Feces-associated pathogenic bacteria (*Salmonella* spp., *Shigella* spp., *E. coli* O157:H7, and others) Pathogenic parasites (*Cryptosporidium*, *Cyclospora*) Pathogenic viruses (hepatitis, enterovirus)
	Plant	Natural toxins: lectins, cyanogenic glycosides, oxalates, trypsin inhibitors
	Livestock	Microbes: *Salmonella* spp., *Campylobacter*, toxigenic *E. coli*, and others Parasites: pork tapeworm, beef tapeworm, *Trichinella* Commensals Drugs: antimicrobials, hormones
	Aquatic animals	Pathogens: *Vibrio* spp. Commensals: *Clostridium* Parasites: trematodes, nematodes Contaminants: *Erysipelothrix*, *Listeria* Spoilage: histamine
Harvest	Plant harvesting	Physical hazards: stones, wood splinters Machine lubricants, cleaning materials
	Slaughter	Contamination of meat with gut contents (common), animal skins, workers, water source, cleaning chemicals, cross contamination among animals from different sources

(Continued)

TABLE 1.1 Food Safety Hazards on the Farm-to-Fork Pathway *(Continued)*

Stage of pathway	Source of contamination	Examples of hazards
	Aquatic capture	Infected workers
Processing	Infected food handler	Infected workers
	Adulteration with harmful substances	Unauthorized dyes, melamine, formaldehyde (as preservative)
	Processing and transportation conditions	Lack of appropriate cold chain control, acrylamide
	Packaging	Packaging migrants, unfavourable conditions leading to microbial growth
	Peri-domestic pests	Flies, rodents, birds
Retail	Infected handlers	Infected workers
	Fomites	Equipment, surfaces, clothes
	Peri-domestic pests	Flies, rodents, birds
	Store conditions	Lack of cold storage
Home	Inappropriate storage	Temperature
	Cross contamination	Use of nonfood-grade containers, lack of hygiene in handling
	Insufficient heating	Kitchen surfaces, lack of stove or fuel

Source: Adapted from Grace 2017.

markets tend to be made up of a diversity of small, medium, and large enterprises with lower rates of attrition, more systematic inspection and reporting, and more coherent links between actors within the chain. The capacity to manage food safety clearly differs across value chains, with consequences for the exposure of the consumers they serve to foodborne hazards.

Consumers can also be exposed to foodborne hazards through imported food that flows into domestic value chains. For this food, much of the value chain lies beyond the importing country, such that the degree to which consumers are exposed to food safety hazards is essentially an issue of preborder, border, and postborder controls, whether applied by governments or businesses operating in the trade and distribution of food.

The exposure of domestic consumers to food safety hazards can have significant economic and social outcomes. FBD contributes to the incidence of malnutrition and erodes food security. The burden of FBD, including the

BOX 1.3 Dietary Changes in Low- and Middle-Income Countries

Many low- and middle-income countries, especially middle-income countries, have seen profound and rapid changes to the structure of diets in recent decades. Figure B1.3.1 shows the change in diet in urban Indonesia from 1998 to 2013. Over this period, the expenditure share on cereals (mainly rice) declined appreciably, while expenditures on prepared food and beverages more than doubled, from 13 percent to 31 percent.

More profound changes to the structure of diets in low- and middle-income countries are expected. In Southeast Asia, for example, it is predicted that more than half the daily calorie intake will continue to come from cereals in 2030, but with much more diversified sources of food contributing to energy, protein, and fat requirements (Jamora and Labaste 2015). While rice and beef consumption are expected to decline in per capita terms, strong demand growth is expected in fruit and vegetables, pork and poultry, dairy products, edible oils, and cereals. This will be reflected in individual diets and in expected aggregate national volumes (figure B1.3.2).

Similar patterns are expected among LMICs more generally. According to IFPRI (2017), LMIC consumption of meat and of fruits and vegetables is expected to grow by 24 and 25 percent, respectively, between 2010 and 2030.

FIGURE B1.3.1 Composition of Food Expenditures in Urban Indonesia, 1998–2013

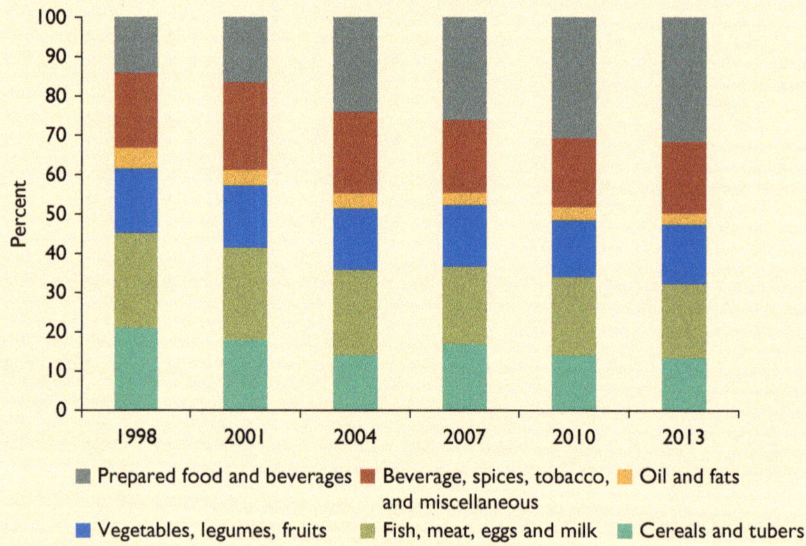

Source: BPS-Statistics Indonesia.

(Continued)

BOX 1.3 Dietary Changes in Low- and Middle-Income Countries *(Continued)*

FIGURE B1.3.2 Estimated Food Demand in Southeast Asia, 2009 and 2030

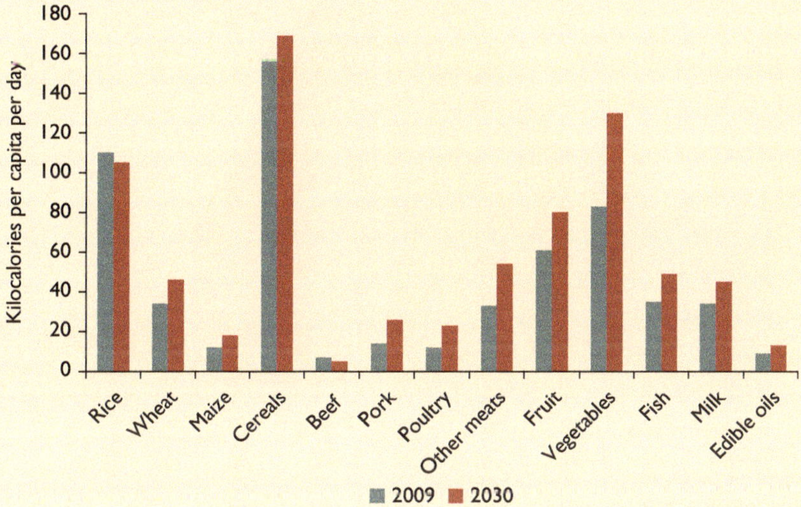

Source: Based on Jamora and Labaste 2015.

costs associated with premature mortality and morbidity, erodes employment and incomes, with consequences for the rate of economic growth and the incidence of poverty. Furthermore, the performance of agri-food businesses can be affected; for example, through loss of consumer trust and the erosion of investor confidence, with consequences for the flow of revenues to governments and secondary impacts on employment and incomes.

THE FOOD SAFETY LIFE CYCLE

While food safety is both a major challenge and an opportunity for all countries, the prominence of food safety issues and their specificity varies significantly among countries. The evidence generally shows that FBD and the incentives for enhancing food safety management capacity vary systematically with the level of economic development. Figure 1.2 presents an indicative profile, or life cycle, of the burden of FBD and failures in relation to countries according to the level of economic development. Four broad stages are presented, from lowest to highest.[2] It is important to note that not only does the scale of the burden of

[2] The precise path of the life cycle will differ among countries in terms of the rate of the incline or decline and the curvature of the turning points.

FIGURE 1.2 Food Safety Life Cycle with Levels of Economic Development

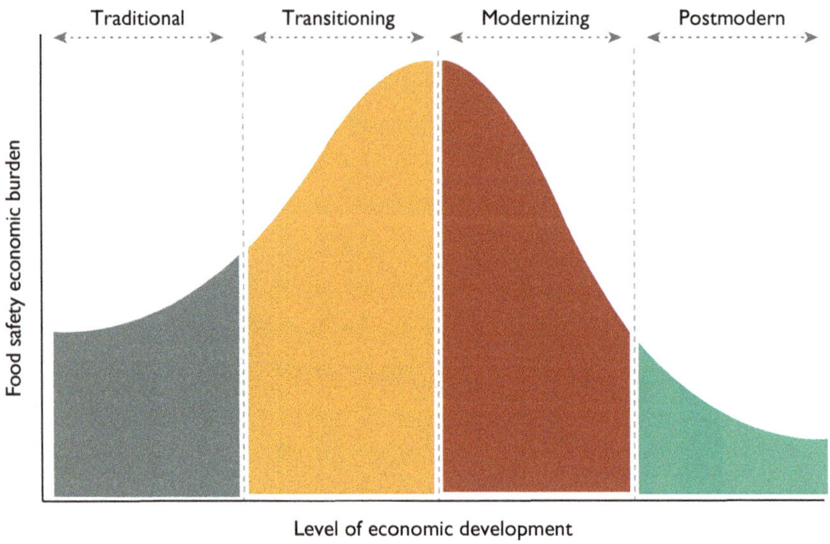

Source: World Bank.

FBD differ quantitatively at these different stages, but the sources of foodborne hazards also change, as summarized in table 1.2.

Traditional Stage

In most low-income countries where many food safety problems are emerging (the traditional stage in figure 1.2), both the supply of and demand for safe food remain underdeveloped, and traditional concerns about national and household food security are paramount. Often, the process of diet transformation has barely commenced or is found only in very isolated urban clusters. The diet predominantly consists of starchy staples produced domestically. A lot of food is produced close to the point of consumption and undergoes limited transformation before reaching households. The predominant FBDs come from microbiological pathogens resulting from low access to clean water and improved sanitation, and naturally occurring toxins, such as mycotoxins. Domestic market drivers or incentives for safer food are often weak. Food safety management systems in low-income countries tend to be rudimentary, with instances of more developed systems being usually geographically concentrated and focused; for example, on high-income consumers (among whom the willingness to pay for safer or certified food might be strong). The agri-food exports of many low-income countries either center on commodities considered to have modest food safety risks (beverage crops) or involve cross-border movements into countries with similarly limited food safety management capacities. For higher-value exports, oases of strong

TABLE 1.2 Sources of Foodborne Hazards, by Stage of the Food Safety Life Cycle

Foodborne hazard	Stage of food safety life cycle			
	Traditional	Transitioning	Modernizing	Postmodern
Naturally occurring food toxins	***	***	**	*
Livestock zoonoses	****	***	***	*
Microbial pathogens	**	****	***	**
Veterinary drug residues	*	**	**	*
Pesticide residues	*	**	**	*
Industrial contaminants	*	**	**	*
Food adulterants	*	**	**	*
Aquatic zoonoses, parasites, and toxins	**	***	**	*
Contaminated or adulterated feed	**	***	**	*
Food additives	*	**	**	*
Heavy metals	*	**	***	*

Source: World Bank.
Note: * = minimal; ** = moderate; *** = significant; and **** = major.

food safety management capacity, usually built around a limited set of lead firms and designated "competent authorities," may emerge, but these tend to be separated from domestic systems.

In terms of figure 1.1, the predominant outcome of FBD in low-income countries may be through impacts on malnutrition, food security, and poverty. These stem from widespread environmental health challenges and low levels of food safety awareness and capacity in the predominant informal food distribution channels. While impacts on incomes and employment may be significant within the informal economy, secondary consequences, in terms of government revenue or investor confidence, are likely to be very limited.

Transitioning Stage

Countries reaching lower-middle-income status have a broader range of and steeply accelerated exposure to food safety hazards. They fall within the transitioning stage of the food safety burden life cycle shown in figure 1.2. For these countries, diets are rapidly transforming beyond starchy staples toward a wider array of plant and animal source foods. In addition, more foods are consumed in processed form and outside the home. As populations become increasingly urbanized, the distances between food production and consumption tend to increase; and as supply chains elongate, they also tend to involve more processes and intermediaries. The intensification of farm production often involves the increased use of agrochemicals and veterinary drugs. Food imports, including perishable foods, often increase, exposing domestic consumers to new foodborne hazards of a microbiological, chemical, and physical nature.

During the transitioning stage, as shown in figure 1.2, agri-food value chains begin to evolve, although the emergence of the formal sector and more organized value chains tend to be geographically concentrated, predominantly in urban areas. Most domestic markets continue to be served by the informal sector. The modern retail sector gradually emerges, but with a focus on urban markets for packaged and processed foods (box 1.4). Overall, food safety management systems remain underdeveloped. Where centers of enhanced food safety capacity exist, they predominantly serve export and urban middle-class markets. Very quickly, the domestic regulatory apparatus becomes overwhelmed by the rising range and incidence of FBD. And because government administrative systems change slowly, it is common to see food safety management capacity being ineffectively used at this stage.

The slow development of food safety management systems in the transitioning stage reflects the weak incentives for investment in these systems in the public and

BOX 1.4 The Link between Supermarket Penetration and Income per Capita

The rapid spread of modern food retailing in Europe and Latin America led to predictions that this model of food distribution would soon predominate (Reardon and Gulati 2008; Reardon, Timmer, and Minton 2012). Supermarkets and other large format outlets have indeed experienced considerable growth in many emerging markets and low-and middle-income countries, reflecting the fairly strong relationship between income per capita and the penetration of more modern food retail formats.

More traditional modes of food distribution remain the predominant outlet in many low- and middle-income countries, especially for fresh produce, meat, and fish. Small convenience stores, meanwhile, have often undergone some of the most rapid growth in the "modern" food retailing segment, as seen in Indonesia (Minot et al. 2015). Here, modern retailing accounts for more than half of urban food spending for many processed foods, yet for less than 5 percent of spending on rice, fish, poultry, tofu, and most vegetables. Shopping in modern food outlets is highly correlated with incomes. It accounts for one-third of food expenditures among the highest-income decile, yet only 8 percent in the fifth decile and 4 percent in the poorest decile. Ironically, there is also a tendency to return to more direct food sourcing at high incomes; for example, through farmers' markets, home delivery, and direct purchases from farms. Moreover, e-commerce is beginning to make inroads into retail food markets.

(Continued)

BOX 1.4 The Link between Supermarket Penetration and Income per Capita *(Continued)*

FIGURE B1.4.1 Link between Supermarket Penetration and per Capita Income

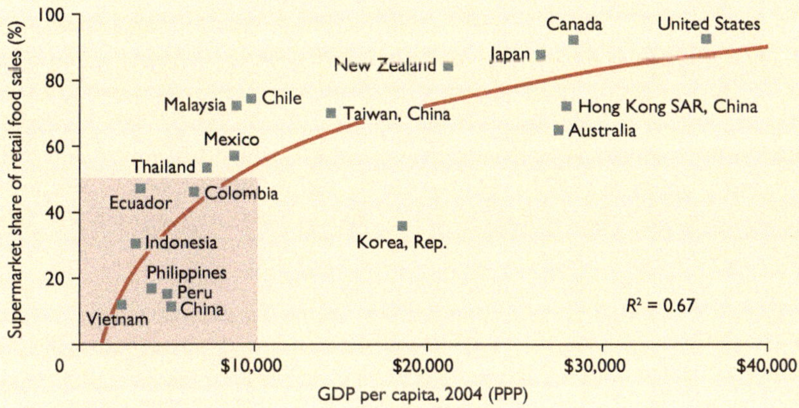

Source: Pacific Economic Cooperation Council 2007.
Note: PPP = purchasing power parity.

private sectors. The polity is slow to respond to the growing burden of FBDs, largely reflecting the inadequacy of surveillance systems, such that the scale and rate of change in the prevalence of FBDs is largely unknown. There is little incentive to allocate scarce public resources to tackle a problem whose impact is largely invisible and predominantly affects the politically weak, such as the poor. Furthermore, market-based incentives are largely missing, except among urban elites. Consumer awareness and concerns about food safety grow (along with increased social media attention), and some consumers are willing to pay extra for food they perceive to be safer (box 1.4). But most consumers continue to focus on value rather than quality in the food they buy. This, and the credibility of "safe food" claims, inhibit private investment in enhanced food safety management systems.

First movers are not always rewarded, especially in circumstances where lower cost and an agile informal sector are prominent, if not dominant. Even so, larger branded food companies will increasingly recognize the business case for investing in improved food safety in their operations and supply chains. But it could take a long time before incentives emerge for investing in enhanced food safety management systems directed at markets serving the poor. So, although levels of investment in enhanced food safety management systems begin to be observed, these tend to be predominately focused on oases that have little or no impact on the broad population.

Lower-middle-income countries often experience an expansion and diversification in their agri-food exports that target both high-income and regional-peer countries. Safety-sensitive, high-value foods may feature more prominently, and many more actors of varying sizes and capabilities test their skills and luck to compete in this trade. This may be reflected in a mixed picture of quality management and compliance with trade-partner regulatory or private standards. Concerns about compliance costs, unfair treatment, and other real or alleged problems tend to come to the fore in these emergent industries.

Figure 1.2 reflects the expectation that countries will experience the highest economic burden of FBD when they transition from lower-middle- to upper-middle-income status. In these countries, consumers will be exposed to a wide range of foodborne hazards as the coexistence of formal and informal markets sends mixed signals to public and private actors to invest in food safety controls. But eventually, as political pressure for change intensifies and awareness and capacity begin to catch up with underlying needs, this burden will peak and start to decline.

During the transitioning stage, food imports often become more prominent, as do exports of higher-value products that are food-safety-sensitive. The economic and social outcomes of FBD begin to multiply and extend across the network of links shown in figure 1.1. Thus, the burden of FBD increases in terms of the costs of medical care and loss of productivity associated with morbidity and premature death. The impact on businesses of food safety failures becomes more significant, both through the erosion of consumer and investor confidence and interruptions in trade flows. Secondary impacts may be more significant through the loss of employment and incomes and lower government revenues. At the same time, the direct impacts on malnutrition and food security may decline, reflecting more powerful and broad-based processes of economic development.

Modernizing Stage

The modernizing stage shown in figure 1.2 is characterized by the increasingly rapid upgrading of food safety management systems in the public and private sectors. Because of administrative change and public investment, regulatory systems become more effective at establishing and enforcing minimum food safety standards, and at promoting and facilitating upgrades in food safety management systems in the private sector. More effective surveillance systems also highlight the burden of FBD, helping the problem gain recognition and making the benefits of upgrading food safety management systems more apparent. Simultaneously, the public administration of food safety becomes more efficient, and is able to respond to the needs and demands of stakeholders.[3] All these changes foster greater public trust in the ability of the agri-food system to deliver safe food (box 1.6).

---

[3] By improving tax revenue, governments have access to more of the resources needed to invest in enhancing food safety management systems in the public sector, and to provide incentives for private investment (or to defray the risks that private investors face). Internationally, government institutions are becoming more involved—and to greater effect—in food safety governance, including through the Codex Alimentarius and the World Trade Organization.

BOX 1.5 Consumer Willingness to Pay for Food Safety

Many consumers in low- and middle-income countries value food safety and, hypothetically at least, show a willingness to pay (WTP) a premium for what they perceive to be safer food. And there is evidence for this, with studies in Asia on WTP for food safety showing the following:

- Studies in China found that consumers were willing to pay a premium for foods with a "safe food" label (multiple sources in Yan 2011). Tian, Yu, and Holst (2011) found that Chinese consumers were willing to pay a premium of 25–50 percent for "green food." Revell (2016) found that consumers in Beijing were willing to pay 20–40 percent more for certified chemical-residue-free products, and many other studies have likewise found that Chinese consumers are prepared to pay more for certified foods, including for food safety reasons.
- Studies in Vietnam found that consumers were willing to pay 10–15 percent more for "safety-labeled free-range chicken" (Ifft, Roland-Holst, Zilberman 2012), and an average of 60 percent more for certified chemical-residue-free greens (Mergenthaler, Weinberger, and Qaim 2009).
- Wongprawmas, Canavari, and Waisarayutt (2014) found that Thai consumers were willing to pay 117–180 percent more for food with safety labels.
- Birol et al. (2015) found that Mumbai consumers were willing to pay more for grapes described to them as having safe-food certification.

In all these studies, trust in labels is a key contributing factor. The actual behavior of consumers often diverges from their stated WTP, and many of the higher premiums reported in these studies are unlikely to be realized. The WTP is estimated more precisely when real alternatives are presented, and consumers make decisions under their usual budget constraints.

Shogren et al. (1999) compared the WTP for food safety across different valuation methodologies, including a direct market experiment for safer poultry meat in the United States. Their results were similar across methods, but actual market behavior revealed the smallest premium for food safety, suggesting that nonmarket methods, such as surveys, may overestimate the potential WTP. In that experiment, the lowest market premium was still greater than the cost of providing safer food, so the certified process was profitable. Even if some of the larger WTP premiums found in the Asian studies could be obtained in the marketplace, they would be competed away over time since they are probably greater than the cost of producing safer food products.

The gap between stated and actual WTP may be explained by multiple factors, including poor study design. Even so, some generalizations are possible from the literature on this issue. Consumers consistently express a desire for safer food and place a positive value on this. The WTP increases with income and varies with socioeconomic factors, such as education and gender. This willingness also depends on the credibility of safe food claims and on consumers' perceived subjective risk, which may differ from objective risk. Leveraging the WTP by providing consistent and credible certification can be one approach to incentivize food safety improvements, and this is discussed in chapter 4.

(Continued)

As markets develop, consumers begin to expect safe food as a matter of course, and thus market incentives more often punish food safety failures rather than reward safer food. Negative market incentives after these failures take the form of lost sales or brand reputation, as well as lost equity value for larger firms. These negative incentives are more important in modernizing economies than in traditional ones.

The modernizing stage is also characterized by a profound and often rapid restructuring of agri-food value chains. Formal sector enterprises come to dominate in both urban and rural areas, and the modern retail sector expands and extends into smaller urban centers and rural areas. Modern retail comes to play a more dominant role beyond processed packaged foods, including in the fresh produce and fresh and semiprocessed animal product sectors. The food service sector begins to emerge and, at later phases of modernization, expands rapidly in urban areas. The branding of food becomes more widespread and even becoming the dominant basis of food marketing and consumer choice. As businesses become better organized, both as individual enterprises and collectively across sectors, they are able to exert greater pressure on government to take actions to enhance public food safety management systems.[4]

Overall in the modernizing stage, the significant enhancement of food safety management systems translates into a lower FBD burden. The rate of decline will reflect the appropriateness, efficacy, and efficiency of the enhancement of food safety management systems. The direction of investments in these systems will reflect the size of market-based and political incentives. Everything else being equal, the role of market-based incentives will probably become more important as consumers are more aware of the potential hazards associated with the food they eat. Furthermore, the "voice" of middle-income consumers and eventually low-income ones will get louder through both market and political channels, such that more investment in the enhancement of food safety capacity will be directed at the supply of foods to poorer parts of the population. Among countries at the modernizing stage, either advanced food safety management systems are adopted by smaller exporting enterprises or exports become consolidated among a limited pool of larger companies with modern facilities that broadly apply international standards.

At this stage, the economic and social outcomes of FBD result predominantly from failures in managing food safety risks in the formal sector directed at domestic and external consumers. The direct burden of FBD, through medical care costs and

[4] Businesses also face market pressure to improve the safety of their products, as consumers become more aware of FBDs and are increasingly able and willing to pay for food they judge to be safer—and suppliers begin to differentiate their products in the eyes of the consumer on the basis of food safety. Thus, broader applications of good agricultural and manufacturing practices, hazard analysis, and critical control points are observed, driven by proactive businesses that yield the private gains necessary to incentivize innovation in their food safety management systems.

BOX 1.6 Personal and Institutional Trust in Food Safety Systems

Trust is an intangible yet vitally important element of a food safety system. The range and depth of trust affect relationships among multiple stakeholders and strongly influence their behavior. The degree of trust strongly influences the relationships between, for example, (1) consumers and food vendors, (2) food manufacturers and their raw material suppliers, (3) consumers and food business operators and public regulatory authorities, (4) exporters and overseas buyers, and (5) public regulatory agencies in different countries. Important attributes of a trustworthy food safety system include competency, transparency, and accountability (WHO 2018).

In traditional and localized food systems, trust tends to be highly personalized. Transactions tend to be repetitive among individuals with whom there may be wider social ties and a sense of moral obligation. As food systems become more complex, trust becomes more institutionalized as interactions increasingly occur among formal institutions, including producing firms, labeling schemes, state agencies, and scientific establishments.

Institutionalized trust relies on, among other things, formal regulations, packaging, brands, and labels. Repeated interactions of the same individuals may happen less frequently, or repeated interactions may become less personal because consumers know that providers are acting as representatives of their institution. Institutionalized trust is more conditional and hence more vulnerable than personalized trust.

Public organizations gain consumer trust by applying results from scientific research, and by involving various types of experts (legal, scientific, and administrative, for example). Private organizations gain trust through brand development, marketing practices, participation in certification schemes, and corporate social responsibility programs, where they try to show that human interest is not subservient to short-term profit considerations. Trust in nongovernment and consumer organizations comes from their absence of commercial interests and expertise in developing standards, information campaigns, and consumer guides. Trust in food is generally stable because food consumption behavior is highly routinized (that is, people buy the same food from the same places). But this can be disrupted by lifestyle changes and food safety scares that cause routines to be changed (Kjaernes, Harvey, and Warde 2007; Zhang et al. 2016).

productivity loses, are high, even though the overall incidence of disease may be declining. Likewise, the costs of consumer market or trade disruptions and product recalls may be considerable. Secondary outcomes on businesses and the economy may also be high, although links between FBD, malnutrition, and food security will generally weaken among countries in the modernizing stage.

Postmodern Stage

Eventually, the burden of FBD declines to much lower and relatively stable levels in the postmodern stage, as figure 1.2 shows, at which point any further improvements in the safety of food occur in smaller increments. While differences persist in the prevalence of particular FBDs across high-income counties, improvements in the aggregate and for particular hazards are slow, especially compared with those observed among a rising number of middle-income countries. This new equilibrium reflects the fact that both market-based and political incentives for improved food safety management capacity remain high and that agri-food value chains are complex. Also reflected in the new equilibrium is that a significant proportion of food is imported, and that "easy wins" from improved capacity will be few. In the postmodern stage, periodic food safety lapses will occur and FBD outbreaks will attract a lot of attention. But the high quality of health services in most high-income countries leads to a situation in which deaths attributable to FBD are comparatively rare.

Table 1.3 summarizes the conditions associated with the different stages of the food safety life cycle, as shown in figure 1.2. The table highlights the degree to which the agri-food sector has transitioned from the informal to the formal sector, and the degree of dietary transformation beyond traditional staples. The level and nature of market-based and political incentives for upgrading food safety management capacity—which underlies the shape of the life cycle in figure 1.2—is not only the level and nature of foodborne hazards but also the extent to which there are incentives for investment in food safety management

TABLE 1.3 Structural Change and Incentives for Enhanced Food Safety Action

Stage (income level)	Agri-food sector formalization	Diet transformation	Market-based incentives	Political incentives	Level and direction of investment in food safety capacity
Traditional (low)	Very low	Very low,	Very low, except in relation to trade	Low	Low, with exceptions of islands or corridors of capacity for export
Transitional (lower middle)	Low	Moderate but accelerating fast	Generally low, but with market segment exceptions and in relation to trade	Medium	Low but increasing, and with a focus on major exports and urban high-income consumers
Modernizing (upper middle)	Medium	Medium	Medium and accelerating fast	High	Medium and rapidly increasing, both for the domestic market and a broader set of export industries.
Postmodern (high)	High	High	High	High	High and stable, with a predominant focus on domestic consumers overall

Source: World Bank.

systems in response to changes in these hazards. This points to the gap that opens between prevailing capacity and the food safety burden faced by certain countries, especially at the transitional and modernizing stages.

SUMMARY

This chapter has shown how safer food supports economic development and the SDGs by improving health and economic opportunity. The specific challenges of tackling food safety in the process of economic development come from the market failures associated with providing safer food and the need to work with all food value chain actors to achieve solutions. This chapter has outlined a model of a food safety life cycle that creates a gap between need and capacity as economies develop. The transformation of the food system during the process of economic development leads to a food safety life cycle for LMICs in which the socioeconomic burden of food safety increases as countries pass from the low- to middle-income stage. As part of this life cycle, there is a lag in the public and private response to emerging food safety challenges. Understanding the evolution of food safety needs during economic development sets the stage for examining the costs of food safety and the state of management capacity in the following chapters.

REFERENCES

Birol, Ekin, Bhushana Karandikar, Devesh Roy, and Maximo Torero. 2015. "Information, Certification and Demand for Food Safety: Evidence from an In-Store Experiment in Mumbai." *Journal of Agricultural Economics* 66 (2): 470–91.

Croes, R., and M. Rivera. 2015. *Poverty Alleviation through Tourism Development: A Comprehensive and Integrated Approach*. New York: Apple Academic Press.

Feglo, P., and K. Sakyi. 2012. "Bacterial Contamination of Street Vending Food in Kumasi, Ghana." *Journal of Medical and Biomedical Sciences* 1 (1): 1–8.

Grace, D. 2017. *Food Safety in Developing Countries: Research Gaps and Opportunities: Feed the Future*. Washington, DC: U.S. Agency for International Development.

Grace, D., A. Omore, T. Randolph, E. Kang'ethe, G. W. Nasinyama, and H. O. Mohammed. 2008. "Risk Assessment for Escherichia Coli O157:H7 in Marketed Unpasteurized Milk in Selected East African Countries." *Journal of Food Protection* 71 (2): 257–63.

Ifft, J., D. Roland-Holst, and D. Zilberman. 2012. "Consumer Valuation of Safety-Labeled Free-Range Chicken: Results of a Field Experiment in Hanoi." *Agricultural Economics* 43 (6): 607–20.

IFPRI (International Food Policy Research Institute). 2017. *Global Food Policy Report*. Washington, DC: IFPRI.

Jamora, N., and P. Labaste. 2015. "Dietary Changes and Implications for Food Demand in East Asia." Unpublished. Washington, DC: World Bank.

Jarquin, C., D. Alvarez, O. Morales, A. J. Morales, B. Lopez, P. Donado, M. F. Valencia, et al. 2015 "Salmonella on Raw Poultry in Retail Markets in Guatemala: Levels, Antibiotic Susceptibility, and Serovar Distribution." *Journal of Food Protection* 78 (9): 1642–50.

Kjaernes, U., M. Harvey, and A. Warde. 2007. *Trust in Food: A Comparative and Institutional Analysis*. Basingstoke, United Kingdom: Palgrave MacMillan.

Lagerkvist, C. J., S. Hess, J. Okello, and N. Karanja. 2013. "Consumer Willingness to Pay for Safer Vegetables in Urban Markets of a Developing Country: The Case of Kale in Nairobi, Kenya." *Journal of Development Studies* 49 (3): 365–82.

Mergenthaler, M., K. Weinberger, and M. Qaim. 2009. "The Role of Consumers' Perceptions in the Valuation of Food Safety and Convenience Attributes of Vegetables in Vietnam." Paper presented at the International Association of Agricultural Economists Conference, Beijing, August 16–22.

Minot, N., R. Stringer, W. J. Umberger, and W. Maghraby. 2015. "Urban Shopping Patterns in Indonesia and Their Implications for Small Farmers." *Bulletin of Indonesian Economic Studies* 51 (3): 375–88.

Ortega, D. L., H. H. Wang, N. J. Olynk, L. Wu, and J. Bai. 2012. "Chinese Consumers' Demand for Food Safety Attributes: A Push for Government and Industry Regulations." *American Journal of Agricultural Economics* 94 (2): 489–95.

Pacific Economic Cooperation Council. 2007. *Pacific Food System Outlook 2007–2008: Linkages to Growing Urban Markets Spur Rural Development*. Singapore: ISEAS Publishing.

Reardon, T., and A. Gulati. 2008. "The Supermarket Revolution in Developing Countries." IFPRI Policy Brief, International Food Policy Research Institute, Washington, DC.

Reardon, T., P. Timmer, and B. Minten. 2012. "Supermarket Revolution in Asia and Emerging Development Strategies to Include Small Farmers." *Proceedings of the National Academy of the United States of America* 109 (31): 12332–37. https://doi.org/10.1073/pnas.1003 160108.

Revell, B. 2016. "Urban Consumer Attitudes to Fresh Produce Safety in China." *Journal of Food Science and Engineering* 6 (1).

Shogren, J. F., J. A. Fox, D. J. Hayes, and J. Roosen. 1999. "Observed Choices for Food Safety in Retail, Survey, and Auction Markets." *American Journal of Agricultural Economics* 81 (5): 1192–99.

Tian, Xu, Xiaohua Yu, and Rainer Holst. 2011. "Applying the Payment Card Approach to Estimate the WTP For Green Food in China." IAMO Forum No. 23, Leibniz Institut für Agrarentwicklung in Mittel- und Osteuropa, Halle, Germany. http://hdl.handle .net/10419/50786.

Wongprawmas, Rungsaran, Maurizio Canavari, and Chutima Waisarayutt. 2014. "Are Thai Consumers Willing to Pay for Food Safety Labels? Choice Experiment on Fresh Produce." Presentation at the European Association of Agricultural Economists Congress, "Agri-Food and Rural Innovations for Healthier Societies," Ljubljana, Slovenia.

WHO (World Health Organization). 2018. *Regional Framework for Action on Food Safety in the Western Pacific*. Manila: WHO.

Yan, Y. 2011. "Willingness to Pay for Safer Dairy Products in China: Evidence from Shanghai Customers' Purchasing Decision of Bright Dairy's Baby Cheese." Nanjing Agricultural University. https://getd.libs.uga.edu/pdfs/yan_yiwei_201408_ms.pdf.

Zhang, Lei, Yunan Xu, Peter Oosterveer, and Arthur P. J. Mol. 2016. "Consumer Trust in Different Food Provisioning Schemes: Evidence from Beijing, China." *Journal of Cleaner Production*, Special volume: Transitions to Sustainable Consumption and Production in Cities 134 (October): 269–79.

CHAPTER TWO

Evidence on the Burden of Unsafe Food in Low- and Middle-Income Countries

INTRODUCTION

A large body of literature provides evidence of the considerable economic costs associated with foodborne disease (FBD) (for example, Hoffmann, Maculloch, and Batz 2015; Thomas et al. 2013; Mangen et al. 2014). While most of this literature relates to high-income countries, recognition is growing that the costs of FBD in low- and middle-income countries (LMICs) are also significant (Grace 2015). As the life cycle concept introduced in chapter 1 suggests, the costs associated with FBD vary both quantitatively and qualitatively according to a country's stage of economic development. In countries at lower levels of economic development, the economic costs of FBD tend to focus on informal domestic food markets. As countries grow and transform, food safety comes to play an important role in the performance of businesses in the formal sector, especially for agri-food exports. And here the costs associated with FBD become more visible, in line with growing economic development. Critically, the degree to which these costs change over time depends on how well emerging food safety challenges are managed.

FBD involves two distinct categories of costs. The first is associated with the public health impacts of unsafe food, including the costs of medical care and productivity losses from ill-health and premature death. The second is the economic and social impacts of food safety failures on consumers, businesses, and the economy as a whole. Examples of economic impacts include reductions in agri-food exports and the deleterious effects on business performance. This chapter examines both categories of costs in LMICs.

THE PUBLIC HEALTH BURDEN OF FOODBORNE DISEASE

The starting point for an analysis of the economic costs of FBD is to examine the associated burden of illness—how many people get sick, how often, and how seriously.[1] Until recently, data on the incidence of FBD and its associated costs were limited to high-income countries and regions, including Canada, parts of Europe, and the United States (Scallan et al. 2011; Thomas et al. 2013; Havelaar et al. 2012; Adak et al. 2005). To address this gap, the World Health Organization's (WHO) Foodborne Disease Burden Epidemiology Reference Group (FERG) has been working since 2006 on global estimates of the incidence of FBD.[2] These estimates cover 31 foodborne hazards in 14 regions, and are expressed in disability-adjusted life years (DALYs) associated with ill-health and premature death, with 2010 as the base year.[3] To prepare this report, the authors had access to FERG estimates of the DALYs associated with FBD for regions and for selected countries, with distinctions made between persons ages above and below five.

The total global burden of FBD in 2010 is estimated at 33 million DALYs, the result of 600 million illnesses and 420,000 premature deaths (table 2.1). As a basis for comparison, in 2015 the estimated global burden of tuberculosis was 40 million DALYs, and of malaria, 66 million DALYS. These estimates starkly illustrate the magnitude of the burden associated with FBD—a finding that is given further credence because FERG estimates are conservative.[4]

Of the total global burden due to FBDs, over 90 percent of illnesses are estimated to be related to diarrheal disease. These cases, however, account for a much smaller proportion of premature deaths due to FBDs (55 percent) and of the total loss of DALYs (54 percent). Invasive disease accounts for only 6 percent of cases of illness due to FBD, but 28 percent of premature deaths.

---

[1] Many LMICs lack robust data on the incidence of FBD. While the most reliable data are derived from systems of active surveillance, these are lacking in most LMICs, especially in low- and lower-middle-income countries. Passive systems for reporting FBD cases and outbreaks can provide an indication of incidence, but these are typically a small proportion of the total cases, the majority of which occur sporadically within a population. And even these systems of case reporting tend to be underdeveloped in many LMICs.

[2] Other sources of global disease-burden estimates include WHO's Global Health Estimates and its Childhood Epidemiology Reference Group, and the Institute of Health Metrics and Evaluation. A direct comparison of FERG results with these sources is difficult because of differences in methods and assumptions that may have an important effect on FBD-burden estimates.

[3] One DALY can be thought of as one lost year of "healthy" life. The sum of DALYs across a population is a measure of the burden of disease, and can be thought of as a measurement of the gap between current health status and an ideal health situation where the entire population lives to an advanced age, free of disease and disability. Estimates of DALYS encompass losses due to premature death and the loss of health status due to illness. For how DALYs are calculated, see http://www.who.int/healthinfo/global_burden_disease/metrics_daly/en/.

[4] For example, the incidence of illness associated with chemical hazards was underestimated in earlier FERG work. Because of data limitations, only four chemicals (aflatoxin, dioxin, cassava cyanide, and peanut allergens) were included in the FERG study. New estimates have been made and are expected to be published in late 2018.

TABLE 2.1 Estimated Global Burden of Disease, by Food-Related Hazards

Hazard group	Illnesses (millions)		Deaths (thousands)		DALYs (millions)	
	Food-borne	All pathways	Food-borne	All pathways	Food-borne	All pathways
All hazards	600	2,050	420	1,170	33	83
Diarrheal disease	549	1,910	230	780	18	59
Invasive disease	36	98	117	380	8	21
Helminths	13	28	45	53	6	7
Chemicals	0.2	0.2	19	19	0.9	0.9

Source: Havelaar et al. 2015.
Note: DALY = disability-adjusted life year.

FIGURE 2.1 The Global Burden of Foodborne Disease, by Hazard Group and Region, 2010

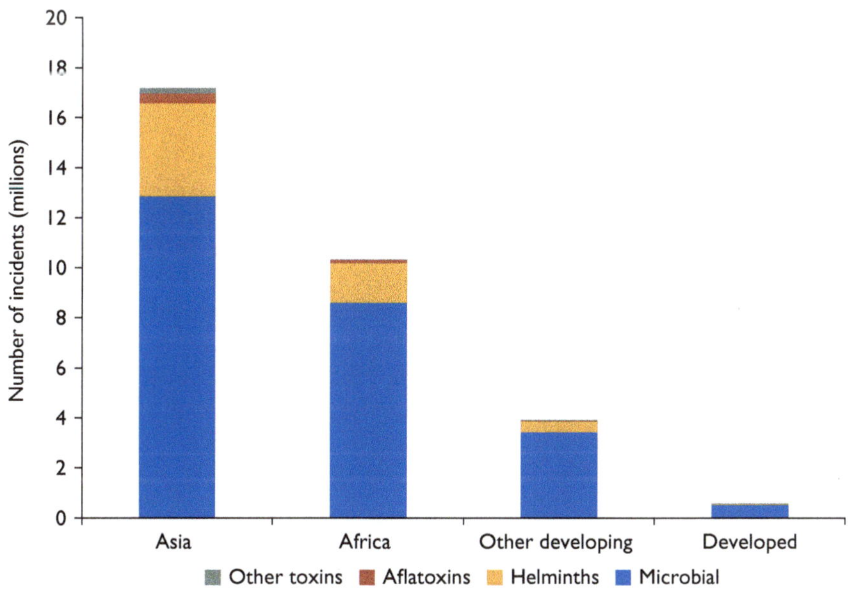

Source: Derived from Foodborne Disease Burden Epidemiology Reference Group estimates.

Globally, Asia and Sub-Saharan Africa have the highest incidence of FBD, along with the highest rate of deaths due to FBDs and the greatest loss of DALYs. LMICs in South Asia, Southeast Asia, and Sub-Saharan Africa are estimated to account for 53 percent of all illnesses due to FBD, 75 percent of deaths, and 72 percent of DALYs related to FBD (figure 2.1). To put these estimates into context, these countries account for 41 percent of the global population. Diarrheal disease accounts for a large proportion of the total burden of FBD in these countries.

Children under five years bear a disproportionate share of the burden of FBD, accounting for 9 percent of the global population, but 38 percent of all cases of illness and 40 percent of DALYs. An estimated 30 percent of premature deaths due to FBD are of children under age five. Children are more exposed to foodborne hazards because of their lack of control over food preparation and a propensity to behaviors that increase the risk of FBD. Children are more vulnerable to the consequences of infection because of their developing immune systems, small body size, and lower levels of stomach acid, among other factors.[5] Geographically, children are most likely to die from FBD in Sub-Saharan Africa, followed by South Asia.

An important question is whether vulnerable consumers, and especially the poor, can reduce their exposure to food safety risks since, as just discussed, the burden of FBD falls disproportionately on the poor and the young. Many studies have found that the poor underinvest in preventive health care (for example, Lucas 2010 and Ozier 2014), and that those who stand to benefit most from preventive action, including avoiding food with high food safety risks, are excluded by higher prices. Thus, consumers who are more susceptible to FBD tend to take on a higher level of risk than is optimal. Furthermore, a differentiated market may lead to hazardous food being concentrated in markets for the poor. This is an important challenge for market-incentive efforts to improve food safety.

Almost 80 percent of the burden of FBD is associated with microbial pathogens. These are estimated to account for 580 million cases of illness, 450,000 premature deaths, and the yearly loss of over 25 million DALYs. The most important microbial pathogens are *Salmonella* spp., toxigenic *E. coli*, norovirus, and *Campylobacter* spp. Foodborne macroparasites are also a significant cause of disease, notably in LMICs. These include tapeworms (particularly pork tapeworm, a cause of epilepsy), fish-associated fluke, and roundworms.

For risk management, it is important to have detailed information on which foods are involved in the transmission of FBD. Unfortunately, very little information on this is available for most countries and regions. A FERG expert elicitation process sought to attribute the FBD burden to different product categories, although that study involved only 11 of the 31 foodborne hazards included in FERG's assessment (Hoffmann et al. 2017). These hazards, however, account for less than half (43%) of the total estimated DALYs. The analysis concluded that several hazards are predominantly attributable to vegetables and fruit, typically with a two-thirds and one-third weighting, respectively.

[5] The elderly are also more vulnerable to FBD because of deteriorating immune systems and chronic conditions. People with primary immune deficiencies, such as a low production of antibodies, are prone to foodborne infections. Patients treated with radiation or with immunosuppressive drugs for cancer and other diseases have a higher vulnerability to FBD.

For several other hazards, attribution was split across several animal product lines (for example, beef, pork, dairy, poultry, and eggs). On the basis of the scientific literature, FERG identified nine other hazards as being completely transmitted by only one food category for each of the hazards.

Because of data limitations and the complexities of tracking the pathways of FBD, the picture of FBD attribution to different product groups is incomplete. In some Organisation for Economic Co-operation and Development countries, animal products were estimated to account for half or more of the burden of FBD, as in studies of the United States (Painter et al. 2013) and the United Kingdom (Tam et al. 2012). Feltes, Arisseto-Bragotto, and Block (2017) estimated that animal products account for more than half of the FBD burden in Brazil. Yet, the pattern for this is likely to vary considerably among countries, given differences in diets, industry structures, environmental health conditions, and other factors. That said, the evidence suggests that animal products, and fruit and vegetables, account for most FBD. In parts of Asia, the burden of FBD from fish is likely to be significant.[6] Current estimates attribute very little of the global burden of FBD to cereals, although the understanding of this may change with the ongoing FERG analysis of chemical hazards. Especially in Africa but also elsewhere, there are widespread concerns over the short- and long-term health effects of aflatoxin exposure (box 2.1).

In collaboration with this report, FERG researchers undertook further detailed analyses of FBDs that can be attributed to animal source foods. The FERG team determined that 14 hazards are closely linked to FBD from animal source foods. Based on the available data, estimates for loss of DALYs from this source were made for more than 100 countries (figure 2.2). While FERG's FBD estimates are for the year 2010, countries are mapped according to average income levels in 2016 because this better reflects today's situation.

The enormous variation among countries, including within regions, is immediately evident from figure 2.2. For this sample of countries, there is very little difference in the unweighted average share of animal source foods in total DALYs among regions. The regional averages range from 40 percent in the Middle East and North Africa, and in Eastern Europe, to 49 percent in Latin America and the Caribbean. The difference is even less in group averages among low- (43.6%), lower-middle- (42.5%), and upper-middle-income (43.2%) countries. Intercountry comparisons, however, show large differences. Within Sub-Saharan Africa, Ethiopia, Kenya, and Nigeria have similar levels of meat consumption per capita, but the DALYs attributed to animal source foods differ by nearly a factor of three. As a result, the shares of animal source foods in the total DALYs for these countries are estimated at 21 percent (Ethiopia), 40 percent (Kenya), and 43 percent (Nigeria).

---

[6] Throughout Southeast Asia and China, eating raw or partially cooked cyprinid fish is common and an important source of hazards from fish-borne zoonotic trematodes. Seafood poisoning from marine toxins is also a significant and increasing problem in Asia, resulting in tens of thousands of cases of illness annually.

BOX 2.1 Aflatoxins, Staple Crops, and Public Health

Aflatoxins are naturally occurring toxins produced by certain fungi, most importantly *Aspergillus flavus* and *Aspergillus parasiticus*. In high doses, aflatoxins can lead to serious illness and even death in humans and animals. Aflatoxins mainly accumulate on crops and grains in tropical regions and contaminate a wide variety of food crops and products, including maize (corn), sorghum, cassava, macadamia nuts, paprika, melon seed, sesame, rice, yam chips, and chili. Aflatoxin-contaminated feed in dairy rations can result in aflatoxin-contaminated livestock products. Children can be affected by aflatoxin through breast milk or from the direct consumption of weaning foods (Mahdavi et al. 2010). The Food and Agriculture Organization estimates that 25 percent of the world crop area is affected by aflatoxins; the U.S. Centers for Disease Control and Prevention estimate that 4.5 billion people in the developing world are exposed to aflatoxins.

Aflatoxins occur most frequently in dry weather when crops are near maturity, when high moisture is present during harvest, and when crop drying and storage are inadequate. Countries in latitudes between 40° north and 40° south are affected by aflatoxins. Thus, Sub-Saharan Africa, South Asia, and Southeast Asia are regions of high potential exposure to aflatoxins. Parts of the Americas also have a high intake of mycotoxins; for example, countries with high maize daily intake, such as Central American countries. The outbreak of aflatoxins in milk in the European Union in 2013, traced to contaminated maize from Serbia and Romania, is an indication of the effects of drought on higher levels of aflatoxin contamination. Climate variability and changes in climate patterns are expected to have implications for aflatoxin production—and ongoing research is trying to understand these implications. The health impacts of aflatoxins are a result of exposure, which is determined by consumption patterns and the incidence of contamination; they are also influenced by an individual's weight and nutritional condition.

Acute exposure to mycotoxins can be lethal. More than 150 deaths were caused by aflatoxin poisoning in Kenya in 2004 and 2005. Chronic exposure, however, is more pervasive. Epidemiological studies carried out in China, Kenya, Mozambique, the Philippines, Swaziland, Thailand, and South Africa showed a strong positive correlation between aflatoxin levels in the diet and cancer (Wu, Groopman, and Pestka 2014). The synergy between exposure to aflatoxins and infection with the hepatitis B virus substantially increases the risk of carcinoma. Every year, about 100,000 new cases of hepatocellular carcinoma, usually always fatal, are attributable to aflatoxin exposure (Liu and Wu 2010; Liu et al. 2012). Aflatoxins are associated with growth retardation and immunosuppression, especially in children (Gong et al. 2002; Khlangwiset, Shephard, and Wu 2011). Even low levels of aflatoxin in animal feed have been found to have significant animal health implications—from reduced productivity and fertility, liver damage, and higher susceptibility to infectious diseases.

A growing set of technological and management solutions have emerged to control aflatoxins. These include using resistant and tolerant crop varieties; applying soil amendments; changing crop densities and the timing of planting and harvesting; biological controls; and using different technologies and practices for drying, storing, and processing crops. Other interventions may affect exposure through dietary diversification and treatments to prevent consumers from absorbing the toxic effects of aflatoxins. There are differential knowledge, cost, institutional, and other constraints on adopting these solutions.

FIGURE 2.2 Foodborne Disease Burden Attributable to Animal Source Foods, by Region

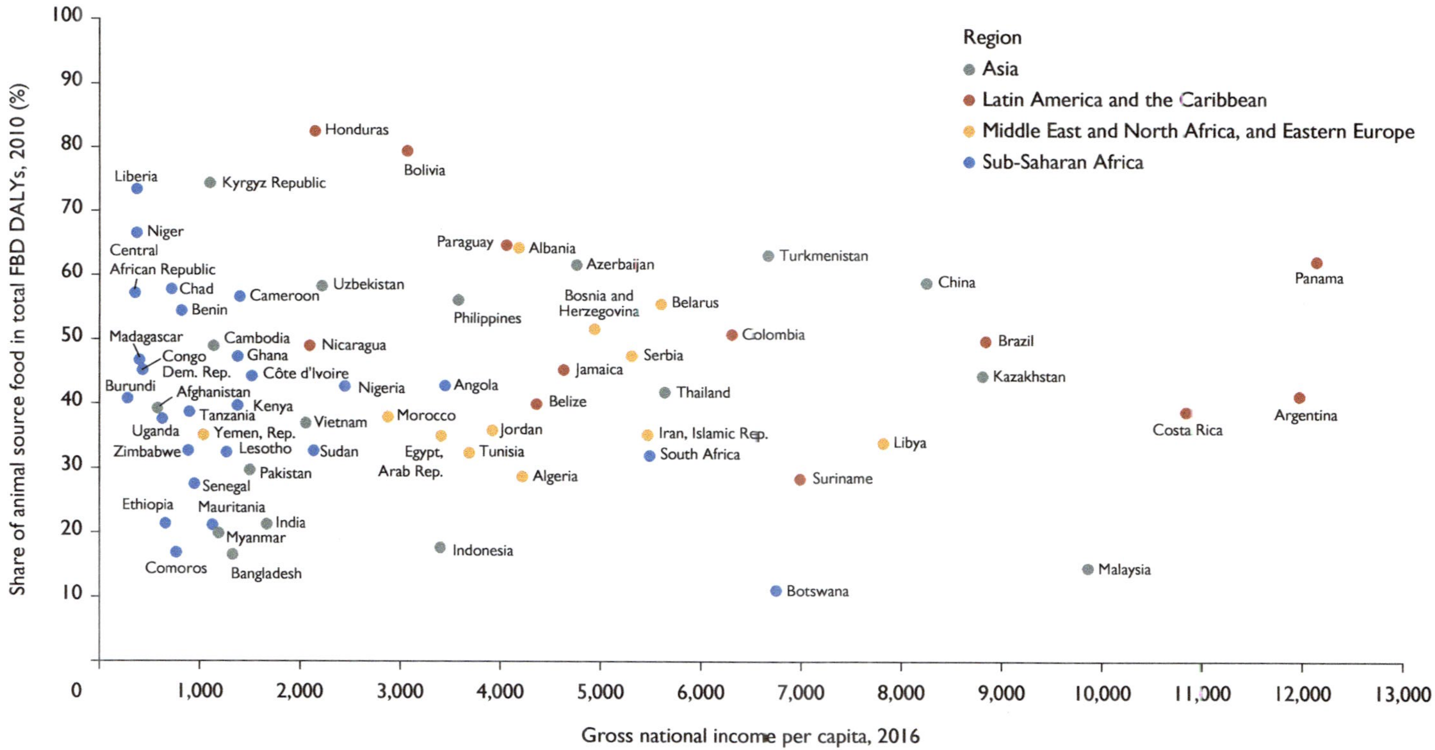

Source: Based on Foodborne Disease Burden Epidemiology Reference Group estimates.

In Asia, Indonesia, Thailand, and Vietnam have similar levels of meat consumption per capita, which is about three times higher than for the three African countries. The share of animal source foods in the total FBD DALYs for the three Asian countries also varies significantly, ranging from 17 percent in Indonesia to 42 percent in Thailand. The picture for India and China appears to be significantly different, with animal source foods estimated to account for only 21 percent of India's FBD burden yet nearly 59 percent of China's. The aggregate burden of FBD in upper-middle-income countries in Latin America is relatively low, but the share of animal source foods in FBD appears to be significant—at 50 percent in Brazil and Colombia. Thus, different country circumstances need to be carefully considered when prioritizing risk management measures, including toward different value chains.

Although FERG estimates give a snapshot of the burden of FBD globally, they do not indicate the extent to which the burden has been changing over time. Data from the Institute of Health Metrics and Evaluation show that the global burden of diarrheal disease declined by 40 percent over 2006–16 (GBD 2017a). This is almost entirely due to a marked reduction in deaths related to diarrheal disease from oral rehydration therapy and other interventions, and reductions in the underlying causes of death, such as malnutrition (GBD 2017b).

Global data on changes in the burden of FBD specifically are not available. Most high-income countries and regions, such as the United States and European Union (EU), have not seen reductions in the incidence of most FBDs (EFSA 2012; CDC 2018). But there is evidence that targeted interventions have achieved marked reductions in the number of cases of certain FBDs; for example, *salmonellosis* in the EU (EFSA 2017) and *campylobacteriosis* in New Zealand (Sears et al. 2011). Against this trend, new foodborne hazards have emerged, such as foodborne cases of norovirus. And the number of reported FBD outbreaks has continued to increase in some Organisation for Economic Co-operation and Development countries, although this probably has more to do with improved surveillance than more outbreaks.

A key factor in the evolution of FBD in LMICs is the change in dietary patterns in populations and related changes in the way food is bought, prepared, and consumed. Thus, the shift from starchy staples toward animal-based foods, for example, leads to qualitative and quantitative changes in exposure to foodborne hazards. Likewise, the degree to which consumer beliefs and norms on food and its safety, and the extent to which these persist or change as diets evolve, can be critical given the extent to which consumers expose themselves to foodborne hazards (box 2.2).

Climate change is another important yet less well understood long-term factor for the spread of FBD. Changing weather patterns will affect pathogens and their hosts in land and aquatic environments, as well as the mobility of food contaminants (Uyttendaele, Liu, and Hofstra 2015; Tirado et al. 2010; Miraglia et al. 2009). For example, shifts in average temperatures, rainfall concentration, and plant geography may change the range of latitudes

BOX 2.2 The "Good" and "Bad" Food Safety Practices of Consumers

It is important to recognize that consumers can be at risk from the food they choose to consume and the way in which they source, store, and prepare food. And as diets change, consumers can expose themselves to greater and different food safety risks.

Eating raw animal source foods is one of the riskiest food safety practices. Fish and seafood products are much more likely to be eaten raw than meat (with a few exceptions, such as beef in Ethiopia). Throughout Southeast Asia and China, eating raw or partially cooked cyprinid fish can cause liver disease and cancer from fish-borne zoonotic trematodes. In high-income countries, the boom in consumption of sushi has reportedly caused a rapid rise in tapeworm infections.

Most new human diseases originate in wildlife. Creating opportunities for humans to interact with and eat wild animals is a high risk for the emergence of novel diseases, as well as being a risk for the transmission of known pathogens. The most devastating pandemics in human history—the Black Death, Spanish influenza, and HIV/AIDS—were all caused by zoonoses from wildlife, and the emergence of major human pandemics is regularly ranked among the top existential threats to humanity.

Consumers can take measures to mitigate the potential food safety hazards they face—for example, by properly cooking food and storing food in a way that reduces cross contamination (for instance, between cooked and uncooked foods)—and the rate of replication of microbial pathogens (for example, through refrigeration). Many traditional eating practices serve this function, and often rapid changes in diet can mean the loss of these practices and the exposure of consumers to potential harm from foodborne disease.

at which certain strains of mycotoxin-producing fungi are able to compete and create opportunities for new fungal toxins to emerge as a public health concern. Climate-related changes in soil properties may favor the build-up in crops of toxic heavy metals, such as arsenic and cadmium. Ocean warming and changes in salinity are affecting the incidence of aquatic microorganisms, such as pathogenic vibrios and harmful algal blooms that cause toxins in consumed shellfish.

Climate change will also influence the efficacy of adaptive farming and supply chain practices, including those related to soil fertility, pests, animal disease, and product quality management. Longer grazing seasons from a warming climate could increase the exposure of livestock to wildlife and outdoor vectors of disease. And moving animals indoors to temperature-controlled facilities could increase the risk of disease transmission. This, in turn, could increase the dependence of farmers on antibiotics and other chemicals, which could find their way into the food system (box 2.3). The disruptive effects of climate change on agroecosystems may favor the emergence or resurgence of certain pests, causing farmers to resort to more and harsher chemicals to control them. This kind of "arms race" could prove problematic from a food safety perspective.

As well as the direct impacts of FBD accounted for in FERG estimates, these diseases can have adverse impacts on nutrition. In LMICs, FBD and

BOX 2.3 Antimicrobial Resistance and Links to Food

Antimicrobial resistance arises when potentially infectious microorganisms—bacteria, viruses, protozoa, and fungi—acquire the capacity to resist the antimicrobial agents used to treat infectious diseases. This occurs through a process of natural selection when antimicrobials are used to prevent or treat infections, even when these drugs are correctly used. Microorganisms with antimicrobial resistance occur in people and animals but also in contaminated food, water sources, and, more broadly, the environment.

Microorganisms with antimicrobial resistance can be transmitted through various pathways, such as person-to-person contact, person-to-animal contact, and contact with human and agricultural wastes. Food plays an important role in the emergence and spread of antimicrobial resistance, especially in the excessive or inappropriate use of antimicrobials in food production systems, including livestock, aquaculture, and crop production. The use of sanitizers and biocides may further exacerbate this resistance.

Foodborne infections caused by resistant bacteria, such as *Salmonella* spp. and *Campylobacter* spp., pose a particular risk to humans because of possible treatment failure. In Europe, resistance to ciprofloxacin, an antimicrobial that is important for treating human infections, is very high in *Campylobacter* spp. As well as antimicrobial resistance in pathogens, microorganisms with this resistance that do not directly pose a health risk may transmit antimicrobial-resistant genes to microorganisms that are more serious human and animal pathogens. For example, resistant commensal bacteria, such as *E. coli* and *Enterococcus* spp., can pose a risk when they carry resistance genes that can be further transferred to pathogens.

The increasing emergence of antimicrobial resistance is creating a global public health threat from its impacts on humans, animals, and the global economy. The toll attributable to drug-resistant microbes is estimated at 700,000 annual human deaths. Microorganisms with antimicrobial resistance in food are an economic risk, because of the potential to affect market access, consumer behavior, and the cost involved in adapting or changing farming practices to reduce the presence of resistant microorganisms.

Managing the risks of antimicrobial resistance in food is complex and requires good practices, from primary production and throughout the food chain to consumption. In practice, managing the emergence and spread of microorganisms with antimicrobial resistance through food is similar to managing other foodborne hazards. But it requires awareness of antimicrobial resistance measures to control microbial populations that harbor resistance determinants, and the risk factors that exacerbate its emergence and spread. Because the use of antimicrobials is key to resistance, the responsible use of antimicrobials is central to the management of related risks.

Large quantities of antimicrobials are being used globally in animal production. One study predicts that consumption could rise by 67 percent by 2030, and nearly double in BRICS countries, essentially driven by the growing consumer demand for animal source foods in middle-income countries and a shift to intensive production systems where antimicrobials are used routinely (van Boekel et al. 2015).

(Continued)

In Vietnam, which uses these systems, antimicrobials are used to prevent infections and increase productivity. Because requirements for a withdrawal period are not being complied with in Vietnam, antimicrobial residues are increasingly found in marketed meat, which can cause allergic and other reactions and gastrointestinal problems. For example, Nguyen et al. (2018) detected residues of sulfonamides, tetracyclines, and macrolides in meat samples from supermarkets and traditional wet markets, with 9.6 percent of samples from wet markets containing residues.

The improper use of antimicrobials on farms in Vietnam appears to be giving rise to multidrug resistance against major foodborne pathogens, such as *Salmonella*. spp. Nguyen et al. (2018) found high levels of resistance against quinolones and β-lactams, with the highest prevalence of multidrug resistance detected in chicken and pork meat. Vietnam is taking steps to tackle this. It has developed a national action plan against antimicrobial resistance, and in 2017 adopted a new regulation aimed at greatly reducing the nontherapeutic use of antimicrobials in livestock.

undernutrition are bidirectionally related.[7] Infectious FBD often manifests as diarrhea, which is strongly associated with child stunting and vice versa (Checkley et al. 2008; Guerrant et al. 2013; Richard et al. 2014).[8] One multi-country study found that 25 percent of the stunting burden was attributable to repeated episodes of diarrhea (Checkley et al. 2008). Each additional diarrhea episode in the first 24 months of life increases the risk of stunting by roughly 5 percent (Black et al. 2008). Studies find a strong peak in diarrhea after the introduction of supplementary foods, with some weaning foods having high levels of microbial contamination (Kumi et al. 2014). About half the burden of infectious disease results from nongastrointestinal manifestations, which can also cause undernutrition through reduced appetite and increased nutrient requirements resulting from inflammation, infection, or other conditions (Tappenden et al. 2013). Environmental enteric dysfunction is estimated to contribute to 40 percent of all global cases of stunting. This has been linked to the ingestion of fecal bacteria in food, as well as zoonotic infections (George et al. 2015).

Aflatoxins are among the most worrying food safety hazards affecting staple food crops and animal source food if livestock feed is contaminated.

[7] See Hasler et al. (2017) for insights into the complexity of food safety and nutrition relationships, and the differences in approaches and foci in food safety and nutritional assessments.

[8] Stunting, or extreme shortness (very low height for age), is the result of a combination of chronic poor dietary intake, both in terms of food quality and quantity, and repeated infectious disease episodes. While stunting is preventable, its impacts are largely irreversible when it occurs within the first 1,000 days of life, a period which is critical for the physical and mental development of infants. Long-term effects of stunting include reduced cognitive and physical development, increased morbidity and mortality from common illnesses, poorer educational outcomes, and decreased productive capacity. Globally, stunting affects some 155 million children ages under five.

These natural toxins are estimated to cause some 90,000 cases of liver cancer each year. A growing body of research shows that high levels of aflatoxin ingestion is strongly associated with stunting and immune suppression in children, although it is not yet possible to attribute causation. Grace et al. (2015) discuss recent studies and the challenges in attributing stunting to aflatoxin. The 83rd Meeting of the Joint Expert Committee on Food Additives of the WHO and Food and Agriculture Organization concluded that "epidemiological data have become available to support the hypothesis that aflatoxin exposure in utero and during early life has negative effects on growth. . . . The available data did not provide evidence for an exposure level at which there is a significant risk for growth faltering" (JECFA 2017). A careful study of doctor-diagnosed children with the most severe stunting (kwashiorkor, marasmus) suggested that daily dietary exposures of 400–1,000 nanograms of aflatoxin per kilogram of body weight leads to stunting (McMillan et al. 2018). Exposure at this range is not uncommon in Sub-Saharan Africa (JECFA 2017; Wild, Miller, and Groopman 2015). For example, evidence shows that diarrheal disease is a significant factor in the high incidence of stunting among the poor in this region. The implications are that FBD has even wider and longer-term development implications for LMICs, and, therefore, for achieving the Sustainable Development Goals.

ECONOMIC COSTS OF FOODBORNE DISEASE

A range of potential economic costs are associated with FBD. These include the harm caused by the disease (for example, lost productivity) and several types of responses (for example, medical treatment and food recalls). These costs are incurred by various economic actors, including consumers, health care providers, agri-food businesses, and governments (McLinden et al. 2014). Food safety failures can also affect export performance, which is discussed later in the chapter.

Valuing the costs associated with FBD is far from easy. Valuation methods are demanding in their data requirements and subject to recognized limitations. This is particularly the case for LMICs, where data are lacking or of poor quality. Indeed, few studies capture national data and those that do often depend on broad assumptions or extrapolations. Despite these challenges, estimates of the cost of FBD can provide valuable insights into the overall economic burden and how this is distributed across society.

The approach used to estimate the economic burden of FBD is summarized in box 2.4. Intuitively, DALYs represent years lost to illness, disability, or death, and this loss to the economy can be crudely represented by gross national income per capita. Using this measure, the total productivity loss associated with FBD in LMICs is estimated at US$95.2 billion. Of this, upper-middle-income countries account for US$50.8 billion, or 53 percent (figure 2.3). Lower-middle-income countries account for US$40.6 billion of the burden,

BOX 2.4 Estimating the Economic Burden of Foodborne Disease

The valuation of health costs using a human capital approach starts with estimated disability-adjusted life years (DALYs). These include years of life lost and years lost to disability, which distinguish between lives lost (mortality) and illness (morbidity). Loss of life typically accounts for the biggest share of the estimated health costs. Narain and Sall (2016) review health valuation methods.

Loss of life can be valued in two ways. The first is the forgone output from the life lost; that is, what a person would have produced if premature death had not occurred. And the second is the value of a statistical life derived from the "willingness to pay" to avoid death. The willingness-to-pay approach typically yields much higher estimates than the forgone-output approach, since the willingness to pay to avoid death is typically higher than income.

Illness or morbidity costs include the direct costs of care and treatment, forgone productivity from days or years of work lost, and the cost of suffering. Because most illnesses have multiple outcomes depending on individual characteristics, tracing these various costs is a challenge for estimating costs from morbidity. For any disease, the number of hospitalizations and days lost from work need to be derived for both mild and more serious infections. Typically, such estimates result in a lower value for years lost to disability than years of life lost.

Given this economic framework, generalizations can be made about the relative economic costs of different diseases. First, those resulting in a higher ratio of years of life lost to years lost to disability are a greater economic burden. Second, illnesses that are a greater burden on children are a greater economic burden, since the premature death of a child results in more years of life lost than the premature death of an adult.

It is difficult in practice to make detailed estimates for the value of either years of life lost or years lost to disability. A frequent shortcut is to use gross national income (GNI) per capita as a measure of lost productivity. Intuitively, for each year lost to illness, disability, or premature death, the economy loses the economic output associated with that year. In this report, we make an approximate estimate of the economic burden of FBD based on this simple measure of lost productivity. While these estimates are crude, they provide insights into the relative economic importance of foodborne disease in low- and middle-income countries and across different levels of development.

The Foodborne Disease Burden Epidemiology Reference Group's 2010 estimates of DALYs per 100,000 people associated with FBD within each region (and by country, where available) are used. Total DALYs for a region and country are calculated by multiplying this estimate by the population in 2016. The economic cost associated with the total DALY burden is then estimated as the value of productivity loss from FBD. This is measured by simply multiplying 2016's GNI per capita by the number of DALYs. The estimate is $VP_i = B_i \times Y_i$ where VP_i is the value of the productivity losses associated with foodborne illness in country *i*; B is the total DALY burden from foodborne illness in country *i*; and Y_i is the GNI per capita for country *i*.

FIGURE 2.3 Productivity Loss from Foodborne Disease, by Income Group and Region, 2016

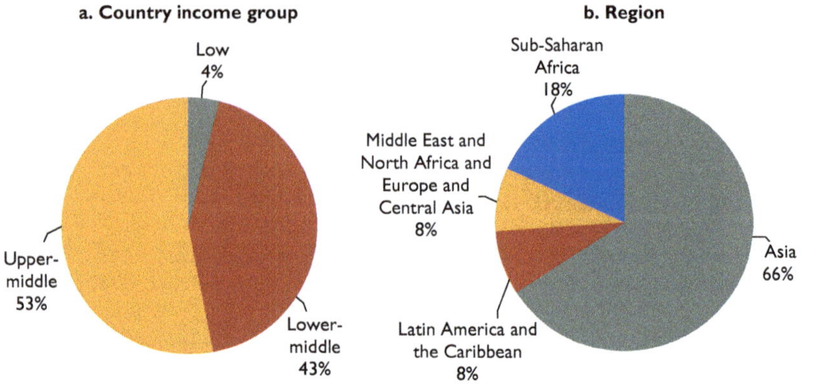

Income group	2016 human capital loss (current US$, billions)
Low	3.8
Low Middle	40.6
Upper Middle	50.8
Total	**95.2**

Region	2016 human capital loss (current US$, billions)
Asia	63.1
Latin America and the Caribbean	7.4
Middle East and North Africa, and Europe and Central Asia	7.9
Sub-Saharan Africa	16.7
Total	**95.2**

Source: World Bank.

and low-income countries account for US$3.8 billion, or 4 percent of the total. The small share of low-income countries is attributable to changes in the World Bank's country categorization. In 2000, 63 countries were classified as low income and accounted for 40 percent of the world's population. By 2016, only 31 countries accounted for less than 9 percent of world's population.

By region, LMICs in Asia account for US$63.1 billion, while those in Sub-Saharan Africa have an economic burden of US$16.7 billion. China alone accounts for over US$30 billion of the total burden of FBD in LMICs, and India for US$15 billion, with these two countries accounting for 49 percent of the total economic burden of FBD in LMICs and for 71 percent of the total burden in Asia. Fifteen LMIC countries have an FBD burden exceeding US$1 billion a year—seven of which are in Asia and three in Sub-Saharan Africa (figure 2.4). While these economies are generally large (for example, China, India, Indonesia, and Nigeria), they include smaller economies (for example, Angola,

FIGURE 2.4 Productivity Loss from Foodborne Disease, by Country, 2016

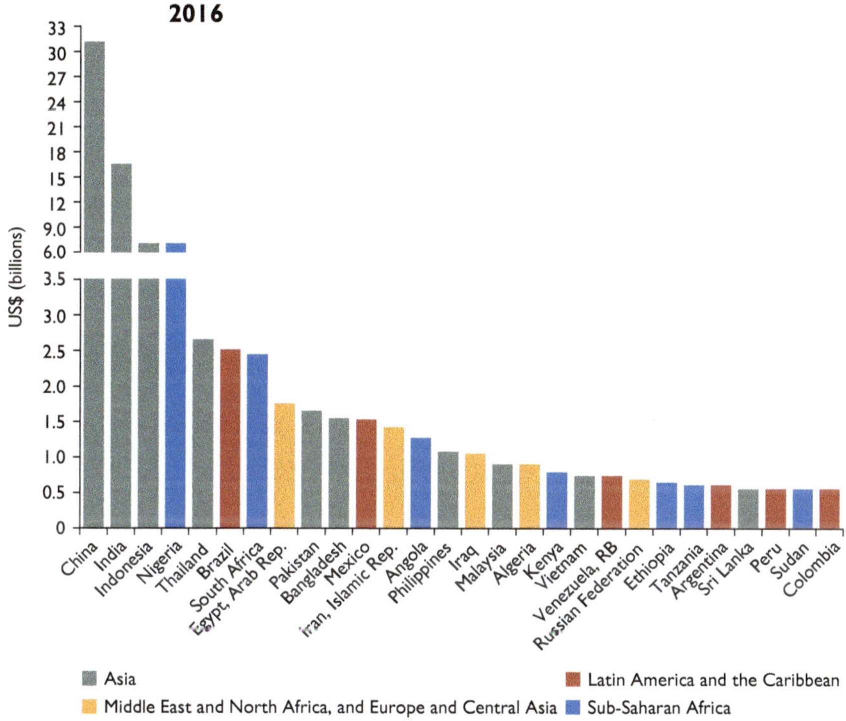

Source: World Bank calculations.

Note: Calculated by multiplying unpublished 2010 Foodborne Disease Burden Epidemiology Reference Group country estimates for foodborne disease disability-adjusted life years by 2016 gross national income per capita estimates from the World Bank's World Development Indicators database.

Iraq, and South Africa). All countries with an FBD burden exceeding US$1 billion a year are lower- or upper-middle-income countries. A further thirteen countries have a burden of between US$500 million and US$1 billion, with all regions included in this group of countries.

To get a better sense of the burden of FBD in LMICs by level of economic development, figure 2.5 plots the loss of productivity as a proportion of total national food expenditures against income per capita. This ratio makes it possible to compare the economic burden of FBD across countries with different population sizes. The ratio was computed for 2010 since data on national food expenditures were not readily available for later years in many low-income countries. While countries, are quite widely scattered in figure 2.5, it is possible to discern a broad pattern in which the relative burden of FBD is highest in middle-income countries, where the processes of market transformation and diet transition are in full swing. The FBD burden is lower in countries with higher levels of income per capita, which is broadly in line with the food

FIGURE 2.5 Relative Burden of Foodborne Disease, by per Capita Income, 2010

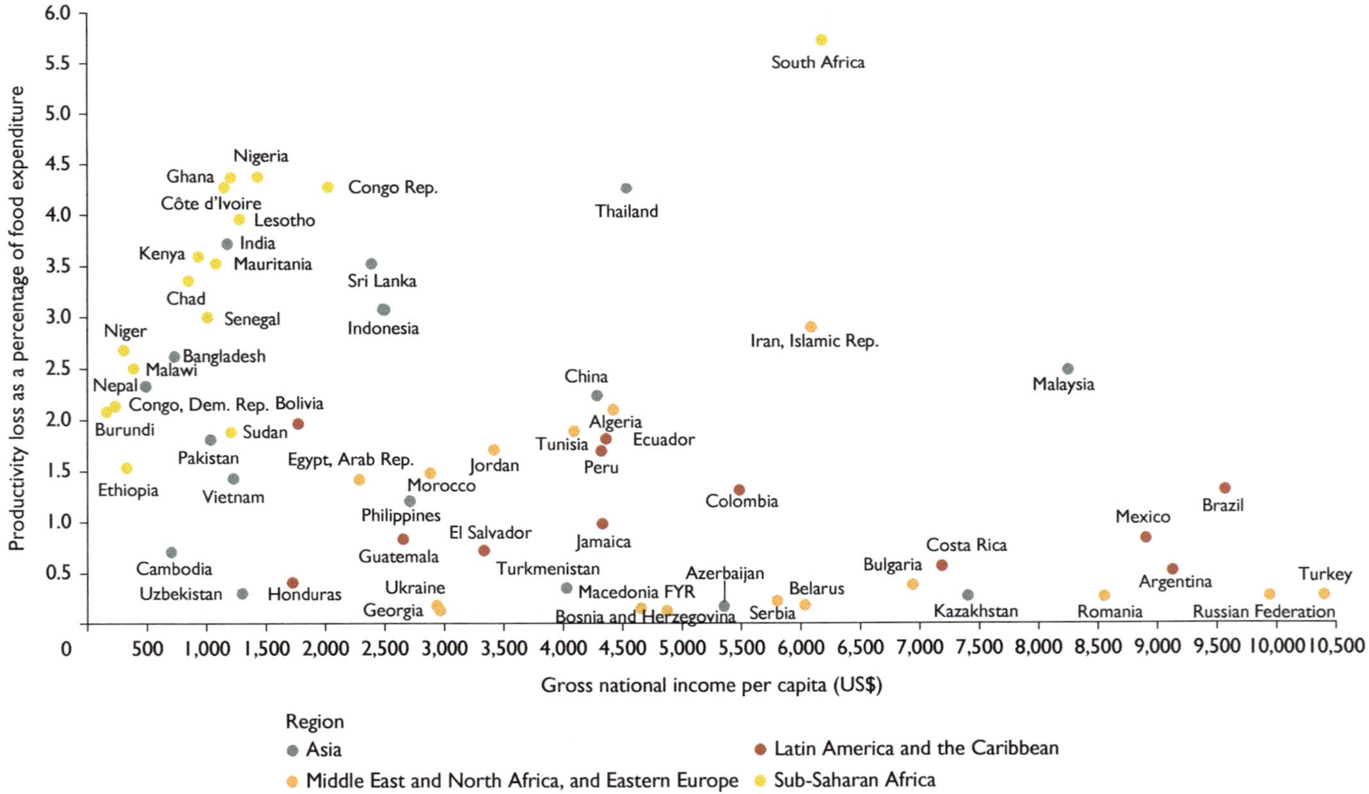

Source: World Bank calculations.

safety life cycle described earlier. Figure 2.5 does not show the relative burden of FBD in high-income countries, which tends to be 1 percent or smaller. For example, the estimated ratio is 0.96 percent for the United States, 0.88 percent for Canada, and 0.48 percent for Japan.

Beyond the broad estimates of productivity loss associated with FBD presented here, there are few estimates of the burden on LMICs. Notable exceptions include more in-depth economic analyses of specific countries, including India (Kristkova, Grace, and Kuiper 2017) and Indonesia (On 2016). In the analysis of India, 100 million cases of FBD were estimated in 2011. The total impact on gross domestic product of avoiding these cases of FBD in India is estimated at 0.5 percent, equivalent to an annual recurring benefit of US$28 billion. This amounts to about US$160 per case.[9]

A small number of cost-of-illness studies that aim to document the actual costs incurred—for example, medical treatment and out-of-pocket expenses—also provide evidence on the economic burden of FBD. Kristkova, Grace, and Kuiper (2017), in a study of FBD in India, estimate these costs at US$20 per case, implying a total cost of US$2 billion. Other cost-of-illness estimates include ILRI (2011) for diarrhea attributable to food in Nigeria (US$10 per case) and Ethiopia (US$40 per case) (Grace et al. 2018). For *shigellosis* in China, Guh et al. (2008) estimate US$28 per case. Although these studies use different methods and provide differing estimates, there is a convergence at about US$27 per case. This can be used to derive a very approximate cost-of-illness estimate for FBD in LMICs of US$15.1 billion, using FERG's estimate of 558 million cases for these countries in 2010. If the "human capital loss" estimate is added to this, the estimate for the public health burden of FBD for LMICs is $110.2 billion.

FOOD SAFETY RISKS IN LMIC DOMESTIC MARKETS

The data just presented give a picture of the aggregate burden of FBD in LMICs for regional and country income groupings and for individual countries. FBD is clearly a heavy burden on LMICs, though the nature and magnitude of this burden varies significantly among countries, most notably with the level of a country's economic development. Such broad trends, however, reflect—and can act to obscure—variations in food safety risks within countries. For example, there are variations across different foods, between rural and urban areas, and within informal and formal agri-food sectors. Identifying where major food safety problems exist in LMICs, and how these vary over time in line with economic development, is essential for developing and implementing strategies to reduce the burden of FBD.

The agri-food systems of LMICs, and especially middle-income countries, are characterized by the rapid evolution of businesses operating in the

[9] Importantly, these benefits are based on a general equilibrium model that takes account of the multiplier effects of the various economic flows created by the avoidance of FBD.

production, processing, and marketing of food and the structure and modus operandi of value chains. Such changes are closely aligned and interrelated with the progressive diversification of diets and with the increased consumption of animal-based foods, fruit and vegetables, and processed foods. Systems for the management of food safety also evolve, although, as chapter 3 shows, these are typically outpaced by the transformation of agri-food systems. This amalgam of changes is a critical driver of the incidence of FBD and the associated economic burden on LMICs.

Despite the progressive modernization of agri-food systems in LMICs, traditional sectors in many of these countries continue to predominate in the production, processing, and marketing of food (Gomez and Ricketts 2013), especially fresh food. In Sub-Saharan Africa, for example, 85–95 percent of the market demand for food is serviced by informal markets (Tschirley et al. 2010). In Vietnam, 97 percent of pork is bought in traditional wet markets; and in Malaysia, where the supermarket sector is much more developed, most meat is sourced from traditional markets (Chamhuri and Batt 2013). Indeed, in many low- and lower-middle-income countries, traditional marketing systems will likely remain the norm for years (Minot et al. 2015; World Bank 2016; Ortega and Tschirley 2017). For Sub-Saharan Africa, the proportion of food bought through the informal sector is expected only to decline to 50–70 percent by 2040 (Tschirley et al. 2014).

Street food is a dominant facet of traditional informal food markets in LMICs. This is food prepared and/or sold by vendors in public places that require no further preparation before consumption. In many Sub-Saharan Africa, street food accounts for over 50 percent of food intake (Steyn et al. 2014), and it is estimated that 2.5 billion people in LMICs eat street food daily (Fellows and Hilmi 2011). The preparation and sale of street food are also a significant source of employment, especially among the poor and for women.

Street food is typically prepared and sold around places of work, schools, hospitals, and transportation hubs, and in local markets. This raises concerns about the safety of street food, reflecting the insanitary conditions in which it is often prepared and sold. The literature on risk factors associated with street food includes Choudhury et al. 2011, Ababio and Lowatt 2015, Sezgin and Şanlıer 2016, and Johnson et al. 2015. The risk factors include:

- Inappropriate and unhygienic locations and surroundings, as vendors target high human-traffic areas that may be exposed to airborne chemicals in dust and vehicle exhaust fumes.
- Low-quality raw materials being bought in open air markets.
- Methods of transportation of food and ingredients, especially inner-city movements of meat and animal carcasses by carts, motor bikes, and on bus rooftops.
- Poor design and construction of street food carts, especially the work surfaces, which inhibit cleanliness and thereby harbor microorganisms.

- Unclean places of preparation—including surfaces, equipment, and utensils—whether at the vending site or in the home, where condiments may be prepared ahead of time.
- Use of contaminated water and ice when noncontaminated sources are not available.
- Use of nondisposable plates, cups, and cutlery.
- Lack of knowledge on temperature control; this is especially problematic when time gaps between food preparation and consumption are long.
- Poor storage practices, including the disposal of leftovers and waste management (most street vendors do not have access to refrigeration).
- Poor personal hygiene practices, either due to a lack of knowledge or a lack of nearby hygienic facilities.
- Low awareness of chemical and microbial contamination.

Comprehensive national or multicountry studies of the safety of street foods are lacking. But the evidence from small-scale studies of street food suggest worryingly high bacterial contamination levels in ready-to-eat food in LMICs (Paudyal et al. 2017; Alimi 2016).[10] Certain street foods are lower risk; for example, those fried immediately before consumption or food that is very salty, sweet, or acidic. Bacterial growth is also minimized when the time between preparation and consumption is short. These exceptions notwithstanding, studies show that street food vendors in LMICs are typified by poor food safety conditions and practices.

In Brazil, Cortese et al. (2016) found that 100 percent of street food vendors in Florianopolis had no access to a water supply, and 12 percent lacked proper cold holding during transport. Twelve percent did not provide ice, 95 percent did not wash their hands, and 91 percent did not have hair covering. Alves da Silva et al. (2014) found that only 38 percent of street vendors in Bahia, Brazil, kept perishable foods in cooling containers, 23 percent did not sanitize their hands, and 80 percent handled food and money simultaneously. In Uganda, Muyanja et al. (2011) found that street food vendors operated in locations with poor hygiene and that, although they tended to be aware of hygienic practices, they did not follow them. The authors concluded that the provision of sanitary facilities at vending sites and vendor education was needed to improve the food safety conditions at the sites under study. Gadaga et al. (2008) found hygienic practices of food vendors in Harare were lacking, and that facilities at vending sites were typically inadequate for safe food handling operations.

Traditional food markets in LMICs extend, of course, well beyond street food to include wet markets for fresh produce, and informal and formal micro and small enterprises engaged in animal slaughtering and processing

[10] The findings include high levels of microbial pathogens in street-vended salads and gravies in Johannesburg (Kubheka, Mosupye, and Holy 2001); salads and traditional fermented foods in Ghana (Mensah et al. 2002); and chicken in Guatemala (Jarquin, Alvaraz, and Morales 2015) and Vietnam (Ta et al. 2012; Nguyen et al. 2018).

animal- and plant-based foods. The safety of this food is potentially a very significant issue for LMICs because much of it is associated with recognized microbiological and other food-based hazards (for example, meat, fish, and milk-based foods). While the literature is not conclusive on this subject, there is evidence that food safety practices in these areas tend to be weak (Macheka et al. 2013; Wambui et al. 2016), and that the incidence of foodborne pathogens can be significant (Chahed et al. 2006; Beneduce et al. 2008; Elgroud et al. 2009; Grace et al. 2011; Nguyen-Viet et al. 2013; Doyle et al. 2015).

Some of these risks can be mitigated by the food preparation and consumption practices of consumers. For example, milk bought from informal vendors is generally boiled before consumption, which minimizes exposure to microbial pathogens (Grace et al. 2008; Makita et al. 2010). Pork from traditional markets in Vietnam is generally cooked very soon after being bought, with time enough to kill most foodborne pathogens (Lapar et al. 2014). In other cases, consumer preparation practices may not be effective in mitigating food safety risks, as in India and parts of Sub-Saharan Africa, where milk is fermented before consumption (Johnson et al. 2015).

It is reasonable to expect that, everything else being equal, the progressive formalization of the agri-food sector will bring about improvements in food safety management practices and capacity. Formal enterprises will tend to process and handle foods in better physical condition, have access to a reliable supply of safe drinking water, and use refrigeration (and have a reliable supply of electricity for this). Furthermore, as food businesses begin to package and brand their products, there are growing market-based incentives to manage food safety effectively. Formalization will make the agri-food system more amenable to regulation. And formal sector and larger businesses should be able to have access to the financial and technical resources to implement and upgrade food safety management systems.

Formalization, however, does not automatically translate into better food safety outcomes.[11] Changes in supply chains, larger facilities, and more modern production techniques must be accompanied by the appropriate management of risks, which will change as supply chains evolve. Investments in physical and human capital will also be needed to manage these risks. Even in more advanced food safety systems, lapses and high-profile outbreaks occur, as illustrated by the outbreak of *listeriosis* in South Africa in 2017[12] and the publication of studies

[11] Several studies highlight circumstances where food sold though formal sector marketing channels was no safer than food sold in the informal sector. Roesel and Grace (2014) report that in Mozambique, levels of microbial pathogens were lower in poultry bought from live bird markets than from formal sector abattoirs; in Kenya, the microbiological quality of beef from a typical local slaughterhouse was no greater than in beef from an improved slaughterhouse selling to supermarkets; and in Assam, India, little or no difference was found in rates of compliance with food safety standards in formal and informal milk value chains.

[12] For a report on the *listeriosis* outbreak, see https://www.reuters.com/article/us-listeria-tiger-brands/south-africa -blames-food-firms-for-worlds-worst-listeria-outbreak-idUSKBN1GH0S9.

showing a much higher rate of product recalls in recent years in the United States and other Organisation for Economic Cooperation and Development countries.[13] But it is not clear whether the rise in product recalls stems from more frequent lapses or—quite the opposite—from improved laws, hazard detection, and product traceability; in other words, from enhanced capacities.

A key characteristic of the transformation of agri-food systems in LMICs is the extension of value chains, both geographically and in the number of participants. These changes reflect the growing distance between the locations of production and consumption, accompanying progressive urbanization and the increasing transformation of food that goes with the rising consumption of processed foods. Many modern value chains involve a "bulking" step, whereby foods are aggregated for transportation, storage, and processing. Examples include chilling tanks for milk, abattoirs for meat, and mills for cereals. Several studies from LMICs indicate that bulking steps in value chains can be a source of contamination.[14] In this way, the transformation of the agri-food system in line with economic development presents new food safety problems. And if these are not effectively managed, the burden of FBD can grow, as in the rapid upward slope of the food safety life cycle in the transitioning stage depicted in figure 1.2 in chapter 1.

Food fraud is a particular food safety problem associated with the modernization of agri-food systems in LMICs, especially adulteration and tampering.[15] Zhang and Xue (2016) suggest that economically motivated food fraud and adulteration is a growing problem in China. There is also evidence of food adulteration in other LMICs. Handford, Campbell, and Elliott (2016) show how milk is frequently the target of adulteration and other forms of fraud in many LMIC because of its high value and the rapid growth in demand for milk. Souza et al. (2011) found that all samples of UHT milk examined in their study in Brazil contained at least one adulterant; 44 percent of samples, for example, were found to contain formaldehyde. Adulteration is not only linked to food produced domestically but also imports. Six percent of milk powder sampled in Dar-es-Salaam, Tanzania, was found to be contaminated with melamine (Schoder 2010). Food can also be contaminated with ingredients that are used

---

[13] For more information on these recalls, see http://www.foodsafetynews.com/2018/04/better-tests-stronger-laws-more-foods-add-up-to-more-recalls/ and https://www.ncbi.nlm.nih.gov/pmc/articles /PMC5201 359/.

[14] For Burkina Faso, Millogo et al. (2010) found that the total bacteria count of milk is lower at the point of production than further along the value chain, suggesting that contamination occurs post-farm-gate and further along the distribution system. A study in Ghana examining the safety of tomatoes before and after milling found that milling increased contamination (Sinayobye and Saalia 2011).

[15] There are many different types of food fraud, and some do not affect food safety, although they have potentially serious impacts on commercial activity. For example, about 20 percent of all fish sold worldwide is estimated to be mislabeled. This often involves less-valuable fish as the fraud is often difficult to detect after filleting. A more specific example is the horsemeat scandal in 2013, when beef sold in Ireland, Germany, and the United Kingdom was found to contain horsemeat from Romania.

purposefully—including food additives, pesticides, and veterinary drugs—but are found at levels that can be injurious to human health. For example, a meta-analysis of studies of acute food poisoning in China found that 10 percent of incidents were related to food additives, accounting for only 3 percent of illnesses but 12 percent of deaths (Xue and Zhang 2013).

THE COSTS OF DOMESTIC FOOD SAFETY FAILURES

Appreciable costs can be imposed on consumers, food businesses, and governments when large-scale food failures occur, and especially where these result in significant cases of FBD as part of an outbreak (table 2.2). In the aggregate, these costs can also be considerable for the economy. The findings from studies of food safety failures in developing countries are in line with the many studies in high-income countries that show how consumers avoid products involved in safety failures. Estimates of the effect of media reports on bacterial contamination of meat in the United States show a modest impact on consumer demand of 1–3 percent of total sales (Lusk and Schroeder 2002; Piggott and Marsh 2004). Similar modest effects were found for the widely publicized recall of peanut butter in the United States in 2007 (Bakhtavoryan, Capps, and Salin 2014). So, while consumer responses to food safety incidents can be dramatic in the short term, the impact on demand tends to taper off over time (Burton, Young, and Cromb 1999; Piggott and Marsh 2004).

In settings where regulatory capacity and associated consumer confidence are high, this is arguably a rational response to the belief that corrective action will be taken and the hazard quickly brought under control. In some cases, however, consumer responses to food safety failures are more dramatic and longer term. Examples of this include the effect on U.S. consumer demand for fresh spinach after an outbreak of *E. coli* in 2005 (Arnade, Calvin, and Kuchler 2009) and U.K. consumer demand for beef after an outbreak of bovine spongiform encephalopathy in the 1990s (Burton, Young, and Cromb 1999). In these and similar cases, consumers clearly lacked trust in food safety management systems and the outbreak was enough to erode any trust that hitherto existed.[16]

Food safety failures can impose significant costs on businesses and industries. These include loss of sales as consumers eliminate foods perceived to be risky and substitute for alternatives, erosion of firm equity, and even the complete loss of business at the firm or market level. Businesses can also face the risk and associated costs of legal action by regulators and private litigation

[16] Risk perception often drives consumer response. In contrast to experts, who tend to base their judgments of risk on the number of mortalities or years lost to illness for a given level of exposure to a hazard, the assessments of the general public are driven by a complex array of factors, including how familiar the hazard is, the level of perceived control, and how potentially catastrophic the consequences might be—no matter how low the probability of these consequences (Slovic 1987). For example, consumers tend to be more concerned about genetically modified organisms and hormones and less concerned about microbial pathogens, even though the objective risks from the latter are much greater (Lusk and Murray 2014).

TABLE 2.2 Potential Market and Economy Costs from Food Safety Problems

Economic unit affected	Types of costs incurred when food safety failures occur	Distribution of costs	Market incentives or regulatory enforcement for food safety	Variations by development level
Consumer	Consumers seek substitutes, limit consumption. May pay higher food prices or incur avoidance costs. May influence dietary patterns with negative nutritional consequences.	Foodborne illness is a greater burden on poor people and children. Both acute and chronic illnesses will reduce labor productivity and incomes.	Consumers may not always identify source of hazard and, as a result, may not be able to avoid them. Consumers will look to certification, media reports, public sector for guidance.	Consumer awareness and access to good information about hazard avoidance will be limited in low-income countries. Information improves with urbanization, but this may not always be reliable. Good evidence for public health burden; mixed evidence on willingness to pay.
Firm	Lower price for products, loss of both domestic and export markets, loss of firm equity and brand reputation, firm failure. Mitigation may require new investments and recurring costs, including certification.	Small firms may evade detection and impact more likely for larger firms. Per unit costs of mitigation likely higher for small firms.	Consumers shun firm or accept product only with lower price. Export markets may be closed. Formal sector buyers require certification. Regulators impose fines or recall products. Equity prices decline.	Unlikely to be detected at low-income levels, except in limited way in informal markets. Buyer incentives more likely as markets urbanize. Export market failures can occur at any income level. Firm equity impacts only in high-income countries with larger firms.
Industry	Loss of product reputation is a cost to all firms, even good actors. Lower price or loss of market share relative to substitute products or import suppliers. Loss of export markets or diversion to lower-price markets. Limited market expansion.	Firm failure for those unable to comply leads to change in industry structure as smallholders more likely to have higher costs of compliance.	Consumers shun domestic product, make substitutions, or accept only at lower price. Export markets may require special certification or approval. Regulators may impose new requirements for entire industry with additional costs. Formal sector may impose certification requirements.	More likely as markets develop and regulators discover problems, which are then reported in the media. More likely if product is also exported, as problems in meeting high-income standards become known.
Food sector	Limited expansion of supply for products associated with failures, with resulting losses for producers.	May bias sector development toward processed or imported products. May bias food safety investments toward high-value exports with little spillover for domestic quality.	Incentives are subtler at this level, and these effects would only appear over time.	More likely to be experienced as countries pass through the middle-income stage of market development.
Economy	Limited food sector development, especially processing and high-value exports. Burden of foodborne illness reduces labor productivity and output across all sectors. Increased food imports and/or reduced exports reduce government revenues.	May limit opportunity for smallholders, women in food processing. May skew direction of structural transformation in agriculture and food with possible negative consequences for income distribution.	Incentives subtler and shift toward fewer high-risk commodities in production and consumption would occur over a long time. Food trade balance impacts also likely to accrue slowly over time. Burden of foodborne illness often hidden and impacts of better health on productivity are hard to measure.	Public health burden hidden but likely more significant at low-income levels. Consequences for structural transformation emerge as countries pass through the middle-income stage.

Source: World Bank.

by victims and their families. Importantly, the costs of food scares unravel in unpredictable ways as the facts surface and different patterns of organizational and consumer behavior occur. In some cases, the distribution costs of food safety failures are poorly aligned with those who are primarily responsible.

While incidents of food safety failure are relatively common in LMICs, their costs and broader ramifications are much less well understood than comparable failures in industrial countries.[17] The best documented cases tend to involve multinational food businesses; examples include sales of outdated Yum Brand meat in China (2012) and high levels of lead in Maggi noodles in India (2015). The Chinese melamine milk scandal of 2008 is also well documented (Wang and Saghaian 2013; Xiu and Klein 2010; Pei et al. 2011), a reflection in part that milk products contaminated with melamine entered international trade. Indeed, some of the better documented cases of more generalized food safety failures in LMICs are in the context of agri-food exports (boxes 2.5 and 2.6)

Impacts of food safety failures by sector or economy are less well documented, even in industrial countries. The limited evidence that exists, however, suggests there are often long-term structural outcomes from persistent food safety failures. The lack of quality certification for infant weaning foods in West Africa, for example, biased consumers toward imported products despite the availability of nutritious and less expensive local substitutes (Masters and Sanogo 2002). Conversely, evidence shows that the contamination of milk products with melamine in China did not drive consumers toward imported products in the longer term (Qiao, Guo, and Klein 2010).

Some evidence of persistent and more generalized structural change in the growing middle-class demand for food safety is found in China. The dairy industry provides insights into the extensive market changes in response to the milk contamination scandal in 2008, and subsequent incidents in 2010. The government reacted to the scandal by instituting new marketing regulations for the industry and promoting centralized dairy production facilities (Jia et al. 2014). These efforts, as well as slumping consumer demand, reshaped marketing channels, with roughly half of milk collection centers going out of business and many smallholders left without market outlets. From this, new models for organizing production and processing emerged, which provided greater oversight and quality control through strengthened vertical coordination (Wang, Chen, and Klein 2015; Jia et al 2014). Another dimension of the market response was the growth in demand for UHT milk, which is seen as providing more reliable quality and safety (Ortega et al. 2012). As a processed branded product, UHT milk allows firms to develop brand reputation and capture returns to better and more reliable quality, but this requires reliable product certification. The dairy market changes adopted in China show how food safety can shape market development and concentration, as well as certified product demand.

[17] Green (2016) reviewed some 900 news articles and other publications on 30 food scares in LMICs from 2000 to 2016 and found only four to be of high quality in terms of providing rigorous evidence of impacts.

BOX 2.5 Sudan Red Dye in Chili Powder from India

The 2005 Sudan Red scandal illustrates the broad ramifications that a food contamination incident can have when food is exported for use as an ingredient in a variety of processed foods. The scandal was triggered when an industrial dye known as Sudan Red was discovered in a batch of Crosse & Blackwell Worcestershire Sauce, then a brand of British food manufacturer Premier Foods.

The industrial dye—normally used in waxes, solvents, polishes, leathers, and fabrics—proved to be carcinogenic when ingested in large or chronic doses in animal studies. Its discovery in a range of branded food products led the British food safety agency to recall several hundred products, which included prepared sausages, noodles, salad dressings, and sauces, many of which used Worcestershire Sauce as an ingredient.

The dye's presence in these food products was traced back to chili powder from India. Unscrupulous spice producers looking to cut production costs allegedly used the dye to restore their chili powder to its characteristically red color after bulking it up with light-colored adulterants, such as stems, seeds, and light-colored pods.

In fact, the dye had already been detected in spice imports to Europe in 2001 (Tarantelli 2017). In 2003, Sudan Red was found in consignments of chili powder sent to France, prompting a much smaller-scale recall that led the Spices Board of India to temporarily suspend the export-registration certificates of five companies (Jaffee 2005). In the same year, the European Union (EU) issued a directive requiring all dried and crushed chili entering the EU to be certified free of Sudan Red, which had been prohibited in food since 1997. As the story unfolded it became clear that what had initially seemed like the misdeeds of a few rogue producers was a widespread problem. Indeed, over 2003–04, the dye was discovered in a growing number of shipments from numerous countries, including China, India, Pakistan, South Africa, the Syrian Arab Republic, and Turkey (Jaffee 2005).

Between 2001 and 2017, the discovery of Sudan Red dye in herbs and spices resulted in at least 429 notifications to the EU's Rapid Alert System for Food and Feed (Tarantelli 2017), though the number of notifications declined in the aftermath of the scandal (ranging from none to three a year since 2012).

In 2005, the widespread use of chilies—and Worcestershire Sauce—as ingredients in processed foods led to a surge in recalls of both, forcing a multitude of businesses across many countries, including restaurant chains with thousands of outlets, to withdraw products that likely contained trace amounts of the dye in sauce packets.

In China, 1,200 KFC outlets suspend menu items sold with affected sauces containing Sudan Red. Beijing's food safety office banned all flavoring products manufactured by the Heinz-Meiweiyuan Food Company after Sudan Red was detected in its pepper sauce (Xinhua News Agency 2005). A wholly owned subsidiary of the South African restaurant chain Nando's Chickenland claimed that it had suffered about US$1 million in costs and damages when its bottled sauces were found to contain Sudan Red, leading to a worldwide recall in 2004.

In all, the recall was estimated to have cost US$150 million (Peter 2012). Overall, costs to the food industry worldwide were estimated to over US$220 million in lost sales, inventory destruction, management and consultants' time, and brand damage.

BOX 2.6 Brazil's Tainted Meat Scandal

A scandal involving some of largest meat processors in Brazil and the world, including JBS and BRF, erupted in 2017, when a federal police investigation pointed to employees of these companies bribing ministry inspectors to approve outdated and adulted products for sale and export. In all, 21 companies were involved in Brazil's tainted meant scandal.

No cases of poisoning were linked to the scandal, despite police reports that flour and cardboard were added to sausages and cold cuts and that the smell of spoilage was masked by chemicals in some cases. The two-year investigation, triggered by a whistleblower, led to hundreds of raids across six Brazilian states and Brasília as part of Operation Weak Meat. Brazil's Ministry of Agriculture, which suspended 33 officials as part of the affair, regarded the incidents as isolated.

The fallout on Brazil's meat exports and reputation was significant. Brazil annually exports over US$12 billion in meat to about 150 countries, accounting for 40 percent of world chicken exports and 20 percent of beef exports. The tainted meat scandal resulted in importers and authorities in Chile, China, the European Union, Japan, the Republic of Korea, Mexico, and South Africa, among other countries, rejecting Brazilian meat shipments and temporarily suspending meat imports from the country, putting perishable products in jeopardy.

According to Bloomberg News (2017), "Chilled meat needs to get from meatpacker to consumer in about 70 days and meat shipped from Brazil uses more than half that time at sea, according to Asian shippers. Inspection times at the receiving port are usually four or five days, but can take two weeks for a thorough examination. Agricultural products that do not pass customs inspections are typically burned at the port, the shippers said."

The full economic impact of the scandal has yet to be determined. One estimate of the cost for Brazil's meat processing industry is US$3.5 billion in lost export revenues, equivalent to 0.2 percent of the country's gross domestic product.

Source: This account of Brazil's tainted meat scandal draws on Reeves 2017; Freitas and Batista 2017; Freitas, Singh, and Gilbert 2017; Freitas and Freitas 2017; Associated Press 2017; and Bloomberg News 2017.

THE COSTS OF FOOD SAFETY FAILURES IN TRADE

Beyond the burden of FBD, food safety is a critical factor affecting the agri-food trade performance of LMICs, with important consequences for formal sector businesses, employment, and incomes. A significant body of literature shows the influence of food safety requirements on agri-food exports. While much of this literature focuses on exports from industrial countries, a growing body of research shows the importance of compliance with food safety regulations and standards for the trade performance of LMICs.

Broadly, these studies show that effectively competing in international agri-food trade may entail considerable compliance costs for the public and private sectors to meet the requirements of food safety regulations or standards in export markets. While this is a well-established issue with exports to industrial countries, compliance with food safety requirements is also becoming the norm for trade between LMICs. The size of these costs is clearly an issue for export competitiveness and is affected by multiple factors, including firm and industry size, the gap between food safety management capacity and the capacity required for compliance with export market requirements, and levels of collective action between exporting firms (World Bank 2005). Such a consolidation occurred in the Indian fish processing industry in the early 2000s after the EU imposed restrictions on the industry's exports.

The fixed costs of meeting stricter food safety requirements in export markets tend to favor established exporters (Anders and Caswell 2009). Food safety challenges generally reenforce or accentuate the broader set of competitive strengths and weaknesses of industries and firms. In some cases, "trade losses" attributed to noncompliance with more stringent standards are more accurately attributable to more entrenched and longer-term competitiveness issues within businesses and sectors (Diaz Rios and Jaffee 2008).

Countries, and businesses and sectors within countries, with lower levels of food safety management capacity often struggle to get into potentially lucrative high-value exports markets. And then there is the specter of exclusion from these markets as food safety requirements are enhanced or when food safety failures occur (Beghin and Orden 2012).[18] Stricter food safety regulations and standards are often portrayed as nontariff barriers to trade. But these can act as powerful catalysts for investments in improved food safety management systems, especially when incentives for these investments are lacking in domestic markets (Jaffee and Henson 2004). The economic returns from these investments, however, are sensitive to the way in which they are made. Significant benefits can come from upgrading food safety management capacity as part of longer-term and strategic efforts to enhance export performance. But they tend to be less beneficial when made as a reaction to immediate crises, such as the loss of a key export market (World Bank 2005).[19]

Some studies have examined the impact of specific and highly publicized food safety events on LMICs export markets. Examples include restrictions on fish and fishery products imported into the EU imposed on Bangladesh, China, and Kenya, among other countries; and U.S. restrictions on raspberry imports

[18] For agri-food products, it is more commonly the case that binding make-or-break constraints are associated with phytosanitary and animal disease issues rather than food safety compliance. It is common for countries to apply absolute restrictions on imports of fresh fruit and vegetables, plants, animal products, and live animals on the basis of the presence of quarantine plant pests and animal diseases, and the absence of adequate information on or effective controls for these pests and diseases. For example, only 28 non–EU member countries are permitted to supply meat products to the EU. Of these, 12 are high-income countries, 15 are upper-middle-income countries, and one is a lower middle-income country.

[19] For example, through case studies on the aquatic products and horticultural sectors, Henson and Jaffee (2008) show that while many LMICs (and export businesses in these countries) tend to upgrade food safety capacity in a reactive mode, those that benefit most make these investments preemptively and as market leaders.

from Guatemala. There is evidence that significant losses were incurred by the sectors affected by these restrictions (Cato and Subasinge 2003; Henson and Mitullah 2004; Calvin et al. 2002; Alavi 2009). In each of these cases, significant investments to upgrade food safety management systems were made in response. Although these investments were successful at regaining market access, not all export businesses survived, and the value of trade took a considerable time to recover. In general, businesses and sectors caught up in high-profile food safety failures, when trade is banned or restricted and strict timelines are set for upgrading food safety management systems, tend to see a heavy consolidation of exports as smaller and less-established actors struggle to upgrade. Such a consolidation followed the EU's restrictions on the industry's exports (Henson, Saqib, and Rajasenan 2004).

Compliance with export market food safety regulations and standards can also bring about changes in the structure and modus operandi of agri-food value chains. In some cases, these changes are a direct and necessary part of upgrading food safety management systems to achieve compliance. For example, for Indian shrimp exporters to comply with EU hygiene requirements, the outsourcing of shrimp peeling was prohibited, resulting in this step being centralized in industrial fish-processing operations (Henson, Saqib, and Rajasenan 2004). In other cases, value chains are restructured because compliance with food safety requirements is easier to achieve and less costly with more consolidated systems of production, processing, and distribution. Concerns have been raised that compliance with stricter food safety requirements might exclude smallholder farmers from value chains for high-value agri-food exports, such as fresh fruit and vegetables. These concerns and the broader issue of smallholder farmer compliance with standards are discussed in chapter 3.

It is probably not possible to know with any certainty the degree to which agri-food exports from LMICs are adversely affected by the challenges of compliance with food safety requirements for export markets or by food safety failures. While the degree to which exports decline because of these factors can be estimated, a nontrivial impact is the loss of potential trade from unrealized exports as a result of firms being deterred from entering a market on concerns that they cannot comply with food safety requirements or that the costs of compliance would erode their competitiveness. In other words, there are certainly cases in which food safety requirements act as a "barrier" to potential trade. It is reasonable to expect that this scenario most commonly applies to smaller and less established enterprises. This then raises the question of whether food safety requirements are really the binding constraint or whether broader competitiveness challenges are the real issue.

The most commonly observed impact on trade from food safety requirements is the rejection of consignments of agri-food products during border inspections at destination export markets (Unnevehr 2007; Buzby, Unnevehr, and Roberts 2008; Baylis, Nogueira, and Pace 2010). While data on border rejections have several limitations, they do provide a picture of recurring issues on compliance with food safety requirements and how compliance issues vary across exporting countries and destinations, and over time.[20] For example, the United Nations Industrial Development Organization provides an analysis of food import rejections for Australia, the EU, Japan, and the United States from 2002 to 2013 (UNIDO 2015, 2017). This analysis has been updated for this report for the EU by examining border rejection data for 2014–16.

Most border rejections in industrial country markets are accounted for by a small number of countries and for recurring reasons. For example, U.S. border rejections are dominated by fresh fruit and vegetables from Mexico due to pesticide residues or adulteration, fish and seafood from China due to microbial pathogens or toxins, and spices from India due to microbial pathogens or toxins. U.S. border rejections of fish and seafood from LMICs due to microbial pathogens have been a persistent problem, but rejections due to veterinary drug residues have declined. Rejections of spices have increased, but rejections of fruit and vegetables from Mexico due to adulteration have declined (Bovay 2016).

A similar pattern of border rejections being dominated by a small number of countries and for recurring reasons can be seen in the EU. A notable recurring reason is the high level of rejections of nuts and nut products and dried fruit due to aflatoxin contamination, especially from the Islamic Republic of Iran (which has an ongoing problem controlling levels of aflatoxins in pistachios). Rejections of fish and fishery products have also been high in the EU, although rejection rates vary widely across exporting countries (figure 2.6). These rejections were due to noncompliance with hygiene requirements in the capture and processing of fish, and restrictions on antibiotic residues, predominantly in fish from aquaculture production. Rejection rates tend to be quite low for countries with income per capita below US$2,000, but the rates rise among countries with income per capita of US$3,000–US$6,000. Border rejections for fresh fruit and vegetables show a similar pattern, where the predominant issue is compliance with EU requirements for pesticide residues (figure 2.7).

A range of factors can explain the patterns of border rejections seen in figures 2.6 and 2.7. At lower income levels, exports from LMICs tend to be dominated by a small number of lead firms that find it easier to comply with strict export food safety requirements. Indeed, the ease and lower cost with which they can comply can be essential to their competitive advantage. As exports increase, however, new exporting firms emerge, many of which struggle to achieve compliance requirements, and they experience rejections of consignments in target export markets. These firms either achieve compliance or are excluded over time, and the sector in which they operate increasingly acts collectively to upgrade standards to achieve a reputation for food safety management. And because of these interventions, levels of border rejections decline.

[20] For example, border rejections only provide an indication of compliance challenges where trade occurs, and where compliance is assessed in the destination export market through the inspection of consignments at the point of entry. Furthermore, these data provide no indication of the challenges faced in complying with voluntary public or private standards.

FIGURE 2.6 Rejection Rates of Fish and Fishery Product Imports to the EU, by Lower-Middle-Income Countries, 2014–16

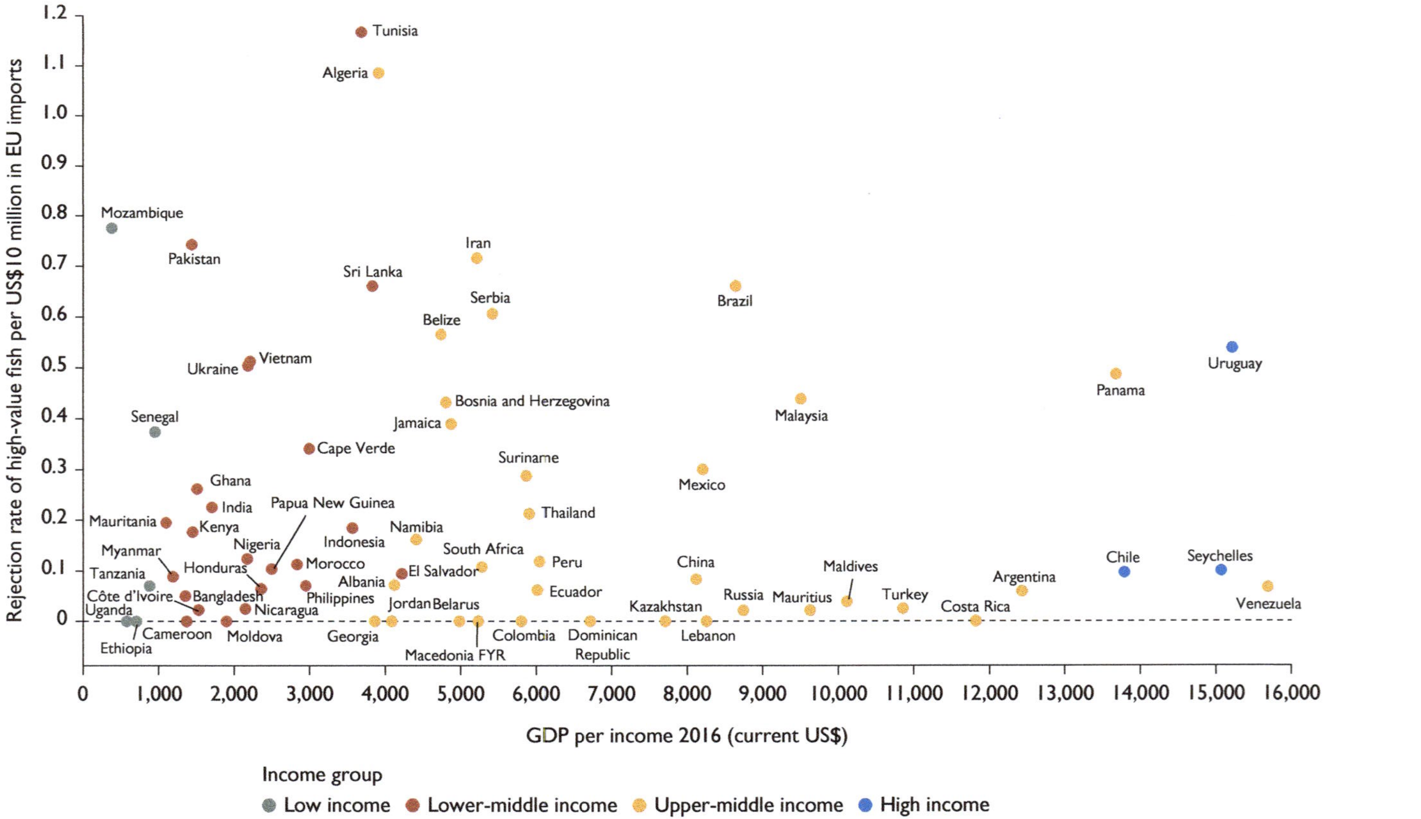

Source: World Bank, based on EU Rapid Alert System for Food and Feed and United Nations Comtrade data.

Note: The rejection rate by country is calculated as the 3-year sum of EU notifications for 2014–16 divided by the 3-year sum of fish and fishery products exports to the EU (in US$10 million) over the same period. The graph shows LMICs with exports of US$25 million or more; it excludes the Arab Republic of Egypt and Zimbabwe, with rejection rates of 3.9 and 18.9, respectively. EU = European Union.

FIGURE 2.7 Rejection Rates of Fresh Fruit and Vegetable Imports to the EU, by Low- and Middle-Income Countries, 2014–16

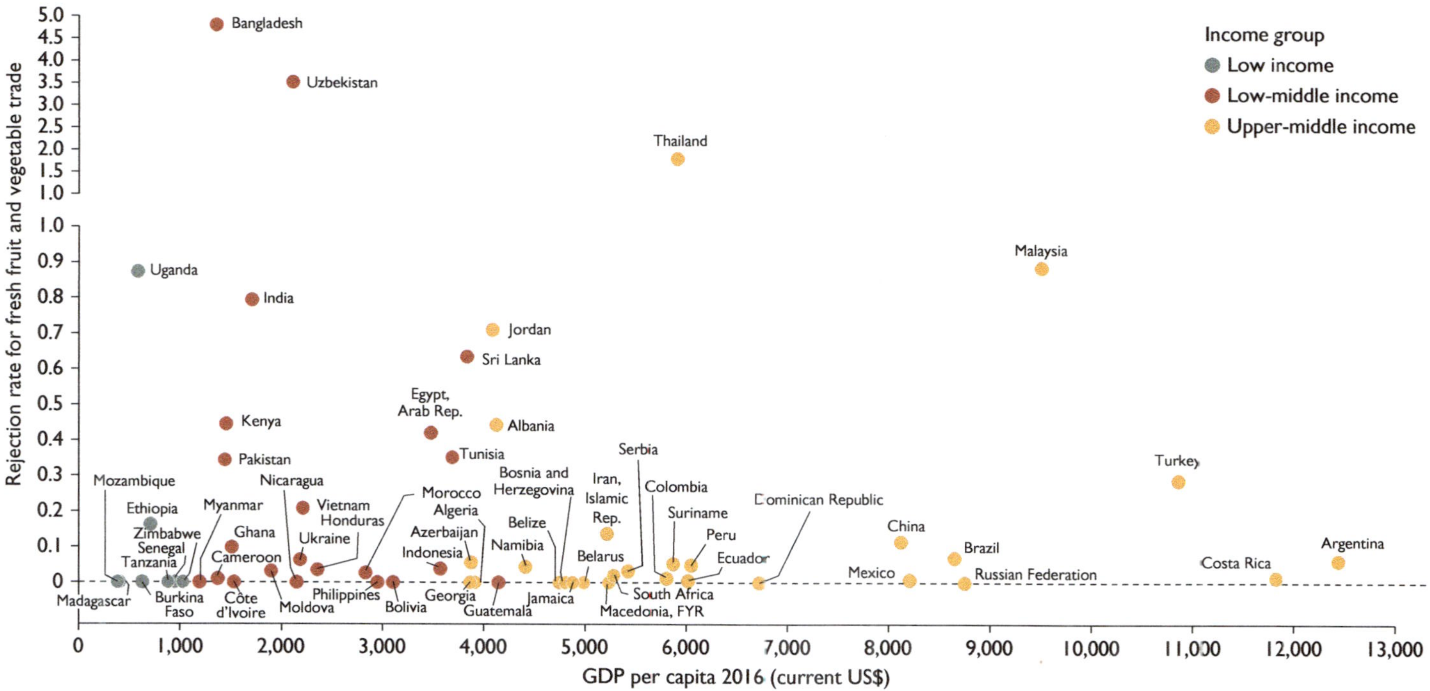

Source: World Bank, based on EU Rapid Alert System for Food and Feed and United Nations Comtrade data.

Note: The rejection rate by country is calculated as the 3-year sum of EU notifications for 2014–16 divided by the 3-year sum of fresh fruit and vegetable exports to the EU (in US$10 million) over the same period. The graph shows LMICs with exports valued at US$25 million or more. EU = European Union.

Beyond this general pattern, it is evident from rejections of fish and fishery products, and fresh fruit and vegetables, that some countries are outliers, which have much higher or lower levels of rejections than most countries at a similar level of development. These countries include Tunisia, which has had a much higher level of rejections of fish and fishery products than most lower-middle-income countries; and Thailand, which has had a much higher level of rejections of fresh fruit and vegetables than most upper-middle-income countries. Clearly, countries face local issues in trying to comply with export food safety requirements that may relate to sector size and structure, degree of cooperation between firms, and food safety management capacity within and across the public and private sectors.

The prominence of many leading LMIC exporters of high-value agri-food products in the border rejection data of the EU and United States suggests that these rejections are merely a bump in the road—or the cost of doing business—in these markets with their export businesses and sectors. Thus, these LMIC countries maintain access to these markets and continue to expand their exports—and, to an extent, they command dominant market shares in some cases. Each of the top ten LMIC suppliers of high-value foods to the EU experienced a reduction in their rate of rejections between 2010 and 2016. Overall, the proportion of LMIC food trade now impacted by border rejections is likely to be in the range of 0.5 to 1 percent in value terms—or about US$2 billion in the aggregate (given that LMIC total food exports and higher-value food safety-sensitive exports were US$475 billion and US$220 billion, respectively, in 2016). For some of the businesses and smaller industries that incur rejections, the costs (and reputation effects) can certainly be considerable—and, in extreme cases, catastrophic. But for many leading industries and larger businesses, the financial and commercial impacts of having some consignments destroyed, reconditioned, or rerouted are much less significant.

As noted earlier, these are not the full trade-related costs or losses associated with unsafe food. Concerns about the ability to comply with regulatory requirements and private standards, together with the financial risks of undertaking significant upfront investments in order to comply, may deter food manufacturers or trading companies from initiating exports in the first place. This deterrent effect probably affects more LMIC trade than actual consignment rejections. Yet, this is primarily a distributional issue rather than one of lost trade for LMICs in aggregate. Some smaller industries and businesses are deterred from exports, while others go ahead and capture those market opportunities. This seems to be what we are witnessing in global LMIC food trade. Food safety (and other sanitary and phytosanitary) challenges are accentuating underlying competitive advantages and disadvantages and contributing to the further consolidation of the LMIC trade in high-value foods.

SUMMARY

This chapter has provided evidence on the costs of food safety for public health, consumer welfare, industry viability, and market growth. Countries today have a better understanding of the public health burden and the nature of food safety risks in transforming food systems, and this is allowing estimates to be made of the productivity costs associated with food safety. Globally, these are annually at least $95 billion, with 28 countries having losses exceeding $500 million. In line with the food safety life cycle trajectory outlined in chapter 1, food safety costs are greatest as a share of food expenditures for lower-middle-income countries, showing the lag in food system capabilities during food market transformation in line with economic development.

In addition to this overall cost to developing counties, evidence is strong that food safety imposes costs on food consumers and the food industry, with possible consequences for market development. Consumers shift their consumption patterns in response to real or perceived risks, thereby increasing their own food costs or changing product selection, which has consequences for food producers. In international markets, potential losses of international sales—or the diversion of sales to lower-value markets—are also evident when food safety is inadequate, and these effects have persisted even as global trade has expanded. Taken together, domestic and international market forces in turn shape structural changes in the food sector, as consolidation takes place in response to perceived needs for better food safety management.

This analysis of costs shows that a lack of capacity to address food safety places burdens on public health, the food sector, and the economy as a whole. The next chapter examines the state of the public capacity to facilitate improved food safety management on several levels.

REFERENCES

Ababio, P. F., and P. Lovatt. 2015. "A Review on Food Safety and Food Hygiene Studies in Ghana." *Food Control* 47: 92–97.

Adak, G., S. Meakins, H. Yip, B. Lopman, and S. O'Brien. 2005. "Disease Risks from Floods, England and Wales, 1996–2000." *Emerging Infectious Diseases* 11 (3): 365–72.

Alavi, R. 2009. "Sanitary Standards in the EU: The Impact on Malaysian Fishing Industry." *Journal of Economic Cooperation and Development* 4: 51–85.

Alimi, B. 2016. "Risk Factors in Street Food Practices in Developing Countries: A Review." *Food Science and Human Wellness* 5 (3): 141–48.

Alves da Silva, S., R. de C. V. Cardoso, J. Â. W Góes, J. N. Santos, F. P. Ramos, R. Bispo de Jesus, R. Sabá do Vale, et al. 2014. "Street Food on the Coast of Salvador, Bahia, Brazil: A Study from the Socioeconomic and Food Safety Perspectives." *Food Control* 40 (June): 78–84. https://doi.org/10.1016/j.foodcont.2013.11.022.

Anders, S. M., and J. A. Caswell. 2009. "Standards as Barriers versus Standards as Catalysts: Assessing the Impact of HACCP Implementation on US Seafood Imports." *American Journal of Agricultural Economics* 91 (2): 310–21.

Arnade, C., L. Calvin, and F. Kuchler. 2009. "Consumer Response to a Food Safety Shock: The 2006 Food-Borne Illness Outbreak of E. coli O157: H7 Linked to Spinach." *Review of Agricultural Economics* 31 (4): 734–50. https://doi.org/10.1111/j.1467-9353.2009.01464.x.

Associated Press. 2017. "Brazil Meat Scandal Deepens as China, EU, Chile Bar Imports." March 20.

Bakhtavoryan, R., O. Capps Jr., and V. Salin. 2014. "The Impact of Food Safety Incidents across Brands: The Case of the Peter Pan Peanut Butter Recall." *Journal of Agricultural and Applied Economics* 46 (4): 559–73.

Baylis, K., L. Nogueira, and K. Pace. 2010. "Food Import Refusals: Evidence from the European Union." *American Journal Agricultural Economics* 93 (2): 566–72.

Beghin, J., and D. Orden. 2012. "NTMs, Agricultural and Food Trade, and Competitiveness." Special issue of *World Economy*.

Beneduce, L., G. Spano, A. Q. Nabi, F. Lamacchia, S. Massa, R. Aouni, and A. Hamama. 2008. "Occurrence and Characterization of Escherichia Coli O157 and Other Serotypes in Raw Meat Products in Morocco. *Journal of Food Protection* 71 (10): 2082–86. http://www.ncbi.nlm.nih.gov/pubmed/18939757.

Black, R. E., L. H. Allen, Z. A. Bhutta, L. E. Caulfield, M. de Onis, M. Ezzati, C. Mathers, et al. 2008. "Maternal and Child Undernutrition: Global and Regional Exposures and Health Consequences." *Lancet* 371 (9608): 243–260.

Bloomberg News. 2017. "Frozen Beef Stranded at Sea as China Shuts Out Brazil's Meat." Bloomberg.Com, March 22. https://www.bloomberg.com/news/articles/2017-03-22/frozen-beef-stranded-at-sea-after-china-shuts-out-brazil-s-meat.

Bovay, John. 2016. *FDA Refusals of Imported Food Products by Country and Category, 2005–2013, EIB-151*. Washington, DC: Department of Agriculture, Economic Research Service.

Burton M., T. Young, and R. Cromb. 1999. "Meat Consumers' Long-Term Response to Perceived Risks Associated with BSE in Great Britain." *Cahiers d'Économie et Sociologie Rurales* 50: 7–19.

Buzby, J., L. Unnevehr, and D. Roberts. 2008. "Food Safety and Imports: An Analysis of FDA Import Refusal Reports." USDA/ERS Economic Information Bulletin EIB-39, U.S. Department of Agriculture, Washington, DC.

Calvin, L., W. Foster, L. Solorzano, J. D. Mooney, L. Flores, and V. Barrios. 2002. "Response to a Food Safety Problem in Produce." In *Global Food Trade and Consumer Demand for Quality*, edited by B. Krissoff, M. Bohman, and J. A. Caswell. New York: Springer US.

Cato, J. C., and S. Subasinge. 2003. "Case Study: The Shrimp Export Industry in Bangladesh." 2020 Vision Briefs 10 No. 9, International Food Policy Research Institute, Washington, DC.

CDC (Centers for Disease Control and Prevention). 2018. Annual Summaries of Foodborne Outbreaks. https:// www.cdc.gov/fdoss/annual-reports/index.html.

Chahed, A., B. China, J. Mainil, and G. Daube. 2006. "Prevalence of Enterohaemorrhagic Escherichia Coli from Serotype O157 and Other Attaching and Effacing Escherichia Coli on Bovine Carcasses in Algeria." *Journal of Applied Microbiology* 101 (2): 361–68. https://doi.org/10.1111/j.1365-2672.2006.02954.x.

Chamhuri, N., and P. J. Batt. 2013. "Factors Influencing Consumers' Choice of Retail Stores for Fresh Meat in Malaysia." *International Food and Agribusiness Management Review* 16 (3): 99–122.

Checkley, W., G. Buckley, R. H. Gilman, A. M. Assis, R. L. Guerrant, S. S. Morris, K. Molbak, et al. 2008. "Multi-Country Analysis of the Effects of Diarrhoea on Childhood Stunting. *International Journal of Epidemiology* 37 (4): 816–30. https://doi.org/10.1093/ije/dyn099.

Choudhury, Manisha, Lipi Mahanta, Jayashree Goswami, Minakshi Mazumder, and Barnali Pegoo. 2011. "Socio-Economic Profile and Food Safety Knowledge and Practice of Street Food Vendors in the City of Guwahati, Assam, India." *Food Control* 22 (2): 196–203. https://doi.org/10.1016/j.foodcont.2010.06.020.

Cortese, R. D. M., M. B. Veiros, C. Feldman, and S. B. Cavalli. 2016. "Food Safety and Hygiene Practices of Vendors during the Chain of Street Food Production in Florianopolis, Brazil: A Cross-Sectional Study." *Food Control* 62 (April): 178–86. https://doi.org/10.1016/j.foodcont.2015.10.027.

Diaz Rios, L., and S. Jaffee. 2008. "Barrier, Catalyst or Distraction? Standards, Competitiveness and Africa's Groundnut Exports to Europe." Agriculture and Rural Development Discussion Paper 30, World Bank, Washington, DC.

Doyle, M. P., M. C. Erickson, W. Alali, J. Cannon, X. Deng, Y. Ortega, M. A. Smith, et al. 2015. "The Food Industry's Current and Future Role in Preventing Microbial Foodborne Illness within the United States." *Clinical Infectious Diseases* 61 (2): 252–59. https://doi.org/10.1093 /cid/civ253.

EFSA (European Food and Safety Authority). 2012. "Poultry Meat Inspection: EFSA Reviews Risks for Public Health." Press Release, June 28. http://www.efsa.europa.eu/en/press/news/120629.htm.

———. 2017. "The European Union Summary Report on Trends and Sources of Zoonoses, Zoonotic Agents and Food-Borne Outbreaks in 2016." *EFSA Journal* 15 (12).

Elgroud, R., F. Zerdoumi, M. Benazzouz, C. Bouzitouna-Bentchouala, S. A. Granier, S. Fremy, A. Brisabois, et al. 2009. "Characteristics of Salmonella Contamination of Broilers and Slaughterhouses in the Region of Constantine (Algeria)." *Zoonoses and Public Health* 56 (2): 84–93.

Fellows, P., and N. Hilmi. 2011 *Selling Street and Snack Foods*. Rome: Food and Agriculture Organization.

Feltes, M. M. C., A. P. Arisseto-Bragotto, and J. M. Block. 2017. "Food Quality, Food-Borne Diseases, and Food Safety in the Brazilian Food Industry." *Food Quality and Safety* 1 (1): 13–27. https://doi.org/10.1093/fqsafe/fyx003.

Freitas, Gerson, and Tatiana Freitas. 2017 "Brazilian Meat Giants Rush to Contain Scandal." Bloomberg.Com, March 20. https://www.bloomberg.com/news/articles/2017-03-20/brazil -meat-giants-appeal-to-family-in-rush-to-contain-scandal.

Freitas, Tatiana, and Fabiana Batista. (2017) "Why Brazil's Tainted-Meat Probe Worries the World: QuickTake Q&A." Bloomberg.Com, March 21.

Freitas, Tatiana, Shruti Singh, and Jonathan Gilbert. 2017. "Brazil's Tainted-Meat Probe Leaves World Hungry for Chicken." Bloomberg.Com, March 22.

Gadaga, T. H., B. K. Samende, C. Musuna, and D. Chibanda. 2008. "The Microbiological Quality of Informally Vended Foods in Harare, Zimbabwe." *Food Control* 19 (8): 829–32.

Global Burden of Disease. 2017a. "Global, Regional, and National Disability-Adjusted Life-Years (DALYs) for 333 Diseases and Injuries and Healthy Life Expectancy (HALE) for 195 Countries and Territories, 1990–2016: A Systematic Analysis for the Global Burden of Disease Study 2016." *Lancet* 390 (10100): 1260–344.

———. 2017b. "Global, Regional, and National Age-Sex Specific Mortality for 264 Causes of Death, 1980–2016: A Systematic Analysis for the Global Burden of Disease Study 2016." *Lancet* 390 (10100): 1151–210.

George, C. M., L. Oldja, S. K. Biswas, J. Perin, G. O. Lee, S. Ahmed, R. Haque, et al. 2015. "Fecal Markers of Environmental Enteropathy Are Associated with Animal Exposure and

Caregiver Hygiene in Bangladesh." *American Journal of Tropical Medicine and Hygiene* 93 (2): 269–75. doi:10.4269/ajtmh.14-0694.

Gomez, M., and K. Ricketts. 2013. "Food Value Chain Transformations in Developing Countries: Selected Hypotheses on Nutritional Implications." *Food Policy* 42 (October): 139–50.

Gong, Y., K. Cardwell, A. Hounsa, S. Egal, P. C. Turner, A. J. Hall, and C. P. Wild. 2002. "Dietary Aflatoxin Exposure and Impaired Growth in Young Children from Benin and Togo: Cross Sectional Study." *British Medical Journal* 325 (7354): 20–21.

Grace, D. 2015. *Food Safety in Developing Countries: An Overview.* London: U.K. Department for International Development.

Grace D., S. Alonso, F. Mutua, K. Roesel, J. Lindahl, and K. Amenu. 2018. *Food Safety Investment Expert Advice: Burkina Faso, Ethiopia, Nigeria.* Nairobi: International Livestock Research Institute.

Grace, D., J. Gilbert, M. L. Lapar, F. Unger, S. Fèvre, H. Nguyen-Viet, and E. Schelling. 2011. "Zoonotic Emerging Infectious Disease in Selected Countries in Southeast Asia: Insights from Ecohealth." *EcoHealth* 8 (1): 55–62.

Grace, D., G. Mahuku, V. Hoffmann, C. Atherstone, H. Upadhyaya, and R. Bandyopadhyay. 2015. "International Agricultural Research to Reduce Food Risks: Case Studies on Aflatoxins." *Food Security* 7 (3): 569–82.

Grace, D., A. O. Omore, T. Randolph, E. K. Kang'ethe, G. W. Nasinyama, and H. O. Mohammed. 2008. "Risk Assessment for Escherichia Coli O157:H7 in Marketed Unpasteurized Milk in Selected East African Countries." *Journal of Food Protection* 71 (2): 257–63.

Green, T. 2016. "What Is the Evidence for Impacts of 'Food Scares' on Nutrition; With a Special Focus on Children in Low and Middle-Income Countries?" Submitted for an MS in nutrition for global health. London: London School of Hygiene and Tropical Medicine.

Guerrant, R. L., M. D. DeBoer, S. R. Moore, R. J. Scharf, and A. A. M. Lima. 2013. "The Impoverished Gut: A Triple Burden of Diarrhoea, Stunting and Chronic Disease." *Nature Review Gastroenterology & Hepatology* 10 (4): 220–29.

Guh, S., C. Xingbao, C. Poulos, Z. Qi, C. Jianwen, L. von Seidlein, C. Jichao, et al. 2008. "Comparison of Cost-of-Illness with Willingness-to-Pay Estimates to Avoid Shigellosis: Evidence from China." *Health Policy and Planning* 23 (2): 125–36.

Handford, C. E., K. Campbell, and C. T. Elliott. 2016. "Impacts of Milk Fraud on Food Safety and Nutrition with Special Emphasis on Developing Countries." *Comprehensive Reviews in Food Science and Food Safety* 15 (1): 130–42. https://doi.org/10.1111/1541-4337.12181.

Hasler, B., P. Dominguez-Salas, K. Fornace, M. Garza, D. Grace, and J. Rushton. 2017. "Where Food Safety Meets Nutrition Outcomes in Livestock and Fish Value Chains: A Conceptual Approach." *Food Security* 9 (5): 1001–17. doi:10.1007/s12571-017-0710-2.

Havelaar, A., J. Haagsma, M. Mangen, J. Kemmeren, L. Verhoef, and S. Vijgen. 2012. "Disease Burden of Foodborne Pathogens in the Netherlands." *International Journal of Food Microbiology* 156 (3): 231–38.

Havelaar, A., M. D. Kirk, P. R. Torgerson, H. J. Gibb, T. Hald, R. J. Lake, N. Praet, et al. 2015. "World Health Organization Global Estimates and Regional Comparisons of the Burden of Foodborne Disease in 2010." *PLOS Medicine* 12 (2).

Henson, S., and S. Jaffee. 2008. "Understanding Developing Country Strategic Responses to the Enhancement of Food Safety Standards." *World Economy* 31 (4): 548–68.

Henson, S., and W. Mitullah. 2004. "Kenyan Exports of Nile Perch: Impact of Food Safety Standards on an Export-Oriented Supply Chain." World Bank Policy Research Working Paper 3349, World Bank, Washington, DC.

Henson, S., M. Saqib, and R. Rajasenan. 2004. "Impact of Sanitary Measures on Exports of Fishery Products in India: The Case of Kerala." Agriculture and Rural Development Discussion Paper 17, World Bank, Washington, DC.

Hoffmann, S., B. Maculloch, and M. Batz. 2015. "Economic Burden of Major Foodborne Illnesses Acquired in the United States." Economic Information Bulletin No. EIB-140, Department of Agriculture, Washington, DC.

Hoffmann, S., B. Devleesschauwer, W. Aspinall, R. Cooke, T. Corrigan, A. Havelaar, F. Angulo, et al. 2017. "Attribution of Global Foodborne Disease to Specific Foods: Findings from a World Health Organization Structured Expert Elicitation." *PLOS One* 12 (9).

ILRI (International Livestock Research Institute). 2011. *Assessment of Risks to Human Health Associated with Meat from Different Value Chains in Nigeria: Using the Example of the Beef Value Chain.* Nairobi: ILRI.

Jaffee, S. 2005. "Delivering and Taking the Heat: Indian Spices and Evolving Product and Process Standards." Agriculture and Rural Development Discussion Paper 19, World Bank, Washington, DC.

Jaffee, S., and S. Henson. 2004. "Standards and Agri-Food Exports from Developing Countries: Rebalancing the Debate." Policy Research Working Paper 3348, World Bank, Washington, DC.

Jarquin, C., D. Alvaraz, and O. Morales. 2015. "Salmonella on Raw Poultry in Retail Markets in Guatemala: Levels, Antibiotic Susceptibility, and Serovar Distribution." *Journal of Food Protection* 9 (September): 1642–50.

JECFA (Joint FAO/WHO Expert Committee on Food Additives). 2017. *Evaluation of Certain Contaminants in Food: Eighty-Third Report of the Joint FA/WHO Technical Report Series 1002* Geneva: JECFA.

Jia, X., H. Luan, J. Huang, S. Li, and S. Rozelle. 2014. "Marketing Raw Milk from Dairy Farmers before and after the 2008 Milk Scandal in China: Evidence from Greater Beijing." *Agribusiness* 30 (4): 410–23.

Johnson, N., J. Mayne, D. Grace, and A. Wyatt. 2015. "How Will Training Traders Contribute to Improved Food Safety in Informal Markets for Meat and Milk?" IFPRI Discussion Paper 01451, International Food Policy Research Institute, Washington, DC.

Khlangwiset, P., G. S. Shephard, and F. Wu. 2011. "Aflatoxins and Growth Impairment: A Review." *Critical Reviews in Toxicology* 41 (9): 740–55.

Kristkova, Z., D. Grace, and M. Kuiper. 2017. *The Economics of Food Safety in India: A Rapid Assessment.* Amsterdam: Wageningen University and Research Center and International Livestock Research Institute.

Kubheka, L., F. Mosupye, and A. Holy. 2001. "Microbiological Survey of Street-Vended Salad and Gravy in Johannesburg City, South Africa." *Food Control* 12 (2): 127–31.

Kumi, J., N. J. Mitchell, G. A. Asare, E. Dotse, F. Kwaa, T. D. Phillips, and N.-A. Ankrah. 2014. "Aflatoxins and Fumonisins Contamination of Home-Made Food (Weanimix) from Cereal-Legume Blends for Children." *Ghana Medical Journal* 48 (3): 121–26.

Lapar, L., R. Deka, J. Lindahl, and D. Grace. 2014. "Quality and Safety Improvements in Informal Milk Markets and Implications for Food Safety Policy." Paper presented at 8th International Conference of the Asian Society of Agricultural Economists, Savar, Bangladesh, February 14–17.

Liu, Y., and F. Wu. 2010. "Global Burden of Aflatoxin-Induced Hepatocellular Carcinoma: A Risk Assessment." *Environmental Health Perspectives* 118 (6): 818–24.

Liu, Y., C. C. Chang, G. M. Marsh, and F. Wu. 2012. "Population Attributable Risk of Aflatoxin-Related Liver Cancer: Systematic Review and Meta-Analysis." *European Journal of Cancer* 48 (14): 2125–36.

Lucas, A. M. 2010. "Malaria Eradication and Educational Attainment: Evidence from Paraguay and Sri Lanka." *American Economic Journal: Applied Economics* 2 (2): 46–71.

Lusk, J. L., and S. Murray. 2014. "New Tool (FooDS) Identifies Consumers' Views on Food Safety. *Choices: The Magazine of Food, Farm, and Resource Issues* 29 (3): 1–7.

Lusk, J. L., and T. C. Schroeder. 2002. "Effects of Meat Recalls on Futures Market Prices." *Agricultural and Resource Economics Review* 31 (1): 47–58.

Macheka, L., F. A. Manditsera, R. T. Ngadze, J. Mubaiwa, and L. K. Nyanga. 2013. "Barriers, Benefits and Motivation Factors for the Implementation of Food Safety Management System in the Food Sector in Harare Province, Zimbabwe." *Food Control* 34 (1): 126–31.

Mahdavi, R., L. Nikniaz, S. R. Arefhosseini, and M. Vahed Jabbari. 2010. "Determination of Aflatoxin M1 in Breast Milk Samples in Tabriz-Iran." *Maternal Child Health Journal* 14 (1): 141–145.

Makita, K., E. M. Fèvre, C. Waiswa, M. C. Eisler, and S. C. Welburn. 2010. "How Human Brucellosis Incidence in Urban Kampala Can Be Reduced Most Efficiently? A Stochastic Risk Assessment of Informally-Marketed Milk." *PLoS One*, December 1.

Mangen, M., M. Bouwknegt, I. Friesema, J. Haagsma, L. Kortbeek, L. Tariq, M. Wilson, et al. 2014. "Cost-of-Illness and Disease Burden of Food-Related Pathogens in the Netherlands, 2011." *International Journal of Food Microbiology* 196: 84–93.

Masters, W. A., and D. Sanogo. 2002. Welfare Gains from Quality Certification of Infant Foods: Results from a Market Experiment in Mali." *American Journal of Agricultural Economics* 84 (4): 974–89.

Mensah, P., D. Yehoah-Manu, K. Owusu-Darko and A. Ablordey. 2002. "Street Foods in Accra, Ghana: How Safe Are They? *Bulletin of the World Health Organization* 80: 546–54.

McLinden, T., J. Sargeant, M. Thomas, A. Papadopoulos, and A. Fazil. 2014. "Component Costs of Foodborne Illness: A Scoping Review." *BMC Public Health* 14. http://www.biomedcentral.com/1471-2458/14/509.

McMillan A., J. D. Renaud, K. M. N. Burgess, A. E. Orimadegun, O. O. Akinyinka, S. H. Allen, J. D. Miller, et al. 2018. "Aflatoxin Exposure in Nigerian Children with Severe Acute Malnutrition." *Food and Chemical Toxicology* 111: 356–62.

Millogo, V., K. Svennersten Sjaunja, G. A. Ouédraogo, and S. Agenäs. 2010. "Raw Milk Hygiene at Farms, Processing Units and Local Markets in Burkina Faso." *Food Control* 21 (7): 1070–74. https://doi.org/10.1016/j.foodcont.2009.12.029.

Minot, N., R. Stringer, W. J. Umberger, and W. Maghraby. 2015. "Urban Shopping Patterns in Indonesia and Their Implications for Small Farmers." *Bulletin of Indonesian Economic Studies* 51 (3): 375–88.

Miraglia, Marina, H. J. P. Marvin, G. A. Kleter, Paola Battilani, C. Brera, E. Coni, and F. Cubadda. 2009. "Climate Change and Food Safety: An Emerging Issue with Special Focus on Europe." *Food and Chemical Toxicology* 47 (5): 1009–21.

Muyanja, C., L. Nayiga, N Brenda, and G. Nasinyama. 2011. "Practices, Knowledge and Risk Factors of Street Food Vendors in Uganda." *Food Control* 22 (10): 1551–58.

Narain, U., and C. Sall. 2016. *Methodology for Valuing the Health Impacts of Air Pollution.* Washington, DC: World Bank.

Nguyen, N., V. Nguyen, C. Nguyen, D. Truong, N. Tran, H. Tran, N. Nguyen, et al. 2018. "Antimicrobial Residues and Resistance against Critically Important Antimicrobials in Non-Typhoidal Salmonella from Meat Sold at Wet Markets and Supermarkets in Vietnam." *International Journal of Food Microbiology* 266: 301–9.

Nguyen-Viet, H., D. Grace, T. T. Tuyet-Hanh, P. D. Phuc, and M. Tanner. 2013. *Risk Assessment for Food Safety in Vietnam.* Evidence for Policy Series, regional edition Southeast Asia 5. Pathumthani, Thailand. http://hdl.handle.net/10568/34009.

On, S. 2016. "Estimate of the Costs of Foodborne Illness in Indonesia." Working Paper prepared for the Global Food Safety Partnership, Washington, DC.

Ortega, D. L., H. H. Wang, N. J. Olynk, L. Wu, and J. Bai. 2012. "Chinese Consumers' Demand for Food Safety Attributes: A Push for Government and Industry Regulations." *American Journal of Agricultural Economics* 94 (2): 489–95.

Ortega, D., and D. Tschirley. 2017. "Demand for Food Safety in Emerging and Developing Countries: A Research Agenda for Asia and Sub-Saharan Africa." *Journal of Agribusiness in Developing and Emerging Economies* 7 (1): 21–34.

Ozier, O. 2014. "Exploiting Externalities to Estimate the Long-Term Effects of Early Childhood Deworming." Policy Research Working Paper 7052, World Bank, Washington, DC.

Painter, J. A., R. M. Hoekstra, T. Ayers, R. V. Tauxe, C. R. Braden, F. J. Angulo, and P. M. Griffin. 2013. "Attribution of Foodborne Illnesses, Hospitalizations, and Deaths to Food Commodities by Using Outbreak Data, United States, 1998–2008." *Emerging Infectious Diseases* 19 (3): 407–15. https://doi.org/10.3201/eid1903.111866.

Paudyal, N., V. Anihouvi, J. Hounhouigan, M. I. Matsheka, B. Sekwati-Monang, W. Amoa-Awua, A. Atter, et al. 2017. "Prevalence of Foodborne Pathogens in Food from Selected African Countries: A Meta-Analysis." *International Journal of Food Microbiology* 249: 35–43.

Peter, K. V., ed. 2012. *Handbook of Herbs and Spices.* Vol. 1. Amsterdam: Elsevier.

Pei, Xiaofang, Annuradha Tandon, Anton Alldrick, Liana Giorgi, Wei Huang, and Ruijia Yang. 2011. "The China Melamine Milk Scandal and Its Implications for Food Safety Regulation." *Food Policy* 36 (3): 412–20.

Piggott, N. E., and T. L. Marsh. 2004. "Does Food Safety Information Impact U.S. Meat Demand?" *American Journal of Agricultural Economics* 86 (1): 154–74.

Qiao, G., T. Guo, and K. K. Klein. 2010. "Melamine in Chinese Milk Products and Consumer Confidence." *Appetite* 55 (2): 190–95.

Reeves, P. 2017. "Amid Massive Tainted-Meat Scandal, Brazil Assures Safety of Its Food Exports." NPR.Org., March 20. https://www.npr.org/sections/thesalt/2017/03/20 /520832729/amid -massive-tainted-meat-scandal-brazil-assures-safety-of-its-food-exports.

Richard, S. A., R. E. Black, R. H. Gilman, R. L. Guerrant, G. Kang, C. F. Lanata, K. Mølbak, et al. 2014. "Catch-Up Growth Occurs After Diarrhea in Early Childhood." *Journal of Nutrition* 144 (6): 965–71. https://doi.org/10.3945/jn.113.187161.

Roesel, K., and D. Grace, eds. 2014. *Food Safety and Informal Markets: Animal Products in Sub-Saharan Africa.* London: Routledge.

Scallan, E., R. M. Hoekstra, F. J. Angulo, R. V. Tauxe, M.-A. Widdowson, S. L. Roy, J. L. Jones, et al. 2011. "Foodborne Illness Acquired in the United States: Major Pathogens." *Emerging Infectious Diseases* 17 (1): 7–15.

Schoder, D. 2010. "Melamine Milk Powder and Infant Formula Sold in East Africa." *Journal of Food Protection* 73 (9): 1709–14.

Sears, A., M. G. Baker, N. Wilson, J. Marshall, P. Muellner, D. M. Campbell, R. J. Lake, and N. P. R. French. 2011. "Marked Campylobacteriosis Decline after Interventions Aimed at Poultry, New Zealand." *Emerging Infectious Diseases* 17 (6): 1007–15. https://doi .org/10.3201 /eid 1706.101272.

Sezgin, A. C., and N. Şanlıer. 2016. "Street Food Consumption in Terms of the Food Safety and Health." *Journal of Human Sciences* 13 (3): 4072–83.

Sinayobye, E., and F. K. Saalia. 2011. "Size Reduction of Food Commodities and Food Safety in Some Accra Markets. *African Journal of Food, Agriculture, Nutrition and Development* 11 (6): 5282–99.

Slovic, P. 1987. "Perception of Risk." *Science* 236 (4799): 280–85.

Souza, S. S., A. G. Cruz, E. H. M. Walter, J. A. F. Faria, R. M. S. Celeghini, M. M. C. Ferreira, D. Granato, et al. 2011. "Monitoring the Authenticity of Brazilian UHT Milk: A Chemometric Approach." *Food Chemistry* 124 (2): 692–95.

Steyn, N. P., Z. Mchiza, J. Hill, Y. D. Davids, I. Venter, E. Hinrichsen, M. Opperman, et al. 2014. "Nutritional Contribution of Street Foods to the Diet of People in Developing Countries: A Systematic Review." *Public Health Nutrition* 17 (6): 1363–74.

Ta, Y. T., T. T. Nguyen, P. B. To, D. X. Pham, H. T. H. Le, W. Q. Alali, I. Walls, et al. 2012. "Prevalence of Salmonella on Chicken Carcasses from Retail Markets in Vietnam." *Journal of Food Protection* 75 (10): 1851–54.

Tam, C. C., S. J. O'Brien, D. S. Tompkins, F. J. Bolton, L. Berry, J. Dodds, and D. Choudhury. 2012. "Changes in Causes of Acute Gastroenteritis in the United Kingdom over 15 Years: Microbiologic Findings from 2 Prospective, Population-Based Studies of Infectious Intestinal Disease." *Clinical Infectious Diseases* 54 (9): 1275–86.

Tappenden, K. A., B. Quatrara, M. L. Parkhurst, A. M. Malone, G. Fanjiang, and T. R. Ziegler. 2013. "Critical Role of Nutrition in Improving Quality of Care: An Interdisciplinary Call to Action to Address Adult Hospital Malnutrition." *Journal of Parenteral and Enteral Nutrition*, 37 (4): 482–97.

Tarantelli, T. 2017. "Adulteration with Sudan Dye Has Triggered Several Spice Recalls." FoodSafetyTech, June 30. https://foodsafetytech.com/feature_article/adulteration-sudan -dye-triggered-several-spice-recalls/.

Thomas, M. K., R. Murray, L. Flockhart, K. Pintar, F. Pollari, A. Fazil, A. Nesbitt, et al. 2013. "Estimates of the Burden of Foodborne Illness in Canada for 30 Specified Pathogens and Unspecified Agents, Circa 2006." *Foodborne Pathogens and Disease* 10 (7): 639–48. https://doi.org/10.1089/fpd.2012.1389.

Tirado, M. C., R. Clarke, L. A. Jaykus, A. McQuatters-Gollop, and J. M. Frank. 2010. "Climate Change and Food Safety: A Review." *Food Research International* 43 (7): 1745–65.

Tschirley, D., M. W. Ayieko, M. Hichaambwa, J. Goeb, and W. Loescher. 2010. "Modernizing Africa's Fresh Produce Supply Chains without Rapid Supermarket Takeover: Towards a Definition of Research and Investment Priorities." Food Security International Development Working Papers, Michigan State University, Department of Agricultural, Food, and Resource Economics, East Lansing.

Tschirley, D., T. Reardon, M. Dolislagar, and J. Snyder. 2014. "The Rise of a Middle Class in East and Southern Africa: Implications for Food System Transformation" WIDER Working Paper 2014/119. Helsinki: UNU-WIDER. http://www.wider.unu.edu/publications /working-papers /2014/en_GB/wp2014-119/.

UNIDO (United Nations Industrial Development Organization). 2015. *Meeting Standards, Winning Markets: Trade Standards Compliance*. Vienna: UNIDO.

———. "A Fisherwoman in Myanmar Benefits from UNIDO's Food Safety Approach." Press Release, March 9.

Unnevehr, L. J. 2007 "Food Safety as a Global Public Good." *Agricultural Economics* 37 (1): 149–58.

Uyttendaele, M., C. Liu, N. and Hofstra. 2015. "Impacts of Climate Change on Food Safety." *Food Research International* 68 (February): 1–6.

Van Boeckel, T., C. Brower, M. Gilbert, B. Grenfell, S. Levin, T. Robinson, A. Teillant, et al. 2015 "Global Trends in Antimicrobial Use in Food Animals." *Proceedings of the National Academy of Sciences* 112 (18): 5649–54.

Wambui, J. M., E. G. Karuri, J. A. Ojiambo, and P. M. K. Njage. 2016. "Adaptation and Mitigation Options to Manage Aflatoxin Contamination in Food with a Climate Change Perspective." *World Mycotoxin Journal* 9 (5): 875–88.

Wang, J., M. Chen, and P. G. Klein. 2015. "China's Dairy United: A New Model for Milk Production." *American Journal of Agricultural Economics* 97 (2): 618–27.

Wang, Xiaojin, and Sayed Saghaian. 2013. "The Impact of the Melamine Scandal and Other Factors Influencing China's Dairy Imports." Paper presented at the Southern Agricultural Economics Association Annual Meeting, Orlando, FL, February. https://ageconsearch.umn.edu/bitstream/142742/2/Eric-SAEA.pdf.

Wild C, J. D. Miller J. D Groopman. 2015. "Mycotoxin Control in Low and Middle-Income Countries." IARC Working Group Report 9, International Agency for Research on Cancer, Lyon, France.

World Bank. 2005. *Food Safety and Agricultural Health Standards: Challenges and Opportunities for Developing Country Exports*. Washington, DC: World Bank.

———. 2016. *Vietnam Food Safety Risks Management: Challenges and Opportunities*. Washington DC: World Bank.

Wu, F., J. D. Groopman, and J. J. Pestka. 2014. "Public Health Impacts of Foodborne Mycotoxins." *Annual Review of Food Science and Technology* 5: 351–72.

Xinhua News Agency. 2005. "KFC Falls Prey to Sudan I." March 17.

Xiu, Changbai, and K. K. Klein. 2010. "Melamine in Milk Products in China: Examining the Factors That Led to Deliberate Use of the Contaminant." *Food Policy* 35 (5): 463–70.

Xue, J., and W. Zhang. 2013. "Understanding China's Food Safety Problem: An Analysis of 2387 Incidents of Acute Foodborne Illness. *Food Control* 30 (1): 311–17.

Zhang, W., and J. Xue. 2016. "Economically Motivated Food Fraud and Adulteration in China: An Analysis Based on 1553 Media Reports." *Food Control* 67: 192–98.

CHAPTER THREE

The Status of Food Safety Management in Developing Countries

FOOD SAFETY CAPACITY

The foregoing discussion highlights how the prevalence of food safety hazards reflects the actions, both individually and collectively, of actors along agri-food value chains, as well as actors that are outside value chains but are part of the wider food system. This reflects the level of food safety capacity within specific value chains and the wider food system.

This perspective shows how food safety capacity is positioned at three levels within food systems. First, it is positioned within the system itself; for example, in the capacity of regulatory agencies and of testing, inspection, and certification services. Second, it is positioned within value chain actors, including input suppliers, producers, processors, distributors, retailers and caterers. And third, it is positioned within individuals handling food products and operating within the wider food system; for example, in the form of knowledge and skills relating to food hygiene.

Integral to this broad definition of food safety capacity is the ability to perform the various functions needed to manage the safety of the food end product. These functions can be thought of as an interdependent and iterative hierarchy of capabilities, as shown in figure 3.1: Food Safety Management Capacities and Functions. At the most basic level, they include awareness and recognition of the importance of food safety, the sources and consequences of food hazards, and the nature and need for food safety practices. The next level is the application of basic good hygiene practices along the value chain to prevent contamination and to eradicate or manage food hazards along the value chain.

FIGURE 3.1 Food Safety Management Capacities and Functions

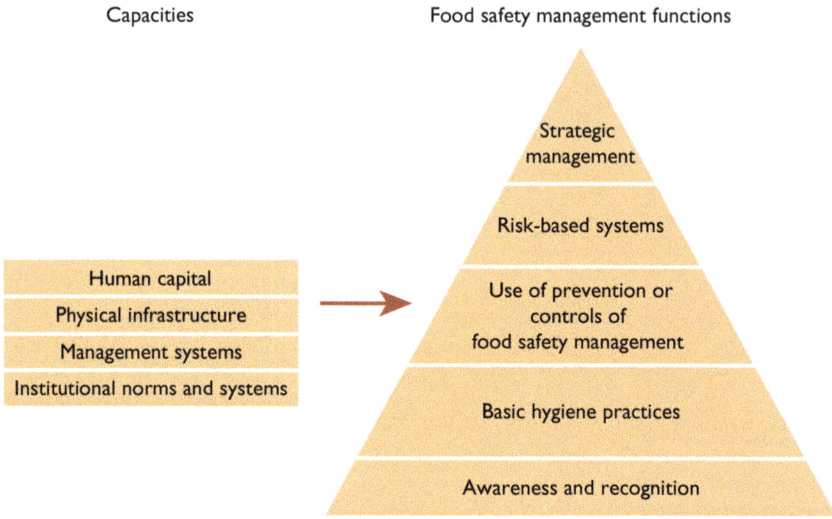

Source: World Bank.

Simple examples include handwashing, cleaning processing tools or machines after use, thorough cooking where needed, and keeping raw and cooked foods separate to avoid cross contamination. These basic functions at the lower level of the hierarchy are often missing in many informal food markets.

The middle of the hierarchy represents the progression to more advanced and technically challenging elements of food safety management, entailing the use of prevention or control measures in informed and purposive ways. For example, in a food-processing plant this means adopting basic sanitary controls, including monitoring incoming ingredients for hazards; monitoring control processes to ensure they are effective (minimum temperatures, for example); and sampling to ensure that basic standards are met. For farm production, this can mean following good agricultural practices—GAPs—for using chemicals and veterinary drugs, and applying manure.[1]

[1] Good agricultural practices are a collection of principles for applying on-farm production and postproduction processes. They are aimed at promoting safe and healthy food and nonfood agricultural products, while taking into account economic, social, and environmental sustainability. There are GAPs related to soil, water, animal husbandry/health, pest management, and other elements of farm production. GAP applications have been developed by governments, nongovernmental organizations, the private sector, and international organizations. GLOBALG.A.P. is an international private sector membership body, which develops and promotes the adoption of a set of specific farm assurance standards involving GAP principles. Farms or businesses applying GLOBALG.A.P. standards can obtain certification.

The top two segments of the hierarchy shown in figure 3.1 involve risk-based and more sophisticated approaches to food safety management. This includes using deliberate steps and procedures to identify sources of hazards and critical control points, and using sampling and testing to verify controls. The approaches also include setting up procedures for handling contaminated or substandard products by destroying or diverting them to lower-risk uses. Within a value chain, risk-based management can mean food value chain actors verifying production processes for raw products, ensuring cold chain control, and providing information to retailers and consumers about control measures taken. Adopting risk-based systems is often accompanied by certification to verify management practices.

Strategic management involves taking a forward-looking perspective on potential and emerging risks, so that proactive measures can be taken to develop control and surveillance. For modernizing economies, new risks may appear with changes in production and marketing practices, as well as changes in diets and consumer expectations. Here, food producers and firms need to be strategic to avoid risks to brand reputation, and public agencies need to be strategic in monitoring risks and carrying out public education.

Achieving the food safety functions shown in figure 3.1 requires establishing, operating, and maintaining a portfolio of four key capacities. The first is human capital across all those involved in the handling of food, as all are potential food safety managers. This has various layers: basic knowledge of food safety hazards and hygiene, appropriate food-handling techniques, and specialized and technically sophisticated expertise in prevention and control. Management and leadership skills are important human capital elements in an effective food safety management system, which often requires coordination along the supply chain. The second capacity is the necessary physical infrastructure, which also has various layers: hygienic market places and distribution centers, food-processing facilities, and laboratory testing and research facilities. Infrastructure to provide clean water, electricity, and sanitation is vital for safe food.

The third and fourth capacities are less tangible than the first two, and often less recognized. The management systems within enterprises handling food—including record-keeping systems, procedures for staff training, methods of verification, and procedures for recalling products—are the third capacity. This also covers institutions involved in food safety controls, such as laboratories and inspection and certification bodies, that require internal management systems for the use of their information to be effective. For example, laboratories can be part of a broader system of surveillance, but this requires an information management system. The fourth capacity is the broader institutional and cultural norms and systems that inform the actions of food system participants. These include regulations and their enforcement, standardization, enterprise and brand reputation, social cues and pressures, and the professionalization of food safety managers. These norms influence the strength (or otherwise) of a food safety culture (box 3.1).

BOX 3.1 Food Safety Culture: What Happens When No One Is Looking

The concept of a food safety culture is gaining ground to explain differences in food safety performance across organizations, as well as the variable effectiveness of training programs. Indeed, the recognition that training and, as a result, food safety knowledge and awareness are poor predictors of safe food handling led researchers to look for other explanatory factors. Some have gravitated toward the concept of food safety culture, which has been described as "what happens when no one is looking."

How does a food safety culture develop, and how can a culture of producing safe food be deliberately fostered? To answer these questions, it is necessary to recognize that a food safety culture is multidimensional. The U.K. Food Standards Agency's work in these areas offers guidance. In 2013, the agency issued an assessment tool for measuring food safety culture in food service organizations, and recommendations on how food safety inspectors can most constructively approach organizations given their prevailing food safety culture.

The tool is structured around eight dimensions: (1) priorities and attitudes (a company's attitudes toward food safety and how much it is prioritized), (2) risk perceptions and knowledge, (3) confidence in food safety systems (including the perceived validity and effectiveness of food hygiene regulations), (4) ownership (whether food hygiene is seen as the responsibility of the firm or the regulator), (5) competence (knowledge and understanding the risks and subsequent risk management), (6) leadership (the extent of a clear commitment from management for food safety), (7) employee involvement, and (8) communications (including the freedom to challenge and discuss practices).

This way of breaking down the concept of a food safety culture suggests multiple entry points for fostering a culture of safe food. It certainly upholds the relevance of training programs. Indeed, training can not only be used to develop knowledge and competence but also to shape attitudes and behaviors, and to show leadership. It also shows staff that food safety is of central importance to a business, thereby increasing their motivation to take food safety seriously. Here, the frequency of training and how it is presented to staff can matter. The level of attendance of training sessions and learning lessons reinforced by managers can also be key.

The hierarchy of food safety capacities shown in figure 3.1 encompasses functions undertaken within agri-food value chains and by other actors, most notably regulators and other the public sector bodies. Recognizing the locus of food safety capacity is important to understand the factors influencing the prevalence of food safety hazards, and for identifying potential points of entry for investment or inducing behavioral change. Understanding the complementarities and interdependencies of these elements of capacity is critical to the design and implementation of efforts to reduce food safety hazards. Thus, many elements of capacity will not work effectively unless they coexist with other elements of capacity.

For example, regulatory limits on microbiological and chemical contaminants in food cannot be enforced unless reliable testing can be done. And this, in turn, requires that laboratory facilities are available and laboratory quality assurance schemes are in place. In some circumstances, capacity weaknesses can be offset by capacity strengths—or at least the ability to tap capacity elsewhere. Laboratory testing capacity in the public and private sectors is an example of how exporting firms can either do their own testing or use private sector providers if public sector capacity is weak (Henson and Jaffee 2008). In the latter case, there are options for where capacity is best situated. Some form of cost-benefit assessment is needed to determine where investments can be best focused given the status of preexisting food safety capacity.

FACTORS THAT MOTIVATE FOOD SAFETY CAPACITY AND BEHAVIORAL CHANGE

Investments in safe food management systems in the public and private sectors, and safe food production and handling practices, are both motivated actions, which can be induced by ethical, commercial, social, political, or other considerations. When accounting for current gaps or lapses, and when considering possible solutions, it is necessary to consider the underlying incentives, drivers, or other motivating factors that apply to specific contexts, and how these are changing or are amenable to change. The motivation for this can come from various sources:

- Primary farm producers can be motivated to change their production practices because this can protect their households against disease and enable them to tap more remunerative markets. Changing production practices can also come from family and social pressure from the community, and whether these producers can use public support programs.
- Businesses may be motivated to invest in enhanced food safety capacity because of fears of the consequences of noncompliance with regulations, to avoid recalls and reputational losses, to reap competitive gains, out of a sense of corporate social responsibility, and from pressure from political leaders.
- Political leaders may be motivated to invest in enhanced food safety capacity in the public and private sectors because of pressure from influential constituencies, such as large firms or vocal urban consumers, and opportunities to tap into additional funding from bilateral or multilateral donors. Other motivations include gaining political advantage and reputation. In some countries, political leaders have business interests in agricultural production, and food production and distribution.

The nature of these incentives and their magnitude in particular contexts need to be explained, as do the reasons why these incentives might be missing or weak in the first place. Effective ways need to be found to enhance these incentives. These include the use of signaling mechanisms in retail food markets that engender consumer demand for safer food, and efforts to raise awareness among exporters of the importance of food safety capacity for international competitiveness. For simplicity, these incentives can be grouped into two types:

- ***Market-based incentives*** through the demands of domestic consumers for the safety of the food they buy and consume, the practices of food suppliers, and the commercial requirements in overseas markets that exporters need to comply with. Critical here is the role of value chains through which market signals are transmitted from end-product markets to food processors, traders, intermediaries, and primary producers.
- ***Political incentives*** through the demands put on governments by citizens, advocacy groups, and businesses domestically; and by trading partners and international agreements for investments in enhanced food safety capacity and for more effective institutions for laying down and applying food safety regulations and norms.

Importantly, these incentives vary both qualitatively and quantitatively, depending on the level of economic of development. It is through changes in the nature and level of these incentives that changes are seen in the level of food safety capacity and, in turn, any variation in the burden of unsafe food across countries. The potential to augment these incentives, individually and collectively, and the degree to which they are complements or substitutes for one another, varies with the level of economic development.

It is also important to recognize the role of a wide range of actors and institutions in creating and transmitting incentives for investment in enhanced food safety capacity. The state of food safety capacity itself is important; indeed, there is a cyclical interdependence—and possibly even a virtuous circle—between food safety capacity across the public and private sectors and the incentives that engender its creation in the first place (figure 3.2). For example, the ability to detect and monitor the prevalence of foodborne illness is a key driver of market-based and political incentives to enhance capacity. Perhaps unsurprisingly, many of the poorest countries are caught in a low-level capacity trap in which incentives to build capacity are weak. This is because many of the critical capabilities that generate and support these incentives, including effective food safety risk assessment and public health reporting, are missing. But actors and institutions well beyond the direct terrain of food safety also play a key role in creating or refining incentives. These actors include the media, consumer organizations, chambers of commerce and other business organizations, and the courts and other aspects of the legal system.

While incentives are important as drivers of the overall level of investment in enhanced food safety capacity, they also steer the direction of investments.

FIGURE 3.2 Cyclical Relationship between Incentives and Level of Capacity

Source: World Bank.

If, for example, the "voice" of exporters or rich consumers is loudest, whether through market or political routes, it is likely that investments directed at the food safety capacity needs of export value chains and formal urban market segments catering to elites will predominate. Likewise, if the "voice" of the poor is muted or weak, there will probably be little political or market-based incentives to invest in enhancing food safety capacity directed at markets catering to them, as in informal food distribution channels. Hence, a "silent" burden of foodborne illness exists among poor and rural populations more generally. There is an evident need for training food handlers in informal markets and informing consumers to induce incentives for behavioral change for improved food safety (box 3.2).

Recognizing the role of incentives can be important to bring about sustained improvements in food safety capacity, and understanding the nature of choice behavior can make regulatory action and other interventions more effective. People often think fast and respond automatically and decisively to social incentives, and use mental models or specific worldviews to interpret information and perceptions. Reflexive methodologies like nudging are gaining attention as a way of triggering desired behavioral outcomes. Instead of changing the conscious decision-making process, nudges alter the environmental context in which a decision or behavior is completed (Marteau et al. 2011). Nudges can take many forms, including environmental cues that engage automatic decision-making processes that are quick and unconscious rather than self-aware, goal-oriented, and controlled decision making. Successful nudges have reduced food waste by 30–50 percent by not offering trays in cafeterias (Thaler et al. 2009), increased positive recycling behavior by 46 percent when footprints led individuals to recycling bins (Hansen 2010), and reduced portion size by serving food in smaller bowls (16 percent) while increasing perceived food intake (7 percent) (Wansink and van Ittersum 2006).

BOX 3.2 Food Handlers, Training, and Behavioral Change

Studies point to low levels of food safety awareness and unsafe food handling practices, including among food handlers in formal and informal micro and small enterprises across a variety of contexts and among consumers. This research often finds that training, education, and information campaigns are needed to increase the food safety knowledge and awareness of both consumers and food suppliers. Training is one of the most common interventions used to improve food handling and related food safety outcomes, but evidence suggests this has a weak record of durably changing food handling attitudes and behavior, let alone food safety outcomes.

The limitations of training in achieving behavior change is not a surprise, at least to the extent that the main purpose of training is to remediate gaps in knowledge and know-how, on the assumption that information is central to behavioral failure and essential to remedying it. Training programs often fail to address what is understood about human behavior. A literature review yields several insights that are now discussed.

Done right, training can enhance knowledge and awareness of food safety risks and risk mitigation practices. Many studies show that trained food handlers have greater knowledge of food safety risks and mitigation practices. For example, improvements in food handlers' post-training knowledge were found in studies by da Cunha, Stedefeldt, and de Rosso (2014) for food handlers in Santos City, Brazil; by McIntyre et al. (2013) for food handlers in British Columbia, Canada; by Baş, Ersun, and Kıvanç (2006) for food handlers in Turkey; by Al-Shabib, Mosilhey, and Husain (2016) for food handlers at a university in Saudi Arabia; by Park, Kwak, and Chang (2010) for restaurant workers in the Republic of Korea; by Soon and Baines (2012) for farm workers in the United Kingdom; by Campbell (2011) for street food vendors in Johannesburg; by Brannon et al. (2009) for food service workers in the United States; and by Choudhury et al. (2011) for street food vendors in Assam, India—to name just some of these studies.

Improved knowledge, however, does not always translate into safer practices among food handlers. Some studies find statistically significant—yet still minor, partial, or time-bound changes in behavior—demonstrating the limitations of training. Singh et al. 2016, in a study of street food vendors in India, showed that training resulted in only partial behavior change, but was not enough for vendors to meet standards. Acikel et al. (2008), in a study of hospital food workers in Turkey, found that wearing jewelry and watches declined after training (self-reported), but that other hygienic behavior remained the same, as did the level of enteric colonies growing on the hands of participants after training. In another study, food handlers in the United Kingdom perceived the effects of training on behavior to be positive yet time-bound and limited (Seaman and Eves 2010).

Some studies find no significant change in behavior. A review of 253 studies showed half of them found "no proper translation of knowledge" into attitudes or attitudes into practices after training (Zanin et al. 2017). Most of the studies were conducted in developing economies.

(Continued)

BOX 3.2 Food Handlers, Training, and Behavioral Change *(Continued)*

The obvious conclusion from this literature review is that training is a necessary but insufficient condition for behavioral change among food handlers. But this requires much more than providing them with knowledge or know-how; it requires attention to economic incentives as well as social norms. Insights from the behavioral sciences—from social psychology, marketing, and behavioral economics—are potentially relevant for designing food safety training programs and other interventions.

Many of these directions are consistent with what are known as social marketing techniques. These often appeal to emotions and social motivations to increase the salience of information, as well as the likelihood that it will be acted on. Social marketing techniques also attempt to harness the power of automatic behavior by providing people with new mental models and behavioral scripts, and by inserting behavioral triggers into their environment.

Given the power of social incentives to change behavior, one promising approach to improving food safety may be to involve consumers and peers in monitoring the behavior of food handlers. One way to do this is to raise awareness among consumers and empower them to make demands on food handlers, thereby shifting social norms surrounding a given behavior.

BENCHMARKING FOOD SAFETY CAPACITY

Benchmarking provides important signals about institutional performance and helps motivate improvements. It can point to specific reform or investment needs and help set and monitor targets. Examples of influential benchmarking abound, including the World Bank's long-standing Doing Business Index, the Enabling Business of Agriculture Index, Transparency International's Corruption Perceptions Index, the Economist Intelligence Unit's Global Food Security Index, and the Barilla Center for Food and Nutrition's Food Sustainability Index.

But no representative and comprehensive benchmark exists for food safety in low- and middle- income countries (LMICs). While detailed assessments have been done on the status of primarily public food control systems in many of these countries, the findings are generally not conducive to quantification and thus comparison. And many of these studies are not in the public domain because of the sensitivity surrounding public food control systems, and perhaps because of concerns about how the media or public would react to documented shortcomings in current systems. Much of the detailed information on food safety management capacity and performance is found in the "gray" literature, which cannot be directly quoted. This situation, together with the underlying weaknesses in the data on food safety hazards and foodborne disease (FBD), exacerbates the inadequate public dialogue on food safety priorities in many LMICs. This is manifested in two separate public dialogues: one involving experts with lead agencies and private companies; the other playing out in social media, informed by a combination of facts, rumors, and myths.

Reviews of food safety technical assessments across countries at similar levels of economic development tend to show many common strengths and weaknesses. For example, a series of food control assessments carried out by the Food and Agriculture Organization in South Asia and Southeast Asia (FAO 2015a, 2015b, 2016) found quite common situations in terms of:

- The lack of a comprehensive national policy, translating into a lack of prioritization of key elements of food safety management capacity.
- Progress on food law modernization, but less on regulations to enable enforcement of the law.
- Food safety laws frequently not being risk-based and covering the whole food chain.
- The presence of many standards, yet lack of clarity on their voluntary versus mandatory nature.
- The absence of effective mechanisms for the accreditation and certification of businesses.
- The categorization of food-processing and -handling enterprises being more frequently based on size and domestic or export market orientation and not on risk considerations. Because of this, inspections of enterprises and facilities were generally not risk-based.
- The fragmentation of institutional responsibilities among lead agencies and ministries with often weak coordination due to overlapping mandates or gaps (these entities also tended to resist giving up their roles so that reforms required policy decisions at higher levels).
- The lack of coordination in monitoring hazards, risks, and illness outcomes.
- Fragmented systems for laboratory testing that do not function as a network and do not yield inferences on food safety.
- Most laboratories not being fully accredited.
- The lack of reliable data to assess the scale and distribution of many food safety problems. Research from different disciplines used different samples and methods that could not be easily analyzed in an integrated way. Although there are some in-depth studies of specific industries or hazards, research tends not to link up with broader changes in the food system and therefore cannot inform forward-looking policy making.

The single dedicated tool for benchmarking food safety management capacities—the Food Safety Performance World Ranking—has been applied only to 17 Organisation for Economic Co-operation and Development countries (Le Vallée and Charlebois 2014). This tool takes a systematic approach to identify and evaluate the elements of food safety management systems related to risk assessment, risk management, and risk communication. Importantly, many of the tool's indicators may not be directly applicable to LMICs. Other examples of benchmarking or comparative tools in which LMICs are included or are the foci include:

- The World Health Organization's International Health Regulations core competency framework. This entails self-reporting related to various laws or institutions. For food safety, however, the "yes" or "no" responses it encompasses often do not give an accurate picture of underlying institutional functionality.
- The Economist Intelligence Unit's Global Food Security Index. This includes ratings for food quality and safety, but it puts more emphasis on dietary quality and diversity indicators, while its three food safety indicators give little information on food safety management capacity.[2]
- The Inter-American Institute for Cooperation in Agriculture's performance of veterinary service (PVS) tool. This covers multiple dimensions of food safety, but it is based on self-reporting and has been systematically applied to only six Latin American and Caribbean countries (and the results are not publicly available).
- The United Nations Industrial Development Organization. It has done a one-time survey of 28 Asian and African countries to gauge the quality of management infrastructure and institutions; coverage included metrology, standardization, certification, and testing.
- Several attempts to use trade rejection data to gauge food safety and wider sanitary and phytosanitary performance. Perhaps the most comprehensive of these being UNIDO (2015); results from this work are cited in chapter 2.
- The International Livestock Research Institute's food safety performance assessment tool. Its first application was in countries in Sub-Saharan Africa, and it shows considerable promise (Grace et al. 2018). But because it relies on secondary data, it only gauges food safety management capacities to a limited extent. Still, it uses other indicators—related to physical, social, and human capital—which would be expected to improve food safety outcomes.

This report took several approaches to gauge levels of food safety management capacity and compare them across countries in different regions and at different levels of economic development. Several restricted databases were used to discern some broad patterns, supplemented by literature reviews on capacity dimensions for which national or comparative data are not generally available. The results, while interesting and suggestive, are not enough, given

[2] These are access to potable water, the presence of modern food retailing, and a dedicated food safety control agency.

the importance of having an accurate reading of food safety management capacity and performance.[3]

THE PUBLIC SECTOR'S CAPACITIES FOR MANAGING DOMESTIC FOOD SAFETY RISKS

A major source of data for this report is the assessment results of the World Organisation for Animal Health–led Evaluation of Performance of Veterinary Services. This is relevant because veterinary services are normally responsible for the safety of animal source foods, typically the riskiest commodities. The organization's PVS tool is used to gauge the status of a broad set of critical competencies associated with national veterinary services. The fundamental components of the assessment pertain to human, physical, and financial resources; technical authority and capability; interaction with interested parties; and measures to ensure market access. The tool's 6th and most recent version covers 38 critical competencies. World Organisation for Animal Health member countries request the organization to undertake evaluations, and expert teams are used for this purpose. The evaluations are often supplemented by gap analyses, in which progress is gauged from the time of earlier analyses. These assessments include a rating system for each competency, ranging from 1 (little or no capacity) to 5 (a very high level of competence or application of best international practice).

The PVS tool has been used in over 100 countries across all country income categories. Most assessments and gap analyses are not public documents, and some have highly restricted access. Development partners, including the World Bank, are being given selective access to many of these assessments because of their role in potentially financing new investments to strengthen service capacities. But there are still limitations on what information from these assessments can be made public, and this includes specific capability assessment ratings for individual countries. Because of this, the information in this report is aggregated or clustered across types of countries.

The relevance of the PVS tool for this report is twofold. First, a subset of the 38 assessment criteria is either directly associated with the food safety of animal products or is likely to influence how well food safety is performed. This report uses the ratings for 18 criteria, including two associated with funding adequacy (operational funding and capital investment); 11 associated with technical capacities and regulatory functions (that is, those related to inspections, veterinary drug regulation, residue testing, the identification

[3] Future work should seek to develop more comprehensive and comparable benchmarks. The authors of this report believe the Inter-American Institute for Cooperation in Agriculture's assessment tool provides a promising start from which adjustments could be made to several of the core criteria. It is important that any comparative tool involve disinterested and expert assessments (rather than self-reporting), and that the results, or at least a stylized summary of those results, be put in the public domain.

and traceability of animals and animal products, laboratory infrastructure, quality assurance, quarantine, border controls, and emergency response); and four related to international market access. Because of the prominence of animal source foods in the incidence of foodborne disease globally and in LMICs, this report's coverage of this more specialized dimension of food safety management is highly relevant and likely indicative of broader patterns.

PVS assessment ratings were obtained for 93 countries where these assessments and gap analyses had been done since 2010. The 93 comprised 20 low-income countries, 35 lower-middle-income countries, 39 upper-middle-income countries, and nine high-income countries. This report focuses on the LMICs.

Table 3.1 highlights the ratings in the PVS assessments for the adequacy of public spending on national veterinary services for operational funding and capital investment. For simplicity, the ratings of 3, 4, and 5 denote adequate funding; ratings of 1 or 2 denote inadequate funding. Spending more of course does not necessarily translate into an effective capacity to perform key functions. Yet, the absence of adequate funding will surely translate into problems for the delivery of regulatory and technical services. Low operational funding restricts the mobility of veterinary and inspectorate staff and their ability to carry out functions, while low capital investment may result in dilapidated or antiquated core infrastructure. The assessed situation is quite serious. Public funding is inadequate across much of the LMIC sample. Only in 15 of the 84 LMICs is funding for operations and capital investment adequate. The situation is much better among upper-middle-income countries (more than a third have adequate funding) than among low- and lower-middle-income countries.[4]

TABLE 3.1 Adequacy of the Finance for National Veterinary Services

Income category	Countries for which data were sourced	Countries with adequate levels of operational funding	Countries with adequate levels of capital investment	Countries with adequate levels of both
Low	20	2	3	2
Lower-middle	35	5	4	3
Upper-middle	29	14	18	10
High	9	8	8	8
Total	**93**	**29**	**33**	**23**

Source: Based on World Organisation for Animal Health performance of veterinary services assessments.

[4] Many of the PVS reports provide detailed estimates on the levels of funding that are needed for effective veterinary system performance.

Figure 3.3 summarizes the frequency of adequate ratings across 13 indicators for different categories of LMICs. Not included are the results for high-income countries, where, almost universally, the ratings are high, except where the capacity is not relevant given some dimension of a country's agriculture or food system. Again, an adequate capacity is one in which the rating is either 3, 4, or 5. Even in the absence of a detailed breakdown, the broad picture is a concern because it points to considerable underinvestment in capacities, especially in low- and lower-middle-income countries. For example:

- Across most LMICs, capacities for disease and food safety surveillance, and production and facility inspections, are very low. This makes risk assessment problematic and, in turn, means that risk management is not readily undertaken.
- Traceability systems for animals and animal products, which are prominent features of disease control and food safety management systems in high-income countries, are virtually absent in LMICs.
- A somewhat larger proportion of LMICs have adequate laboratory infrastructure, but laboratory quality assurance systems are generally weak.
- A much larger proportion of upper-middle-income countries have adequate capacities across most functional areas considered here. But most upper-middle-income countries have strong capacity only for a minority of functions.

FIGURE 3.3 Indications of Underinvestment in Animal Product Food Safety Capacity

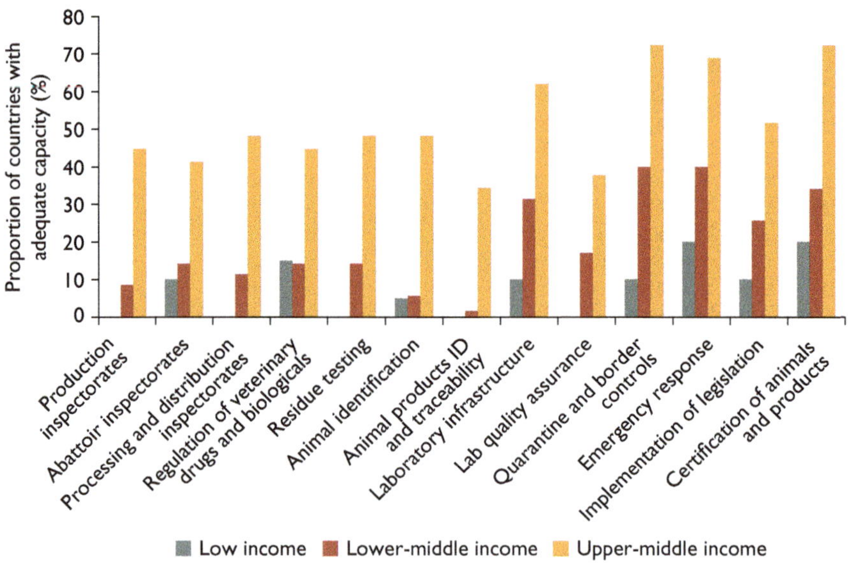

Source: Based on World Organisation for Animal Health country performance of veterinary service assessments and gap analyses.

The ratings for capacities relevant to the management of food safety related to animals and animal products are brought together to develop a simple unweighted Animal Products–Related Food Safety Capacity Index. Figure 3.4 shows the comparative results by country and region. Several observations can be made. The highest capacities tend to be clustered among countries in Latin America, several of which are major exporters of animal products. For these countries, market position has undoubtedly been a major driver of investments in veterinary controls and food safety. Animal products–related food safety capacity is also generally stronger among countries in North Africa, the Middle East, and Eastern Europe, either stemming from their existing or aspired trading relations with the European Union (EU) or Russian Federation, or because of the importance of commercial livestock production in these countries. Capacity patterns vary considerably in Asia and Sub-Saharan Africa, with some better-performing outliers (for example, Botswana, Malaysia, South Africa, Thailand, and Uganda); yet many other countries in these regions have comparatively low capacities.

The capacity to manage the food safety risks associated with animal products needs to be considered in relation to the need to do so. Livestock and animal products are vital to the agricultural economies of some countries, yet not to others. The importance of animal products in diets also varies widely. Some countries are prominent or at least minor exporters of livestock and animal products, while others are not. Exporting countries tend to have more advanced capacities to oversee external trade in animal products, yet this may not spill over to improved risk management for these products in domestic markets. Demographic factors, such as level of urbanization, might be expected to influence the need for effective food safety management, given its impact on the length of animal product distribution channels or the greater possibility of disease transmission in densely populated areas. Taking these factors into consideration, a Food Safety Management Capacity Need Index was constructed.[5]

Figure 3.5 maps the Animal Products–Related Food Safety Capacity Index against the Food Safety Management Capacity Need Index for countries for which data are available. Countries in the top right quadrant have high capacity needs and high-rated capacities. Those in the bottom left quadrant have low capacity needs given their dietary, agricultural structure, and demographic conditions. Countries in the lower right quadrant have high capacity needs relative to capacity and, consequently, are those of greatest concern.

It is the relationship between need and capacity that should influence food safety outcomes. Figure 3.6 ranks countries according to their apparent

[5] This is based on a series of the following proxies: (1) the economic importance of the livestock sector measured by livestock production as a proportion of the value of agricultural output (35 percent weighting), (2) level of consumption of animal-based foods measured as the proportion of total food consumption accounted for by these foods (35 percent weighting), (3) importance of exports measured by the value of livestock and meat exports as a proportion of total agri-food exports (15 percent weighting), and (4) the extent of supply chain restructuring and degree of separation of production and consumption measured by the proportion of the population living in urban areas (15 percent weighting).

FIGURE 3.4 **Animal Products–Related Food Safety Capacity Index, by Country and Region**

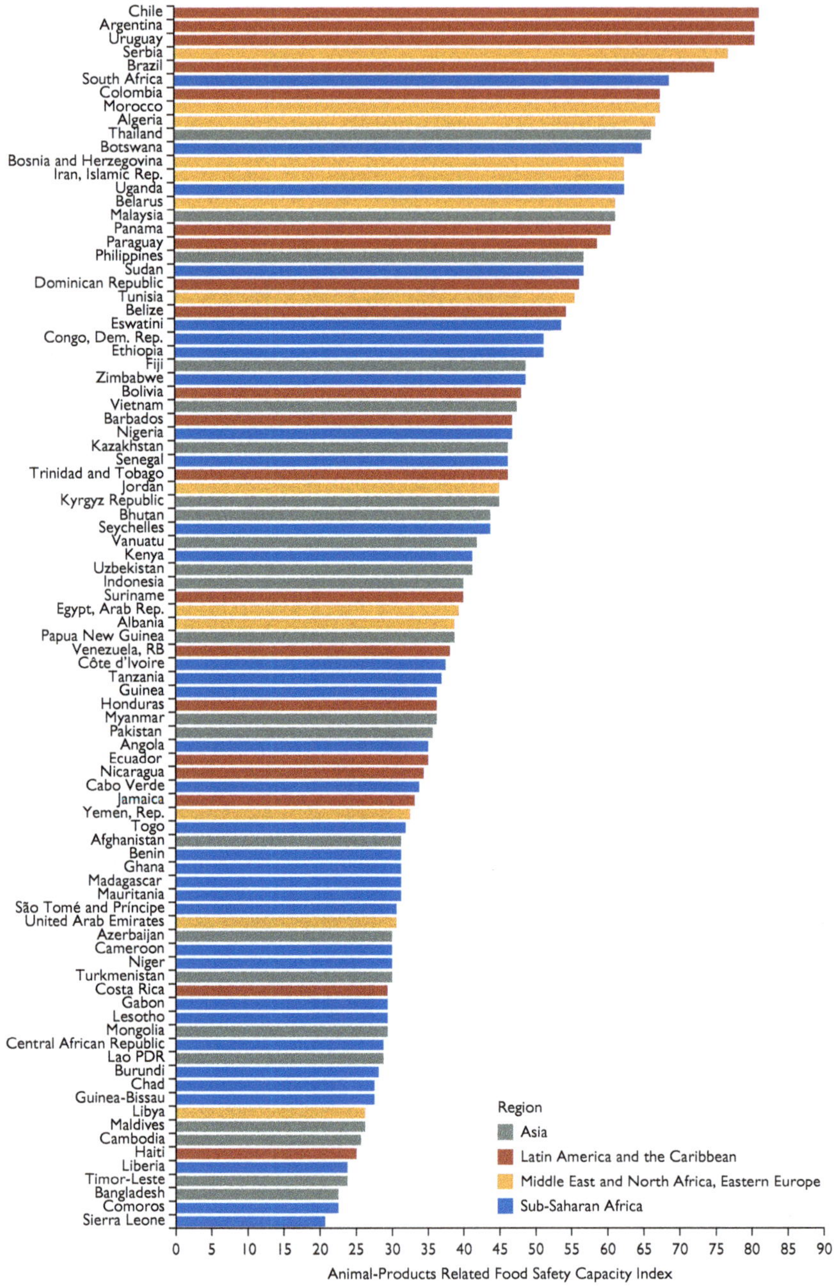

Source: Based on World Organisation for Animal Health country performance of veterinary service assessments and gap analyses.

FIGURE 3.5 Animal Products–Related Food Safety Capacity Index versus Food Safety Management Capacity Need Index, by Income Group

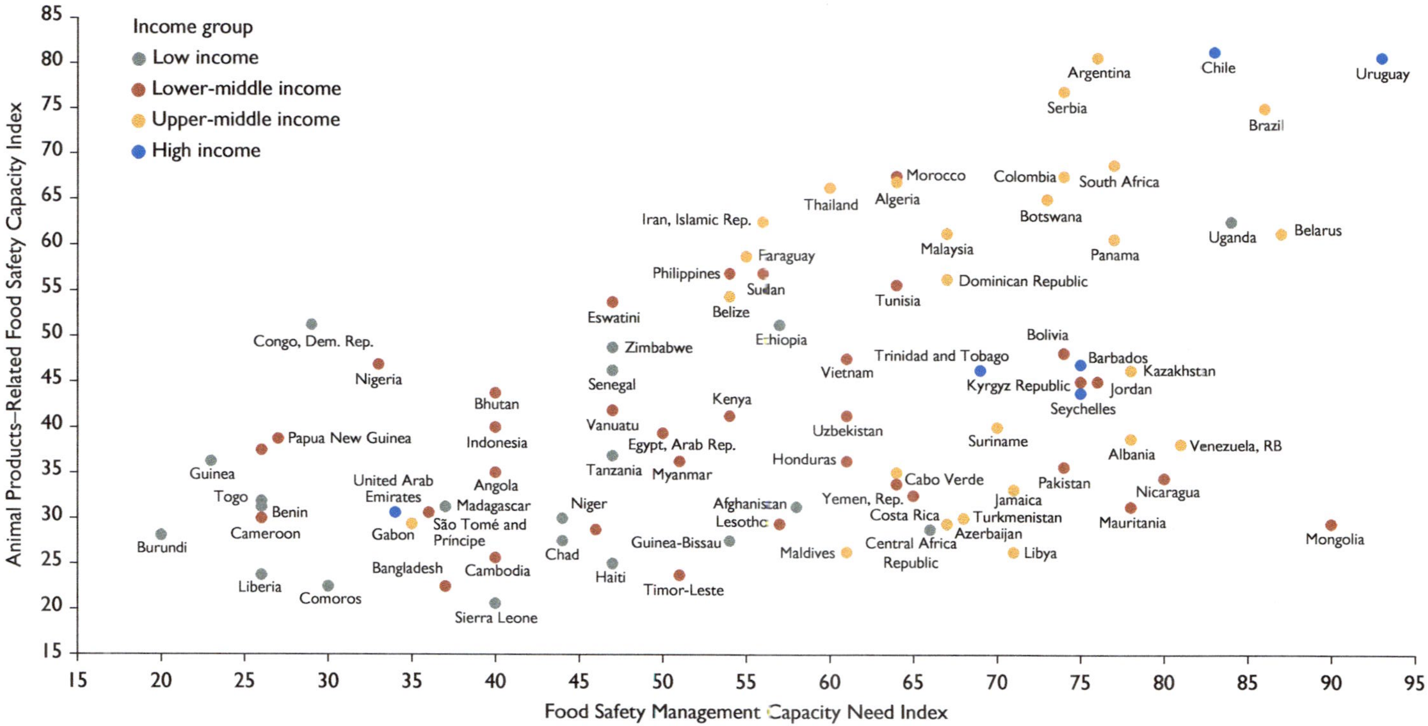

Source: Based on World Organisation for Animal Health country performance of veterinary service assessments and gap analyses; FAOSTAT; World Bank, World Development Indicators.

FIGURE 3.6 Gap between Animal-Based Food Safety Need and Capacity, by Country and Income Group

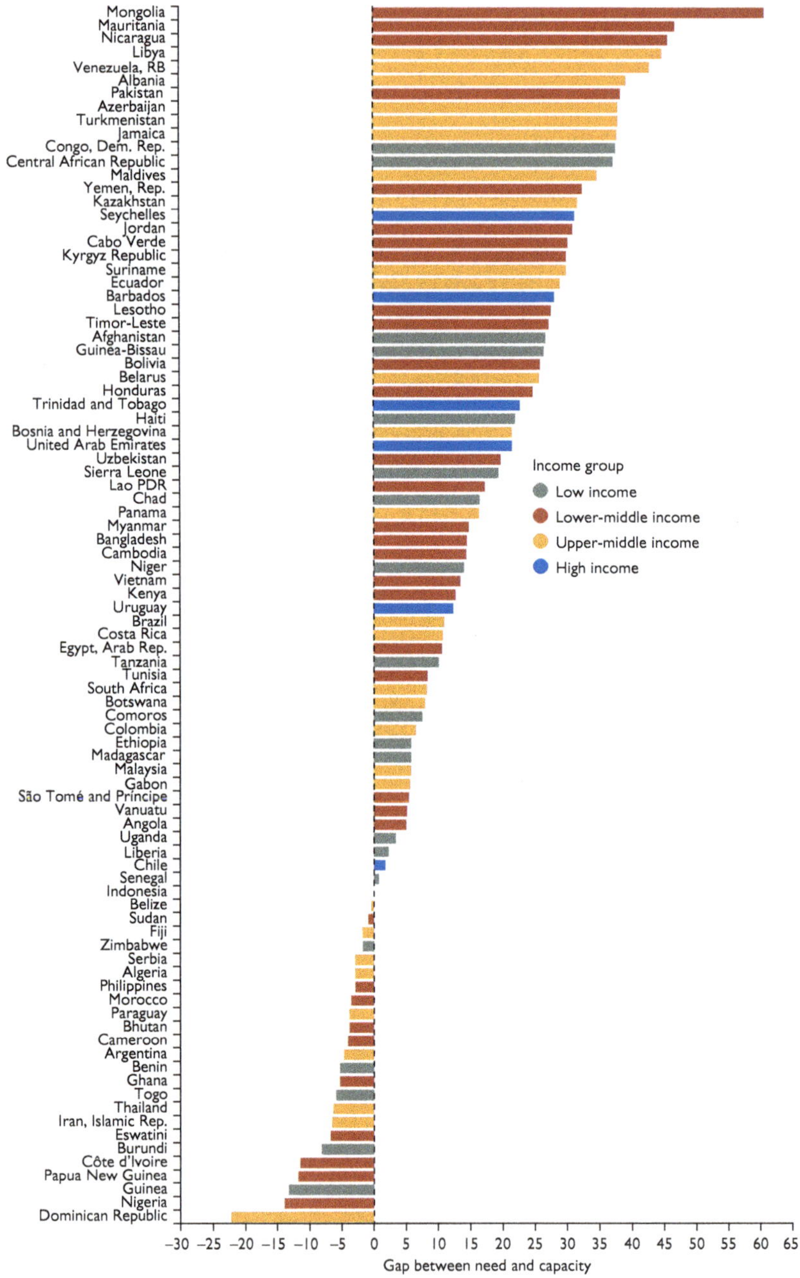

Sources: Based on World Organisation for Animal Health country performance of veterinary service assessments and gap analyses; FAOSTAT; World Bank, World Development Indicators.

"capacity gap" in managing animal-based food safety—that is, the gap between need and capacity as shown by the relative position of the two indexes. Most of the countries with especially high gaps are middle-income countries, a pattern consistent with the life cycle concept highlighted in chapter 1. The largest gaps appear to be for Mauritania, Mongolia, and Nicaragua. Countries having more than adequate capacity are either those with very strong animal-based food safety management systems (for example, Argentina, the Islamic Republic of Iran, and Thailand) or those not yet requiring strong capacities because of their position on the agricultural and dietary transformation pathway. An example of efforts to address this gap in food safety management capacity for animal-based foods is given in box 3.3.

Multiple factors contribute to FBD from animal-based foods. Among bad conditions and practices are poor husbandry practices, inappropriately administered veterinary drugs, mishandled animals during transport, insanitary slaughter facilities and inappropriate slaughtering methods, and recontaminated meat during storage and distribution. Weak capacities to regulate and deliver technical support services undoubtedly exacerbate the widespread nature and persistence of these conditions and practices.

BOX 3.3 Tackling Risks from Animal-Based Foods in Vietnam

The World Bank–supported Livestock Competitiveness and Food Safety Project aims to increase the competitiveness of livestock production in 12 provinces in Vietnam, while reducing the environmental footprint of livestock and enhancing food safety along the entire value chain.

The project supports disease-free livestock production and the adoption of good animal husbandry practices, combined with the collective action of livestock farmers, the modernization of slaughterhouses to comply with environmental and food safety standards, and upgrading traditional wet markets, where most fresh food in Vietnam is bought. The project also aims to strengthen the capacities of central and local governments to undertake disease and food safety control measures.

The project has already effectively applied a One Health approach on a fairly large scale. Significant attention has been given to upgrading slaughterhouse and market infrastructure, as well as influencing the behavior of farmers, food operators, and consumers toward safer animal husbandry, food handling, and food preparation practices.

The project has been instrumental in changing the minds of policy makers about the role and ability of smallholders and small and medium enterprises to participate in modern agri-food value chains, and in demonstrating practical examples of how to improve the management of food safety in the context of a relatively fragmented farm sector, informal trade practices, and consumers' preference for buying fresh meat in wet markets. The prevailing thinking had been that production and distribution channels must be consolidated to realize improved food safety.

Everything else being equal, countries with more adequate levels of food safety management capacity will likely have a lower incidence of FBD. To test this assumption, the burden of FBD attributable to animal source foods, as estimated by the Foodborne Disease Burden Epidemiology Reference Group, was examined in relation to the Animal Products–Related Food Safety Capacity Index. Countries with a higher value on the index have a lower burden of animal-based FBD.[6] For particular elements of the index, capacities for inspection and the regulation of veterinary drugs and residue testing have the strongest negative correlation with the burden of animal-based FBD.[7] The status of laboratory infrastructure is the element of animal-based food safety capacity that is least strongly correlated with the burden of animal-based FBD.[8]

An especially noteworthy finding is the enormous difference among low- and lower-middle-income countries in the apparent FBD burden between countries that are and are not adequately funding their veterinary services. This is summarized in table 3.2. Only seven of the 55 low- or lower-middle-income countries in the sample were rated in the World Organisation for Animal Health's PVS assessments as providing adequate operational funding for their veterinary services. For the seven countries, the average disability-adjusted life years (DALYs) burden of FBD from animal source foods is 192

TABLE 3.2 Average Animal Source Food DALYs Burden, by Country Category and Funding Adequacy

Income category	Countries in sample	Countries with adequate levels of veterinary service operational funding	Average animal source food DALYs per 100,000 people for countries with adequate funding	Average animal source food DALYs per 100,000 people for countries with inadequate funding
Low	20	2	228.1	597.7
Lower middle	35	5	177.1	293.2
Upper middle	29	14	116.1	81.0
High	9	8	46.0	41.9
Total	**93**	**29**	**115.1**	**333.0**

Sources: Based on World Organisation for Animal Health performance of veterinary services assessments and Foodborne Disease Burden Epidemiology Reference Group estimates.
Note: DALY = disability-adjusted life year.

[6] Correlation coefficient is –0.57.

[7] Correlation coefficients are inspection and regulation of veterinary drugs = –0.52, residue testing = –0.51.

[8] Correlation coefficient is = –0.37.

per 100,000 people. For the 48 countries using inadequate public resources, the estimated DALYs burden is 407 per 100,000. The difference between the two is equivalent to four or five times the total FBD DALYs from animal source foods per 100,000 people in most high-income countries.

Figure 3.7 shows the diverse pattern of estimated FBD DALYs from animal source foods among several Sub-Saharan African countries. Countries are split between those with adequate and inadequate levels of operational funding for veterinary services. The averages for the former are a loss of 208 DALYs per 100,000 of the population; for the latter, the average is 569. For an indicative country of 20 million people that has a gross national income of US$2,000 per capita with adequate funding, the annual productivity loss would be US$83.2 million. The loss for inadequate funding using the same measure would be US$227.6 million. For Nigeria, a large country, the difference between having adequate and inadequate finance implies a productivity loss of US$749 million rather than US$2.05 billion. Conversely, by adequately investing in veterinary services, a country the size of Ethiopia would have a burden of US$415 million rather than US$1.1 billion. These results provide a compelling case that moderate levels of investment in enhancing food safety management capacity—and specifically for animal-based FBD—can have significant public health and economic benefits.

FIGURE 3.7 Foodborne Disease Attributable to Animal-Based Foods among Sub-Saharan African Countries with Adequate vs. Inadequate Veterinary Service Funding

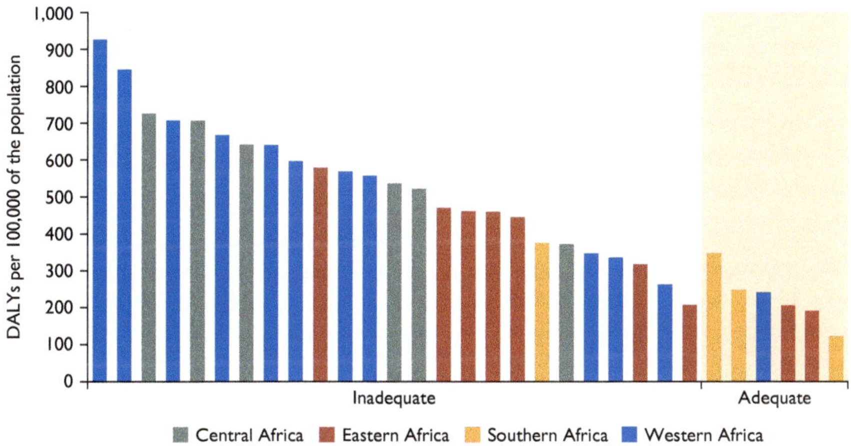

Sources: DALY estimates by Foodborne Disease Burden Epidemiology Reference Group; funding adequacy based on the World Organisation for Animal Health performance of veterinary services assessments.

Note: Country-specific burden of disease estimates are not published by the WHO and hence the countries are not individually labeled in this graph. DALY = disability-adjusted life year.

THE ALTERNATIVES TO PUBLIC REGULATION

Because public food safety management capacity tends to be inadequate in LMICs, interest is growing in alternative approaches to regulation envisaging a new relationship between the private sector as the "regulated" and the government as "regulator" (box 3.4). Thus, co-regulatory approaches and other forms of public-private partnerships are seen to provide opportunities to achieve greater efficiency in the management of food safety through the adoption of approaches that are practicable and more amenable to available resources, prevailing capacities, and incentives within agri-food value chains (Martinez et al. 2007; Narrod et al. 2009).

For alternatives to direct regulation, the public sector can support the development and application of voluntary codes of practice or private standards, provide information to businesses and consumers about risk management, and engender market-based incentives for better risk management. Regulatory approaches can be made more flexible to allow businesses to comply in ways that are more efficient and effective. Initiatives for this include industry inputs to the design of regulatory standards, flexibility in applying and enforcing process standards, and industry collaboration on enforcement.

BOX 3.4 Shifting Paradigms and Responsibilities in Food Safety Regulation

Regulatory systems for delivering public goods have traditionally been aimed at changing or controlling the behavior of businesses in a way that will either avoid damage or help create desired public goods, including the protection of public health. The trend toward a new regulatory paradigm, most notably in industrial countries—such as Australia, New Zealand, the United Kingdom, and the United States—involves establishing a partnership between the public and private sectors, and moving away from the strict policing function of government. The aim is to ensure that regulatory systems are effective in what they aim to deliver (in other words, how they perform in terms of desired outcomes), rather than in how they are designed and the enforcement functions applied.

For food safety, there is a strong link between this trend and the more preventive approach. Rather than ex post sanctioning for a food safety failure, the focus has progressively shifted to ex ante identification of a hazard, and measures are then taken to prevent potential damage. Thus, the focus is essentially on managing risk. For example, the European Union adopted a preventive approach through its General Food Law Regulation of 2002. In 2011, the United States adopted a preventive approach through its Food Safety Modernization Act, and spent six years developing the implementing regulations and preparing staff, businesses, and markets for this new approach to food safety regulation.

The United Kingdom has perhaps advanced farthest, with the Food Standards Agency actively promoting the concept of "regulated self-assurance and earned recognition" through its Regulating Our Future proposal. This includes measures

(Continued)

BOX 3.4 Shifting Paradigms and Responsibilities in Food Safety Regulation ***(Continued)***

to (1) develop an enhanced registration system to gather more data on food businesses and to try to ensure that each business is sufficiently compliant from the start; (2) develop the agency's segmentation model of food businesses, which is still based on risk but is moving most of the sector into regulated self-assurance; (3) develop a system of regulated self-assurance for businesses that have demonstrated their compliance; (4) maintain inspection and enforcement systems at the local government level; (5) maintain a surveillance system for emerging risks; and (6) aim for full cost recovery of regulatory activities, including the Food Standards Agency's running costs and the costs of intervention.

A key element of co-regulatory approaches to food safety regulation is the recognition of private assurance systems. These involve food safety standards that are established by private entities, which have compliance with regulatory requirements as their starting point and compliance ascertained through private auditing systems. In the United Kingdom, the Red Tractor Scheme is an on-farm assurance facility with separate standards for different agricultural commodities. Red Tractor, run by the nonprofit company Assured Food Standards, sets standards and assesses compliance with these standards at various points on the value chain. Certificates of conformity permit products to display the Red Tractor logo at the point of sale. For organic foods in the United Kingdom, the charity Soil Association certifies food products against its own organic standards, which comply with European Union norms.

Co-regulatory approaches to food safety have progressed most dramatically in industrial countries, though there are signs of a shift toward this approach in low- and middle-income countries. China uses the preventive model at the legislative level through its Food Safety Law of 2015, although the country has a long way to go to implementing this approach. The Association of Southeast Asian Nations, also in in 2015, adopted the Food Safety Policy and Regulatory Framework for its member states, which has proactive prevention at its core. And India is striving to engage consumers in raising food safety standards as an alternative and supplement to conventional enforcement.

Because of the weak regulatory capacity of many LMICs, especially low- and lower-middle-income countries, considerable interest is growing in the role of co-regulatory approaches and other forms of public-private partnerships for food safety. These approaches offer opportunities to offset weaknesses in public systems in promulgating and enforcing food safety regulations by leveraging private incentives for safe food. This, however, greatly contrasts with the strict regulatory function of government in LMICs and will require a significant cultural shift by regulatory agencies and their personnel.

Importantly, adopting co-regulatory approaches does not imply that governments simply stand back and let agri-food markets function unimpeded. Active engagement is needed between the public and private sectors, and explicit recognition of where private food safety governance mechanisms do or do not accord with regulatory requirements. Indeed, a role remains for more traditional modes of regulatory enforcement where private mechanisms of food safety assurance are too weak or market-based incentives for businesses to upgrade their food safety management capacity are missing. Co-regulatory approaches also require capabilities within businesses and across sectors, including the ability and willingness of value chain actors to coordinate their activities for food safety management. In nascent and rapidly evolving sectors, and in the informal sector, it is unlikely that conditions will be conducive to this approach.

In industrial countries, markets have emerged for foods on the basis of food safety, either through the branding of food (for example, many retailers' brands are marketed on their safety and quality) and labels attached to systems of certification with voluntary public or private standards, especially the latter. In principle, market-based initiatives might offer potential for the private governance of food safety in LMICs, but these countries face various constraints that are likely to limit their role in practice.

Market-based incentives for compliance with voluntary food safety standards are highly reliant on consumer demand for certified foods. There is evidence that consumers in LMICs are unable or unwilling to pay for these foods because of a lack of awareness or poor understanding of what certification represents. Yin et al. (2010) found that low awareness of organic food was one of the main reasons for the lack of consumer demand for these products in China. A study carried out in urban centers of southern Vietnam found that consumer familiarity with food quality certifications went hand in hand with higher levels of income and education, younger ages, and increased supermarket shopping. Overall, this study found survey respondents were unfamiliar with leading food labels; under 10 percent, for example, had heard of VietGAP or GLOBALG.A.P. (Nguyen et al. 2017).

Consumers in LMICs vary in the level of trust they have in labels associated with food safety. The literature on certified food in China shows generally low levels of trust in these labels (Liu, Pieniak, and Verbeke 2013). Jin and Zhao (2008) found that many Chinese consumers who would be willing to pay more for food with safety guarantees did not have enough trust in China's "green" and "organic food" labels to pay premiums for these foods. This mistrust in part relates to certification programs rarely providing actual evidence that these foods are safer (lower levels of pesticide residues, heavy metals, and microbial pathogens, for example). This reflects the fact that statistically relevant sampling and testing certified products are almost never carried out in China or other LMICs.

Evidence shows that consumers are sensitive to the actors behind food safety labels. Studies show that consumers largely accept these labels if the country of origin is trusted, whether or not they are backed by government. For example, Wu et al. (2014) found that Chinese consumers were willing to pay higher premiums for infant milk formula manufactured in China but certified by a U.S. or European organic certification scheme rather than a Chinese one. Evidence shows that Chinese consumers have more trust in government food safety measures than the private certification schemes of civil society (Zhang et al. 2016). A study in Indonesia found that 60 percent of consumers preferred organic food certification to be overseen by the central government (Maghraby et al. 2013).

The availability of certified products in LMICs can be a significant limiting factor, both in terms of the ability of consumers to buy these products and their familiarity of and exposure to them. In many LMICs, certified products are mainly distributed through supermarkets and are rarely available in traditional markets and local stores. This has been observed in China (Li 2007; Qing et al. 2006; Tang Li, and Jiang 2010), the Russian Federation (Bruschi et al. 2015), and Thailand (Wongprawmas and Canavari 2017). In many cases, labels are specific to individual distribution channels. In Thailand, for example, the Carrefour Quality Line private label is only found in supermarkets operated by Carrefour, while the City of Clean Food label is specific to wet markets in Bangkok (Schipmann and Qaim 2011).

Although niche markets exist for foods certified to voluntary food safety standards directed at rich consumers in urban areas of LMICs, there is probably little scope for these initiatives in informal markets for the poor and in rural areas. Thus, efforts to promote certified foods, in effect, segment food markets into those with higher and lower standards of food safety. This is especially so where public regulatory systems are weak. These actions could also further undermine food safety in markets for the poor as substandard food is diverted from markets in which consumers demand higher food safety standards. This could happen with contaminants over which producers have limited ability to control in the context of traditional production technologies and where controls are costly. In these cases, there may be incentives for foods simply to be sorted and for contaminated products to be diverted into low-income markets. Certification works best when it leads to overall improvements in food safety management and risk reduction, rather than simply in the market segmentation of high- and low-risk food.

The public sector can play a vital role in establishing and maintaining private governance mechanisms for food safety in LMICs in four main ways. First, public infrastructure is essential for upgrading food safety management capacity (for example, a reliable supply of electricity and running water). Or public infrastructure may be undersupplied by the private sector, especially when demand is nascent (for example, laboratory testing facilities) and for which there are significant public good elements (for example, cleaning up environmental contaminants).[9] Second, public oversight may be necessary to prevent consumers from being mis-sold products that are falsely labeled as certified; this strongly reflects the credence nature of many aspects of food safety, as outlined in box 1.2

[9] For example, new landing facilities were required for Kenya's Lake Victoria fisheries to meet hygiene requirements for exports to the European Union. These were provided with donor and government support (Henson and Mitullah 2004).

in chapter 1.[10] Third, there may be little incentive or it may be too costly for the private sector to support upgrading food safety management capacity by more vulnerable value chain actors; for example, smallholder farmers and micro and small enterprises. Because these actors are important for achieving the Sustainable Development Goals, governments have an important role to play in training, engendering collective action by small farmers and businesses, and providing storage facilities. And fourth, the public sector can play a key role in defraying the risks and costs associated with nascent private initiatives to enhance food safety (for example, through public procurement of certified foods). The public sector can also provide a convening function for collective action by businesses, give direct financial support, and disseminate information that lends credibility to the efforts of businesses to communicate the food safety benefits of their products.[11]

Examples are emerging of private initiatives aimed at enhancing the safety of food directed at domestic markets in LMICs. In some cases, these are predominantly driven by the private sector; and in others, they are part of public-private partnerships that vary in the level of formality of the relationship between the public and private sectors. For example, in Kenya, Aflatoxin Proficiency Testing for East and Central Africa is a private certifier that approves the testing protocols of millers and tests randomly selected duplicate samples. Another example relating to enhanced controls for aflatoxins is a pilot project in Nigeria that is promoting the adoption of new aflatoxin-control technology through the public's support of a price premium in domestic markets for commercial feed (IITA 2013). The private sector is also involved in adapting international private standards to local market conditions and training suppliers to achieve compliance. Examples include local GAP programs for producers selling into markets that are being promoted by GLOBALG.A.P. and the Global Food Safety Initiative's Global Markets Programme for small processors, which provides defined paths for making progress on food safety management.

But what about the scope and limitations of market-based approaches for improving food safety in informal markets or in circumstances where these markets still account for most marketed product? The International Livestock Research Institute has participated in multiple initiatives focusing on farmers and informal market operators. The institute provides training, introduces low-cost technologies, and occasionally offers incentives for behavioral changes. Some of the better documented examples are summarized in table 3.3. Box 3.5 is a case study of aflatoxins in maize in Kenya.

[10] Another issue is that private firms have incentives to "game" compliance. In other words, it may be cheaper to invest in the appearance of compliance rather than actual compliance. Here, private firms may have quality control systems and even laboratory facilities, but in practice are tempted to avoid compliance. There is anecdotal evidence that this occurs in the formal dairy industry, where large-scale firms blend down milk with antimicrobial residues to below limits, and the meat industry, where companies pressure veterinary inspectors to classify meat as fit for consumption. Brazil's 2017 tainted meat scandal is a case in point.

[11] Zhou, Huo, and Peng (2004) found that 20 percent more consumers were willing to buy "green pork" when given detailed information on production and processing requirements, and they indicated a willingness to pay a significantly higher price for it. In a controlled experiment, Birol et al. (2015) found that consumers in Mumbai were willing to pay more for GLOBALG.A.P.-certified grapes if they were given information on the food safety practices underlying the label.

TABLE 3.3 Training and Certification in Informal Markets: Selected Cases

Particulars	Kenya	Ibadan, Lagos	Assam, India
Value chain	Informal milk sector	Butchers	Informal milk sector
When	1997–2006	2009–11	2009–13
Number of traders	25,000–30,000	About 900	About 300 traders and 600 producers
Number of trained market actors	In 2010, 4,200 traders registered nationally In pilot areas, 85% of traders	80 directly by the project and about 420 by peer-to-peer training	265 traders and 480 producers trained
Consumers reached	About 500,000 to 5 million	About 360,000	About 1.5 million
Intervention	Training in hygiene and business practices, providing hygienic dairy cans with wide necks, certificates given to successful trainees, which reduced harassment by officials.	Peer-to-peer training on basic hygiene, provision of boots, hats, aprons, fly-proof netting, and food-safe disinfectants; banners and promotional material; using butchers' associations to monitor performance and ensure compliance.	In-depth training needs analysis; training of trainers, training covered hygiene and business skills; traders motivated by better relations with officials and positive publicity, and farmers by visible reduction in mastitis.
Documented impact	Improved milk safety after training (reduction in unacceptable coliforms from 71% to 42%). High economic benefits from the initiative of US$33.5 million a year.	Reduction of unacceptable meat from 97.5% to 78.5% ($p < 0.001$). Significant improvements in KAP after training. Cost of training US$9 per butcher and estimated gains through diarrhea averted was US$780 per butcher.	Improved knowledge attitude and practice (KAP) after training. Significantly higher milk production after training and tendency for reduced mastitis. Sector-level benefits in Kamrup at least US$5.6 million a year.
Current status of the initiative	Training and certification episodic and project-led, but trained vendors have an important share of the market.	Pilot intended to investigate efficacy and acceptability, but did not have a strategy for sustainability.	Training and monitoring ongoing and supported by government.
Information sources	Omore and Baker 2011 Kaitibie et al. 2010	Grace, Dipeolu, et al. 2012 Grace, Olowoye, et al. 2012	Lapar et al. 2014 Lindahl et al. 2014

Sources: Works cited in the table.

BOX 3.5 Limitations of Market-Based Incentives: Aflatoxin Controls in Kenya

Kenyan maize is frequently contaminated with aflatoxin, a hepatotoxic carcinogenic metabolite produced by certain fungi. The level of dietary exposure to aflatoxin in Kenya is among the highest in the world because of a combination of high maize consumption and agro-ecological conditions. The level of awareness and concern over aflatoxin contamination in Kenya is high among consumers, the private sector, and policy makers. Various interventions have been undertaken to address the problem, including introducing various technologies, such as Aflasafe and mobile dryers; improved product testing; and experimental studies gauging farmer, consumer, and miller responses to incentives and information.

Much of the maize consumed in Kenya is produced by small-scale farmers and never traded. Marketed maize consists of grain sold on the informal market; branded (sifted) maize flour processed in large-scale, formal sector roller mills; and unbranded flour processed by small-scale, often unregistered, hammer mills. These market structure characteristics are important for understanding the scope and limitations of market-based incentives to tackle aflatoxin contamination.

Hoffmann and Jones (2018) find that farmers producing maize for sale take fewer actions to prevent aflatoxin contamination than those producing for only household consumption. For the latter farmers, investing in aflatoxin control is purely an investment in household health. The current market structure does little to encourage aflatoxin control at its source on the farm. Instead, millers make their brands safe by rejecting contaminated lots of grain. But this grain invariably finds another buyer, typically serving a lower market tier. In this way, the safety premium for maize concentrates aflatoxin exposure among poor consumers, who typically buy low-cost brands or buy their maize from the informal sector.

Despite a growing capacity for food safety testing in Kenya, firms are reluctant to label their food as "aflatoxin safe." One reason is fear of attracting increased regulatory scrutiny. A randomized study of consumer responses to this labeling showed an initially large impact on sales, but the effect faded by the third week of active marketing (Hoffmann, Moser, and Herrman 2017). Millers investing in food safety are therefore more likely to be driven by fears of negative publicity or regulatory action than by consumer demand for food safety certification.

Simultaneously building the testing capacity of mills in high-contamination areas and the regulatory capacity of local authorities, and strengthening the links between millers and local farmers, will be essential for bringing down aflatoxin levels in maize sold through the market.

Providing premium prices to producers for safe maize has been shown to increase the use of on-farm aflatoxin control technologies. But this strategy is mostly limited to experimental studies and donor sourcing of food aid subject to local procurement mandates. For the market premium for safe maize at retail to be an incentive for reducing aflatoxin in the food supply, it will be necessary to link farmers in affected regions directly to millers. Doing this will require public intervention, which should focus on geographic areas where aflatoxin contamination is most severe.

The scope for market-based approaches for improving food safety in informal markets is highly context-specific and needs to be carefully adapted to fit particular food systems. The incentives for behavior change, which are key to long-term sustainability, have also been difficult to generalize. In Kenya, where the approach was first developed in the dairy sector, informal traders were prone to harassment by the authorities, and a main motivation for training was to get a certificate protecting them from this (Kaitibie et al. 2010). In Assam, by contrast, traders were motivated by the good publicity they received after being trained and the opportunity to enter a dialogue with government dairy development partners (rather than being regarded as a nuisance by them). In none of the three evaluated pilots in India, Kenya, and Nigeria were trained traders able to charge a premium for selling higher-quality products, which was initially considered to be a promising incentive.

ENABLING SMALLHOLDER FARMERS TO BE FOOD SAFETY COMPLIANT

The participation of smallholder producers in LMICs in value chains directed at predominantly export markets for higher value and differentiated agri-food products is recognized as a vital opportunity to enhance and diversify farm incomes and generate rural employment. Yet, concerns are widespread that these opportunities go unrealized because smallholder farmers lack the technical ability and financial means to meet evolving regulatory requirements and private standards, especially for food safety. Even where smallholder farmers have production cost advantages over larger producers, these can be outweighed by the potentially high transaction costs associated with facilitating, monitoring, and certifying compliance with these standards. There are concerns, too, that efforts in LMICs to upgrade food safety management capacity for high-value foods, whether for export or domestic markets, could be detrimental to the livelihoods of poor farmers, and thus for achieving the Sustainable Development Goals.

Concerns about the potential for smallholders to be excluded from export value chains dominated the academic literature in the early 2000s, and contributed to a wave of development assistance programs, especially in Sub-Saharan Africa.[12] More recently, it is being recognized that the process of including or excluding smallholder farmers, especially in the context of strict food safety standards, is more nuanced. For example, the assumed dichotomy between low- and high-value markets represent an unduly simplistic image of the market choices available to small-scale producers. In reality, a continuum of alternative supply chains exists with different levels of stringency and the specificity of domestic or trade-oriented buyer requirements (figure 3.8). Thus, there is, in effect, a progressive enhancement of the methods by which the safety of

[12] The basis for these concerns, and the nature and efficacy of government and donor-assisted programs, are assessed by Jaffee, Henson, and Diaz Rios (2011).

FIGURE 3.8 Smallholder Farmers, Agricultural Markets, and Varied Conformity Requirements

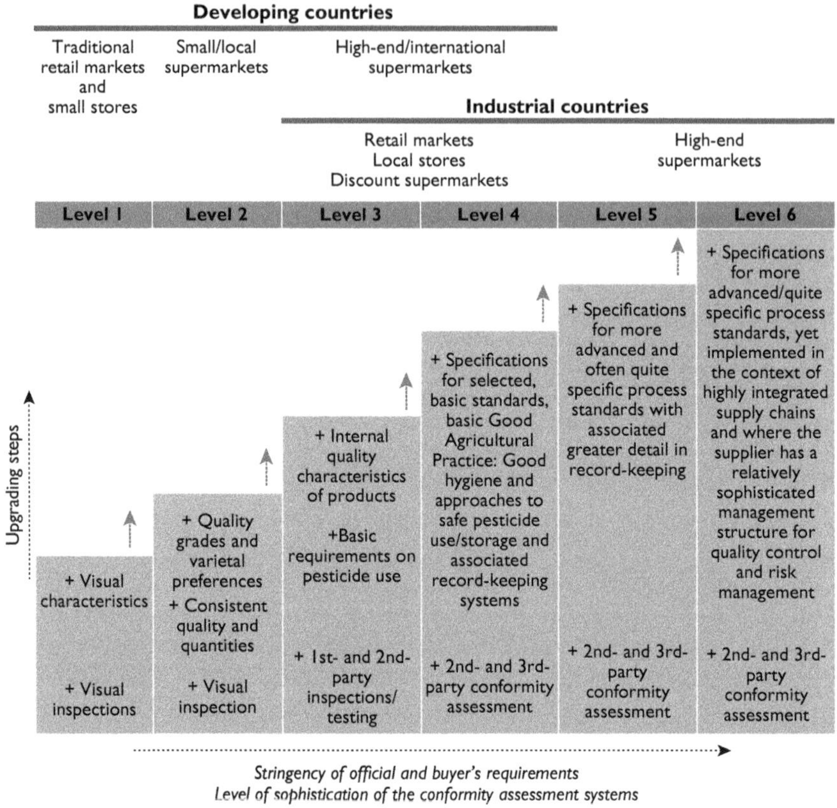

Source: Jaffee, Henson, and Diaz Rios 2011.

food products are assessed and communicated.[13] Most concerns about the exclusion of smallholder farmers focus on one market segment, which is often represented in the literature by GLOBALG.A.P. certification requirements for export and domestic high-end supermarkets. In most LMICs, however, by far the biggest market opportunities for smallholder farmers are markets where less stringent product, process, and documentary requirements are the norm.

Two factors mainly explain the success or not of interventions to strengthen smallholder participation in value chains in the context of stricter food safety standards. The first is the degree of upgrading and change required by smallholder farmers in the context of prevailing practices and the capabilities of farmers, service providers, and commodity buyers. Incremental upgrades

[13] From visual inspection at one extreme to intensive documentation of practices and outputs based on second- and third-party conformity assessment at the other extreme.

involving technical learning, institutional coordination, and increased record-keeping are often very successful (Jaffee, Henson, and Diaz Rios 2011). But radical shifts that involve costly investments and exposing smallholder farmers to much higher levels of market risk are rarely successful or sustainable.

The second factor is the strength and capabilities of lead firms that engage directly with smallholder farmers—and this is critical for success. If these firms are well-managed and well resourced, and have a competitive position within domestic or focal international markets, interventions are more likely to achieve strong and sustained traction for getting smallholder farmers to upgrade (Jaffee, Henson, and Diaz Rios 2011). Indeed, lead firms tend to drive the adoption of improved standards by smallholder farmers through the requirements they set, and from their advisory and procurement oversight systems. Conversely, programs that try to bypass lead firms and upgrade weaker enterprises, and poorly organized smallholder farmers, do not have a good track record.

Various market institutions have evolved in the context of stricter food safety standards to overcome the transaction costs faced by smallholder farmers. The participation of smallholders in contract production, and especially production-based contracts that include inputs on credit before producers are trained and intensive monitoring begins, was found to facilitate compliance in Zimbabwe (Henson, Masakure, and Boselie 2005), Kenya (Okello and Swinton 2007), Peru (Lemeilleur 2013), and Senegal (Maertens and Swinnen 2009). In Kenya and India, farmer groups play an important role in facilitating compliance by providing extension and group monitoring (Roy and Thorat 2008; Okello and Swinton 2007). Direct sourcing that offers scope for the compliance monitoring of buyers can also play an important role, as found by Ding et al. (2015) for Chinese fruit and vegetable growers supplying supermarkets. Cost-sharing by exporters and public agencies facilitated farmer compliance in several countries (Kersting and Wollni 2012; Handschuch, Wollni, and Villalobos 2013; Leimeilleur 2013; Subervie and Vagneron 2013; Henson Masakure, Cranfield 2011). In Thailand, exporters and donors pay for over 90 percent of all costs of GLOBALG.A.P. certification (Kersting and Wollni 2012).[14]

THE STATE OF CAPACITIES FOR MANAGING TRADE-RELATED FOOD SAFETY RISKS

The application of strict food safety requirements, both through regulatory reforms and private standards, is a concern in many LMICs. But there is little evidence that this trend has adversely affected agri-food exports.

[14] Compliance with higher regulatory or private standards may give rise to a wider set of benefits over and beyond higher or more stable prices for farmers. Unnevehr and Ronchi (2014) summarize the findings from about dozen studies and countries on this subject. Some of the additional benefits cited include adopting improved technology with spillover benefits for staple crops (Minten, Randrianarison, and Swinnen 2009), higher or more stable labor incomes (Maertens and Swinnen 2012; Minten, Randrianarison, and Swinnen 2009), or improved health through reduced on-farm exposure to pesticides (Kersting and Wollni 2012; Asfaw, Mithöfer, and Waibel 2009; Okello and Swinton 2009).

Indeed, many LMICs have recorded impressive growth in agri-food exports, with total food exports from these countries rising from US$113 billion in 2001 to US$475 billion in 2016. This included a fourfold increase (to a level of US$220 billion) in LMIC exports of high-value food that are more food-safety-sensitive, including fish, animal products, fresh fruit and vegetables, spices, and nuts (figure 3.9).

LMIC exports of high-value food are dominated by upper-middle-income countries, accounting for 69 percent of the total of these exports in 2016. Twenty-eight percent of high-value food exports were from lower-middle-income countries and 2 percent were from low-income ones. While exports from low-income countries grew at 8.6 percent a year over 2001–16, they were valued at less than US$5 billion, and mainly consisted of niche products to specific markets.

Many LMIC countries are participating in the rising trade in high-value food, although 10–15 countries account for most of this expansion. In 2016, the 10 largest LMIC exporters accounted for 66 percent of total high-value food exports, compared with 59 percent in 2001. The top five (Brazil, China, India, Mexico, and Thailand) accounted for 46 percent, compared with 40 percent

FIGURE 3.9 LMIC Exports of High-Value Foods, by Product Group, 2001–16

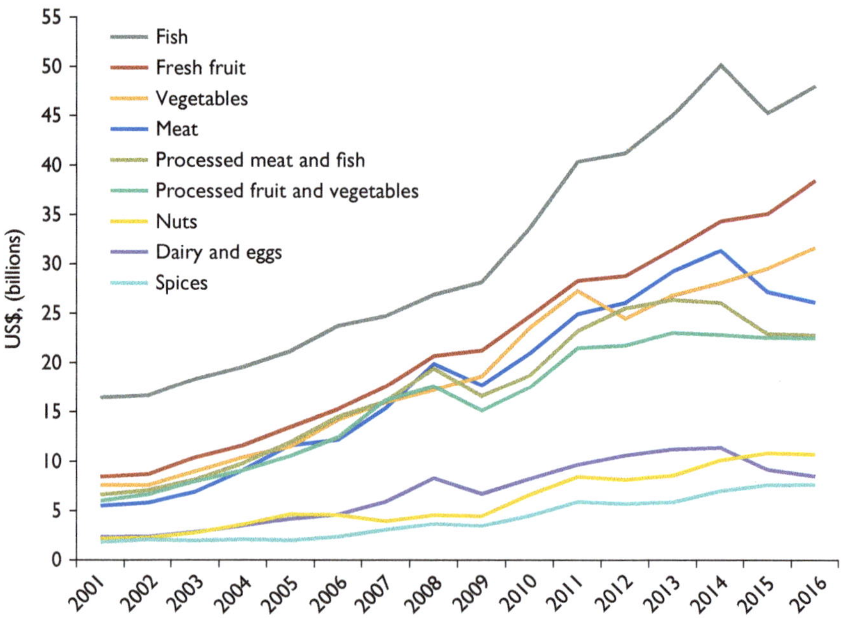

Source: International Trade Centre Trade Map Database.
Note: LMIC = low- and middle-income country.

in 2001.[15] Nine of the top 10 exporters in 2016 were also among the leaders in 2001; Vietnam was the new entrant (figure 3.10).

The trade in individual categories of high-value foods is typically more concentrated than for high-value food in the aggregate. For example, the 10 largest LMIC exporters of fresh vegetables accounted for 78 percent of total LMIC exports of high-value food, with two countries, Mexico and China, accounting for half. The top 10 countries also accounted for 84 percent of LMIC spice exports. Meat exports are even more concentrated, with the top 10 exporters accounting for 91 percent of the total, with two-thirds of this from Brazil and India.

Proxy indicators can be used to show the status of trade-related food safety management capacity in LMICs. These indicators—three of which are discussed here—suggest that considerable advances in capacity were made in recent years, but these are concentrated among a small number of larger middle-income economies.

FIGURE 3.10 High-Value LMIC Food Exports, by Income Group, 2001–16

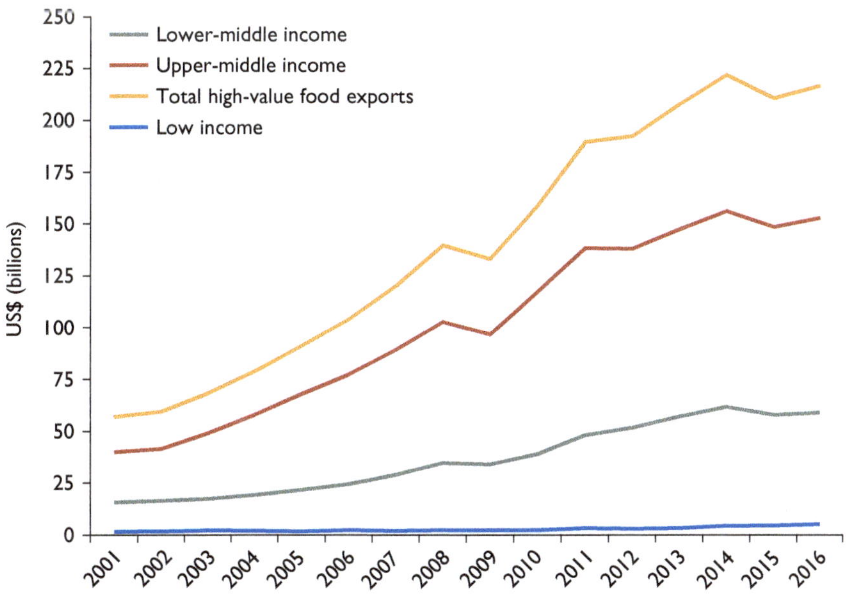

Source: International Trade Centre Trade Map Database.
Note: LMIC = low- and middle-income country.

[15] The concentration level would have been even higher if Chile had not attained high-income status in 2012.

The first relates to adopting GAPs. Table 3.4 shows the area of GLOBALG.A.P.-certified fruit and vegetable production.[16] Globally, growth has been impressive in the certified areas since 2010, largely because of the private sector's response to evolving market requirements in industrial countries, especially in the EU. The largest expansion in certified area was in high-income countries. The certified area in LMICs increased from 700,000 hectares in 2010 to 1.86 million hectares in 2017. Most of this growth has been in upper-middle-income countries, primarily in Latin America and the Caribbean, but also in China, the Philippines, and South Africa.

Among LMICs, 15 countries account for 89 percent of the area of fruit and vegetable production certified to GLOBALG.A.P. (table 3.5). These countries account for 59 percent of LMIC fresh fruit and vegetable exports, but accounted for more than 80 percent of the LMIC trade directed at high-income countries.

TABLE 3.4 Area of GLOBALG.A.P.-Certified Fruit and Vegetable Production, by Region and Income Group, 2010 and 2017

Hectares (thousands)

Area	2010	2017
Region		
Asia	92.7	325.6
Europe	868.6	2,735.5
Latin America and the Caribbean	519.4	1,344.4
Middle East and North Africa, Eastern Europe	111.6	195.7
North America	130.9	371.2
Sub-Saharan Africa	192.2	278.4
Total	**1,915.6**	**5,250.9**
Income group		
Low income	4,648.8	23.6
Lower-middle income	134.4	340.3
Upper-middle income	560.6	1,501.7
High income	1,215.9	3,385.1
Total	**1,915.6**	**5,250.8**

Source: Based on GLOBALG.A.P. data. secretariat.

[16] GLOBALG.A.P. certification would normally only be undertaken for export-oriented horticulture, but this is the only proxy for GAP for which data could be obtained. Many national GAP schemes are running, but information on area coverage is difficult to find and of uncertain reliability. GLOBALG.A.P. data, while accurate, convey only a partial picture.

TABLE 3.5 GLOBALG.A.P.-Certified Area for Fruit and Vegetables in LMICs, 2017

Country	Total certified area (2017)		Total fresh fruit, vegetable exports (2016)			Fresh fruit, vegetable exports to high-income countries (2016)		
	Hectares	Share (%)	US$ ('000)	Share in LMICs with certified area (%)	Share in LMICs (%)	US$ ('000)	Share in LMICs with certified area (%)	Share in LMICs (%)
South Africa	201,237	15.5	3,086,363	4.3	3.7	2,257,245	4.8	4.5
China	153,509	11.8	16,030,742	22.1	19.3	6,970,928	14.7	13.9
Mexico	106,231	8.2	12,148,599	16.8	14.7	11,831,093	24.9	23.7
Costa Rica	95,963	7.4	2,221,518	3.1	2.7	2,117,545	4.5	4.2
Peru	87,371	6.7	2,679,460	3.7	3.2	2,404,449	5.1	4.8
Ecuador	75,725	5.8	3,011,083	4.2	3.6	1,922,275	4.0	3.8
Egypt, Arab Rep.	73,425	5.7	2,163,247	3.0	2.6	1,433,728	3.0	2.9
Argentina	66,936	5.2	1,737,314	2.4	2.1	807,734	1.7	1.6
Brazil	58,167	4.5	860,027	1.2	1.0	767,545	1.6	1.5
Philippines	54,946	4.2	1,146,205	1.6	1.4	879,093	1.9	1.8
Colombia	50,593	3.9	1,055,240	1.5	1.3	1,045,233	2.2	2.1
Morocco	43,652	3.4	1,644,846	2.3	2.0	1,427,096	3.0	2.9
Guatemala	37,458	2.9	1,448,972	2.0	1.7	1,381,736	2.9	2.8
India	21,822	1.7	2,756,906	3.8	3.3	1,870,628	3.9	3.7
Turkey	19,950	1.5	4,814,706	6.6	5.8	2,957,617	6.2	5.9
Other LMICs	149,468	11.5	15,763,950	21.7	29.0	7,407,540	15.6	14.8
LMICs with certified area	—	—	*72,569,178*	*100*		*47,481,485*	*100*	
LMICs with no certified area	—	—	*10,347,172*		*12.5*	*2,497,692*		*5.0*
Total LMICs	**1,296,452**	**100**	**82,916,350**		**100**	**49,979,177**		**100**

Source: Based on GLOBALG.A.P. data.
Note: Area of coverage corresponds to GLOBALG.A.P.-certified area for first quarter, noncovered crops' first harvest. LMIC = low- and middle-income country; — = not available.

This is indicative of the far greater importance of GLOBALG.A.P. certification for food exports to high-income countries.

The second proxy measure of trade-related food safety management capacity is the adoption of certified organic production systems. Successfully using these systems is an indicator of capacity to adopt process controls and related certification, which requires sophisticated management and well-developed monitoring and record-keeping through the supply chain. Organic certification is a good indicator of growing capacity for managing quality and safety, even though it does not specifically address food safety.[17]

For fruit, vegetables, cereals, and pulses (legumes), most of the certified organic area is in high- and upper-middle-income countries (table 3.6). For oil crops, nuts, and beverage crops, low- and lower-middle-income countries account for a greater proportion of the certified area. For nuts and beverage crops, low-income countries have over 500,000 hectares under organic production, equivalent to more than 15 percent of their total land area for these crops.

For fruit and vegetable production, Mexico and China account for almost 57 percent of the total harvested area under organic certification in LMICs (table 3.7). The Arab Republic of Egypt and Turkey account for a further 12 percent. Over 11 percent of Mexico's total harvested area of fruit and vegetables is organically certified. Other countries with a high proportion are Bulgaria and the Dominican Republic.

TABLE 3.6 Organic Production Area, by Commodity and Country Income Group, 2017

Commodity	Low income	Lower-middle income	Upper-middle income	High income
Fruit and vegetables				
Organic area (hectares)	40,237	140,169	664,111	828,966
Share of organic area in total area (%)	0.22	0.21	0.86	5.62
Cereals and pulses (legumes)				
Organic area (hectares)	57,170	367,231	1,394,879	2,800,959
Share of organic area in total area (%)	0.07	0.13	0.53	2.08
Oil crops				
Organic area (hectares)	107,227	677,779	762,584	772,593
Share of organic area in total area (%)	0.69	0.70	0.67	1.18
Nuts and beverage crops				
Organic area (hectares)	571,559	353,368	784,691	222,167
Share of organic area in total area (%)	15.60	1.85	6.87	12.16

Source: FiBL 2018.

[17] Some lower-income countries have tried to take advantage of a situation in which there is very little use of purchased inputs and therefore only modest changes are needed to convert to organic production systems. These "organic by default" strategies have been used in some African countries. The mixed experience with this strategy is reviewed by Jaffee, Henson, and Diaz Rios (2011). In circumstances where the initiative centered only on certification and product marketing, the gains were temporary, compared with initiatives that also aimed to raise productivity through improved agronomic and postharvest practices.

TABLE 3.7 Certified Organic Fruit and Vegetable Production Area in LMICs, 2017

Country	Harvested area (hectares)	Organic harvested production area (hectares)	Organic area as proportion total harvested area (%)	Proportion of LMIC organic harvested area (%)
Mexico	2,208,609	253,448	11.48	30.01
China	49,634,732	224,621	0.45	26.60
Turkey	2,251,820	54,359	2.41	6.44
Egypt, Arab Rep.	1,556,705	43,749	2.81	5.18
Dominican Republic	210,856	26,473	12.55	3.13
Kenya	606,174	25,778	4.25	3.05
Ecuador	528,634	19,590	3.71	2.32
Vietnam	2,403,979	19,350	0.80	2.29
Madagascar	840,405	19,161	2.28	2.27
Bulgaria	119,663	19,068	15.93	2.26
Other LMICs	100,887,981	138,923	0.14	16.45
Total	**161,249,558**	**844,519**	**0.52**	**100**

Source: Research Institute on Organic Agriculture annual survey.
Note: LMIC = low- and middle-income country.

The third proxy measure of trade-related food safety management capacity in LMICs relates to the number of businesses and food-processing facilities that have shown an interest in exporting to high-income countries. In the United States, for example, facilities that process or handle food and beverage products must be preregistered with the U.S. Food and Drug Administration (FDA), and provide information about their facilities, including the categories of food being manufactured and types of activity within the facility. As of January 2018, 213,441 companies were registered with the FDA, of which 118,270 were based outside of the United States.[18] Of these companies, 30 percent were in upper-middle-income countries, 10 percent in lower-middle-income countries, and only 1 percent in low-income countries. China and Mexico accounted for 37 percent of total FDA registrations in LMICs (table 3.8). Fifteen LMICs collectively accounted for 75 percent of registrations, and these same countries accounted for 85 percent of high-value exports to the United States.

[18] In October 2012, 273,000 foreign food companies were registered with the FDA. Many companies, however, have not chosen to recertify, and some were still registered but had gone out of business.

TABLE 3.8 LMIC Food Businesses Registered with U.S. Food and Drug Administration, January 2018

Country	Number of valid registrations	Share of total valid registrations (%)	HVF exports to United States in 2017 (US$)	Share in total HVF exports to United States 2017 (%)
China	9,994	20.7	4,856,230	10.4
Mexico	8,291	17.1	16,857,494	36.2
India	3,585	7.4	3,136,250	6.7
Brazil	1,975	4.1	1,158,774	2.5
Colombia	1,500	3.1	383,223	0.8
Argentina	1,469	3.0	739,454	1.6
Vietnam	1,467	3.0	3,128,254	6.7
Thailand	1,416	2.9	2,145,821	4.6
Peru	1,348	2.8	1,945,749	4.2
Russian Federation	1,203	2.5	483,134	1.0
Turkey	1,200	2.5	408,165	0.9
Ecuador	973	2.0	1,463,616	3.1
Indonesia	960	2.0	2,293,579	4.9
South Africa	911	1.9	212,651	0.5
Philippines	713	1.5	646,998	1.4
Total Top 15 LMICs	*37,005*	*76.5*	*39,859,392*	*85.6*
Other LMICs	*11,383*	*23.5*	*6,689,857*	*14.4*
Total LMICs	**48,388**	**100**	**46,549,249**	**100**

Source: Based on data provided by the U.S. Food and Drug Administration.
Note: HVF = high-value food; LMIC = low- and middle-income country.

For a wide range of food products of animal origin in the EU, processing facilities are required to be inspected and approved for export by a recognized competent authority in the country of origin. These facilities must have hygiene standards equivalent to the EU. Table 3.9 details the countries with facilities approved for the export of chilled or processed fish to the EU. Nearly 1,900 processing facilities in 28 lower-middle-income countries were approved to export to the EU in 2018. Nearly all upper-middle-income countries have EU-approved fish-processing facilities, with nearly 2,100 approved facilities. Only eight low-income countries have fish-processing facilities approved to export to the EU, but their ratio of approved facilities to the value of exports is greater than for all other country income groups.

TABLE 3.9 Processing Facilities Approved for Chilled and Processed Fish Exports to the European Union

Country income group	Total fish production, 2013–15 (tons)	Number of countries with approved facilities, 2018	Number of approved chilled facilities, 2018	Number of approved processed fish facilities, 2018	Approved facilities per 100,000 tons of production	Value of fish exports to EU, 2014–16 (US$)
Low income	3,924,474.8	34	--	--	3.77	507,030.3
with approved facilities	1,815,046.8	8	16	132	8.15	505,069.7
Lower-middle-income	56,403,544.6	47	--	--	3.47	4,177,411.7
with approved facilities	54,850,217.9	28	102	1,855	3.57	4,176,711.7
Upper-middle-income	99,975,353.7	56	--	--	2.15	5,968,850.3
with approved facilities	99,172,226.0	37	103	2,051	2.17	5,948,309.3
High income	33,415,466.0	80	--	--	7.75	12,073,774.7
with approved facilities	20,666,836.1	20	377	2,212	12.53	2,342,717.3

Sources: Food and Agriculture Organization, FishStatJ; European Commission, Directorate General Health and Food Safety; UN Comtrade International Trade Statistics.

Note: Fish production includes captures and farming outputs from marine and inland fisheries. Data from the European Commission is the number of establishments from non–European Union (EU) countries from which imports of fishery products into the EU were permitted at January 27, 2018.

The impressive performance of LMIC food exports since 2000, especially for high-value food, testifies to the advances made not only in production capacity and efficiency but also in upgrading food safety management capacity. Many LMICs have undertaken administrative reforms and increased investments in the public and private sectors to facilitate market access and respond to changes in food safety requirements in export markets (see box 3.6, which looks at Ukraine's efforts to secure new food markets). These investments have in some cases been made strategically as part of efforts to establish or enhance exports for businesses or sectors. In many cases, however, these investments were stimulated by acute food safety problems, including temporary restraints on trade, subpar grades on inspection visits by trade partner regulators, and significant numbers of border rejections.

Instances of noncompliance with export market food safety requirements have in some cases imposed heavy costs on businesses and sectors. For businesses and sectors that are large and well established, however, this often means little more than a bump in the road. Here, trade disruptions tend to be short-lived and these businesses and sectors often emerge from these episodes stronger and with greater displays of industry collective action, maintained or even enhanced reputations for management of food safety, and more effective instances of public-private collaboration (box 3.7). These businesses and sectors have also been able to achieve economies of scale in upgrading their capacity and collective infrastructure (for example, fish landing sites, inspection systems, and laboratories), and by applying industry norms and standards.

There are examples of small sectors—often in smaller countries—that were able to differentiate themselves on the basis of high product quality and best practices in food safety management. Often, this has involved collective action within the private sector or across the public and private sectors to overcome logistical disadvantages and to establish a market presence. Notable examples are Kenya's and Peru's fresh vegetable export industries. There are also instances where efforts by even very small countries to upgrade food safety management capacity were successful at gaining access to export markets. Smaller players in the global high-value food trade, however, have tended to struggle to recover from food safety lapses. Often, a "one and done" situation prevails, whereby one lapse or even a suspected problem tarnishes the industry's reputation, causing buyers to flee to alternative sources. A case in point is the cyclospora outbreak in the late 1990s in the United States, which was traced to raspberries from Guatemala, and which put the sector out of business.

Almost all the attention given in LMICs to agri-food exports and the importance of food safety management capacity has focused on high-income country markets, with the growth of South-South trade and the role of food safety being largely ignored. While this growth seems to reflect the relatively favorable position of LMICs for complying with food safety requirements in high-income

BOX 3.6 Investing in Ukraine's Food Sector to Secure New Markets

The International Finance Corporation (IFC), the private sector arm of the World Bank Group, has worked over the past several years at all levels of Ukraine's agribusiness value chain and with the government's food safety authority to improve competitiveness. The goal is to diversify markets, either through exports or access to new domestic markets, and to attract investments in Ukraine's food sector. As part of the public sector component, IFC helped the government to draw up food safety legislation that meets international norms, streamline food safety regulations, and introduce inspection systems equivalent to European Union (EU) standards. IFC is working with industry to identify market barriers, and to develop inspection training programs.

IFC's partnerships with the private sector enabled the identification of priorities and proved to be essential in gaining public support for regulatory changes. Because of these and other efforts, the EU opened up for Ukrainian poultry in 2013, with three firms being initially certified. Ukrainian dairy products got market access to China in 2015 and to the EU in 2016. New export markets are continuing to open for Ukraine's food sector, most recently Saudi Arabia and Turkey.

IFC also helped Ukraine's private sector to secure new markets by providing on-site consulting services to over 90 large and small firms in the food sector. The partnerships of Ukrainian firms with multinational retailers, including Metro Cash & Carry and Auchan, were a strong driver for better food safety practices for these firms, encouraging 75 small and medium enterprises in processing and eight horticulture growers to improve food safety practices.

A survey of small and medium enterprises that participated in the IFC support program showed several benefits from improved food safety management, including better product quality, reduced waste, higher productivity, and more retained sales. Firms found that the benefits of increased revenue exceeded the costs of improving food safety. And they were most successful when food safety was part of a corporate strategy and employees were involved in the planning process.

For the Ukrainian dairy-processing industry, results like these confirm an ex ante analysis of the potential costs and benefits of using the hazard analysis and critical control points (HACCP) approach for the industry. The costs included capital investments, HACCP design and implementation, and the recurring costs of using the HACCP approach. The benefits included higher sales, less waste and other efficiencies, and increased attractiveness to investors. The costs of using the HACCP management system were estimated based on expert opinion and resulted in assumed increased sales of 15–25 percent. The payback period for investing in HACCP was estimated at only one to two years, though this depends on the age of firms' capital equipment.

Sources: IFC (2011, 2016); Tetyora, Osmochescu, Onul (2017).

BOX 3.7 Training of Trainers: Bangladesh Aquaculture and India Spices

The Joint Institute for Food Safety and Applied Nutrition, which is supported by the U.S. Food and Drug Administration, has carried out long-term "train the trainers" programs in Bangladesh and India. Both programs have given intensive training to an initial cadre of experts, who then adapt them in local languages and provide training to value chain actors through training centers. The Bangladeshi program started in 2009 and the Indian one 2012. Long-standing problems with import rejections and market access prompted the programs, motivating public-private partnerships and local matching funding to help counter the problem.

One indicator of the programs' success is a decline in U.S. import rejections for Bangladeshi shrimp and Indian spices. In both countries, the train-the-trainers approach resulted in broad impacts in terms of the number of trainees who were trained and the subsequent training of supply chain actors. In both countries, thousands of individuals were trained using this approach, including farmers, food-processing and laboratory staff, and public inspectors. The resources needed for these successful training programs were modest compared with the value of the exports involved.

A key factor for the success of the training programs was their use of public-private partnerships for promoting exports. Training was one programmatic element among several strategic, complementary efforts to promote exports, and training was a major component, strengthening public accreditation in both countries. In Bangladesh, demonstration farms were set up to reach smallholder farmers, which led to improved safety and productivity. In India, industrial parks were set up to support private investments in processing and value-added products for spices. These examples show that training did not occur in a vacuum, but supported and furthered a public-private partnership strategy to enhance exports.

Source: Background paper prepared by C. Narrod, X. Dou, and C. Wychgram.

countries, the evidence suggests that South-South trade suffers from significant transactional and quality barriers (UNIDO 2015).[19] For example:

- Middle-class consumers in growing middle-income country markets are increasingly aware of food safety and seek out safer products. Many of the highest-profile food safety incidents have taken place in some of the most

[19] UNIDO (2015) explores several cases where standards are potential barriers in growing South-South trade. One example is imports into South Africa from the rest of Africa. Countries in Sub-Saharan Africa have trouble competing with established suppliers in Latin America and the Caribbean in the South Africa market. UNIDO concludes that even regional harmonization will not tackle some basic cost and quality issues in Sub-Saharan Africa's supply of food products, including for tea, bananas, nuts, and maize. UNIDO also examines Argentina's fruit exports to Brazil. In Brazil, market segmentation is emerging mainly based on quality, with high-end retailers demanding the same quality as the EU and lower-quality produce going to smaller retail chains at a discount. It is by no means clear that the lower-quality product is unsafe. Other examples are found in fruit exports from Malaysia, Myanmar, and Vietnam to China and other Asian countries. This trade encounters phytosanitary barriers because of differing requirements and inconsistent border practices.

important LMIC markets. In the growing urban areas of middle-income countries, retailers are also increasingly using the same private standards as in high-income markets to attract consumers.

- LMIC governments are just as concerned about plant and animal health protection as high-income countries when it comes to imports. LMICs often have large and economically important agricultural sectors and want to protect their animal and plant health. Examples of countries with both growing high-value imports and important agricultural sectors include China and South Africa.
- In many ways, South-South trade is subject to greater barriers than trade with high-income countries. Often, this trade has higher border costs due to noncompliance with sanitary and phytosanitary principles. These include a lack of transparency for import requirements, discriminatory practices that impose different requirements on exporters, and high transaction costs for entry, including long waits at borders and corruption.

Taken together, these issues highlight the need for LMICs to tackle trade barriers related to food safety and other sanitary and phytosanitary issues. And, more widely, they highlight the need to take advantage of the growth in demand for food products in other LMIC markets.

Regional initiatives to harmonize standards and streamline border procedures are often proposed to promote South-South trade. Examples of regional trade alliances include the Association of Southeast Asian Nations (ASEAN) GAP, the Common Market for Eastern and Southern Africa Green Pass, and East Africa Community dairy standards. Humphrey (2017), however, concludes that progress has been slow in implementing these regional standards. Furthermore, harmonization does not address other transaction costs (for example, corruption and road tolls). ASEAN GAP, a voluntary standard promoted by member-state governments to facilitate trade, may be the one modest success story of these efforts. ASEAN GAP allows one standard for ASEAN members trading with larger regional countries, such as China or India, and is generally in line with or moving toward more stringent GAP standards for high-income markets. The ASEAN GAP standard also provides a common basis for government extension efforts with farmers. Conceivably, initiatives such as this could support growth in South-South trade, while complementing efforts to strengthen the safety of domestic food supplies.

MOVING TOWARD RISK-BASED IMPORTED FOOD CONTROLS

The progress being made by LMIC agri-food exports tends to overshadow trends in the scale and composition of agri-food imports. LMICs on average are showing double-digit growth in agri-food imports, especially imports of high-value foods, which in value terms are about a third of LMIC agri-food imports (and 20 percent of the agri-food of low-income countries). From 2001 to 2016, LMIC imports of agri-food products rose from US$89 billion to US$414 billion, with imports of high-value food rising from US$30 billion to US$149 billion in the same period.

The most rapid growth in high-value food imports has been in meat, fish, dairy products, and fresh fruit and vegetables (figure 3.11). Historically, most LMIC imports of high-value food have come from high-income countries, but this is rapidly changing. Half of LMIC high-value food imports come from other LMICs. In the case of low-income countries, 60 percent of high-value food imports are from other LMICs.

Among LMICs, 10 countries accounted for two-thirds of high-value food imports in 2016 (table 3.10). These tend to be larger and rapidly developing middle-income countries in which the size of the middle class is expanding at a fast pace (for example, China, Mexico, and the Russian Federation). Many of these countries are also leading agri-food exporters, reflecting differences in domestic production and the demand patterns of the population for type and quality of food products.

Importantly, the rapid growth in imports of some high-value foods reflects the concerns of LMIC consumers over the safety of domestically produced foods. A case in point is the explosive growth in imports of dairy products,

FIGURE 3.11 LMIC High-Value Food Imports, by Product Group, 2001–16

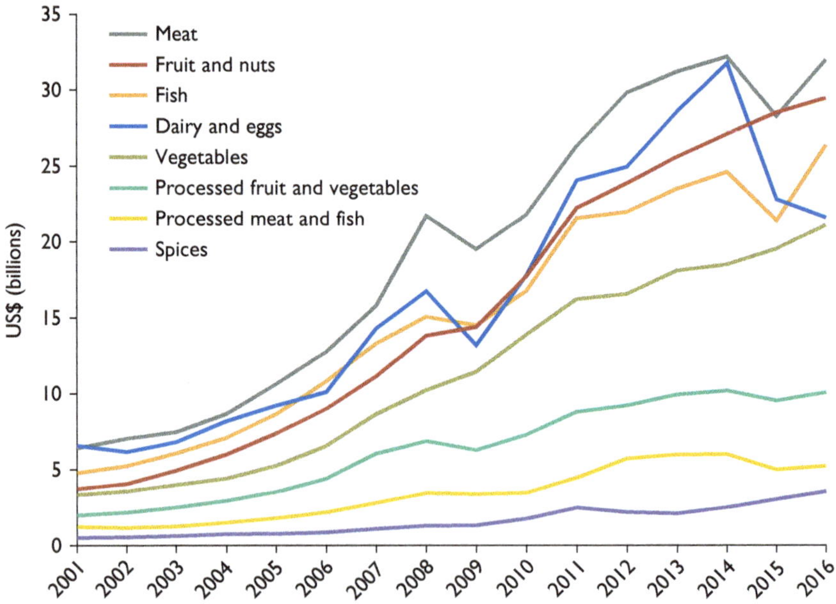

Source: International Trade Centre Trade Map Database.

TABLE 3.10 Largest LMIC Importers of High-Value Food, 2006 and 2016

	2006				2016			
	Country	Value (US$)	Percent LMIC	Percent world	Country	Value (US$)	Percent LMIC	Percent world
1	Russian Federation	11,762,546	17.2	3.4	China	29,651,926	19.6	5.0
2	China	6,151,661	9.0	1.8	Vietnam	15,348,910	10.2	2.6
3	Mexico	5,740,605	8.4	1.7	Russian Federation	12,570,855	8.3	2.1
4	Poland	3,186,166	4.7	0.9	Mexico	8,576,822	5.7	1.5
5	Thailand	2,303,197	3.4	0.7	India	7,618,310	5.0	1.3
6	Malaysia	2,088,382	3.1	0.6	Thailand	5,822,059	3.9	1.0
7	India	1,856,772	2.7	0.5	Malaysia	4,739,234	3.1	0.8
8	Nigeria	1,533,803	2.2	0.4	Brazil	4,268,894	2.8	0.7
9	Brazil	1,378,709	2.0	0.4	Egypt, Arab Rep.	3,907,502	2.6	0.7
10	Ukraine	1,303,013	1.9	0.4	Indonesia	3,569,083	2.4	0.6
Subtotal (top 10 LMICs)		*37,304,854*	*54.6*	*10.7*	*Subtotal (top 10 LMICs)*	*96,073,595*	*63.6*	*16.3*
Subtotal (top 10 LMICs)		*30,960,787*	*45.4*	*8.9*	*Subtotal (top 10 LMICs)*	*54,940,626*	*36.4*	*9.3*
Subtotal LMICs		*68,265,641*		*19.6*	*Subtotal LMICs*	*151,014,221*		*25.7*
Subtotal HICs		*279,176,466*		*80.4*	*Subtotal HICs*	*437,204,313*		*74.3*
World total		**347,442,107**				**588,218,534**		

Source: International Trade Centre Trade Map Database.
Note: HIC = high-income country; LMIC = low- and middle-income country.

which not only reflects the rapid expansion of consumer demand but also specific instances of adulteration and other food safety issues. In 2008, 20 businesses in China were involved in the deliberate adulteration of milk and infant formula, with the scandal resulting in 300,000 hospitalizations, including 54,000 children. Concerns over the safety of domestically sourced milk are not isolated to China. Hanford, Campbell, and Elliott (2016) review the impacts of numerous cases of milk fraud during the latter part of the first decade and the early part of the second decade of the 2000s, including in Brazil, East Africa, India, and Pakistan.

Growing agri-food imports pose new challenges for the effective management of food safety in LMICs, especially when these imports are from other LMICs that themselves have weak food safety management systems or whose trade is carried out through informal channels across borders. These challenges are especially acute for smaller countries with significant agri-food imports. It is generally not possible to have oversight of food production and processing in exporting countries, which means that border inspections are the only protection. It is of course not possible to check all or even a high proportion of consignments imported into a country. Furthermore, the import inspection systems of most LMICs are underresourced or ineffectively organized. The low pay of many inspectors can also blunt their efforts to be proactive in detecting hazardous foods and makes them prone to corruption.

To ensure that rising food imports enhance rather than reduce domestic food safety, risk-based import controls need to be developed and applied in LMICs. These typically require the categorization of food safety risks on the basis of product type and country of origin, among other factors, and the combined application of preborder, border, and postborder measures (FAO 2016). The following briefly describes these different types of controls:

- *Preborder controls.* This is a way of trying to ensure that controls in an exporting country—for example, for food production, processing, and exports—lead to safer imported food. Preborder controls cover the profiling of exporters, manufacturers, imported products, country of origin, consignment source country and port of entry, agreements with importing countries, controls put in place by importers on their suppliers, and any other initiatives that can increase confidence in the safety and quality of the product being imported.
- *Border controls.* These cover the application of import permits by food businesses, and the processes for admissibility and inspections of consignments and importer inspection.
- *Postborder controls.* These refer to activities in an importing country after a product has been imported into that country. Postborder controls cover two basic types of controls. The first is any control of the importer; for example, assessing the importer's due diligence arrangements to ensure the safety of imported food and the standard of the importer's

warehouses. The second are actual controls over specific imported food products, which are either still in the importer's warehouses or already in the domestic market. This type of control may involve market surveillance and product recalls.

Facilitating trade while ensuring the safety of agri-food imports requires adhering to practices and principles that are consistent with Codex Alimentarius Commission guidelines. As well as having decisions that are risk-based and guided by robust evidence, these good practices include:

- Transparency in legislation and operating procedures
- Clearly defined institutional roles and responsibilities
- Consistency and impartiality in the application of controls
- Harmonized standards, guidelines, and recommendations
- Recognition of other food control systems, including equivalence, among trading partners

Among LMICs, these principles are often not applied to food safety import controls, and import control policies are generally not based on scientific evidence. Information on food safety requirements and procedures is often difficult to find, operating procedures change frequently, and coordination is often lacking among the multiple agencies involved. Although a systemic picture of the "state of the art" in LMIC food safety import controls is not available, a recent Marshall School of Business study, based on a survey of companies, gives a sobering picture of declining tariffs being replaced by a growing array of protectionist technical barriers to trade measures, which are applied as "on/off valves" in response to domestic market conditions (APEC Business Advisory Council 2016). Furthermore, food safety and other sanitary and phytosanitary measures are often ambiguous and inconsistent, and are enforced in a discriminatory manner.

Table 3.11 compares the scores for applying transparent rules and practices for agri-food imports in middle- and high-income economies that are members of the Asia-Pacific Economic Cooperation forum. The scores range from 1 for lowest to 5 for highest. Scores of 4 or 5 signal proximity to international best practice; scores of 1 or 2 indicate significant shortcomings. Country scores are considered in relation to five criteria: the clarity and suitability of technical barriers to trade, sanitary and phytosanitary measures, the state of information and the administrative burdens pertaining to food import controls, and the consistency of enforcement measures among stakeholders, and locations.[20]

---

[20] None of these five areas should be affected by an economy's level of development. The Marshall School of Business study also considers other criteria, including transportation and information and communication infrastructure.

High-income economies generally get mixed scores for applying technical barriers to trade and sanitary and phytosanitary measures. Yet these economies often score well for information disclosure, enforcement consistency, and administrative matters. New Zealand and Singapore score highest among high-income economies. The Marshall School of Business survey found that high-income economies apply stringent food standards, but do this in a transparent and fair way.

The situation for middle-income economies that are members of the Asia-Pacific Economic Cooperation forum is rather different than for high-income economies. High scores for middle-income economies are rare for any of

TABLE 3.11 Scores for Applying Transparent Rules and Practices for Agri-Food Imports in Middle- and High-Income Economies

Economy	Technical barriers to trade	Sanitary and phytosanitary measures	Information	Administrative burdens	Enforcement consistency	Total
Middle income						
Peru	3	3	5	3	3	17
Mexico	4	3	4	2	2	15
Malaysia	2	2	4	3	3	14
Philippines	3	3	2	2	1	11
Vietnam	3	3	2	2	1	11
Thailand	2	2	3	2	1	10
Russian Federation	2	2	2	1	3	10
Papua New Guinea	3	2	2	1	2	10
China	2	2	3	1	1	9
Indonesia	1	1	1	1	1	5
Average	**2.5**	**2.3**	**2.8**	**1.8**	**1.8**	**11.2**
High income						
Singapore	5	5	5	5	5	25
New Zealand	5	4	5	5	5	24
Taiwan, China	4	3	5	4	5	21
Japan	3	3	5	4	5	20
Australia	3	3	5	4	5	20
United States	3	3	5	4	4	19
Chile	4	4	3	3	5	19
Canada	3	3	4	4	4	18
Korea, Rep.	3	2	3	3	3	14
Average	**3.7**	**3.3**	**4.4**	**4.0**	**4.6**	**20.0**

Source: APEC Business Advisory Council 2016.

table 3.11's five rated areas. Some economies, including Peru and Mexico, scored much better than others. Indonesia received the lowest score on each of the five criteria. Among LMICs, the worst situations relate to administrative burdens and enforcement consistency. More common than not, the prevailing situation is one of (1) multiple agencies with overlapping responsibilities, (2) redundant documentation, (3) frequent policy changes, (4) lack of adequate technical and human capital, (5) facilitation payments often not being required, (6) lack of or frequently changing protocols and document requirements, and (7) discriminatory behavior on the basis of economy, business, or mode of delivery.

These result in higher costs, affecting suppliers to these markets as well as domestic consumers, yet do not contribute to safer food. The Marshall School of Business study argues that micro, small, and medium enterprises are especially hard hit by administrative burdens and inconsistent enforcement because of the costs involved, the lack of a dedicated staff to deal with these matters, and discriminatory treatment, as these enterprises are powerless to exercise "voice." This type of situation either drives down the involvement of these enterprises in trade or leads them to find informal cross-border channels that are detrimental for the control of food safety.

SUMMARY

This chapter has explored the state of food safety management capacity in LMICs, using a wide variety of indicators. Capacity has several dimensions, which naturally evolve as economies develop and the motivation for safety from food system actors strengthens. The available evidence on the state of this capacity reinforces the conclusion that there are significant gaps between food safety management capacity and food safety needs in LMICs.

The most comprehensive measure of capacity from the World Organisation for Animal Health shows large gaps in basic elements of the public food safety system in most LMICs. Furthermore, a clear relationship exists between a greater burden of FBD and lower capacity. Many LMICs have a clear need for greater capacity, whether measured through trade indicators or domestic market trends. But they have relatively little capacity to meet their needs. Other indicators of capacity are more tentative, but also point to a gap.

The chapter has examined examples of LMIC governments that partner with the private sector (for example, to support food safety certification) and to facilitate smallholder inclusion in high-value food chains. There are successful examples of these efforts, but too few of them.

The international trade arena provides more concrete evidence of food safety management capacity in LMICs, but it also reinforces the gap between need and capacity. As expected, the private sector, especially in well-established exporting countries, has made major investments to certify improved production practices, both in farming and processing. But the scope of these investments is not wide, which means they are probably having only a limited effect on domestic food safety in LMICs. The public sector in LMICs has only a limited capacity to facilitate international trade by providing transparent and consistent border controls. This gap will become more important as many LMICs source more high-value food imports from other LMICs. The following chapters explore how to tackle the gap between capacity and need.

REFERENCES

Acikel, Cengiz Han, Recai Ogur, Hakan Yaren, Ercan Gocgeldi, Muharrem Ucar, and Tayfun Kir. 2008. "The Hygiene Training of Food Handlers at a Teaching Hospital." *Food Control* 19 (2): 186–90.

Al-Shabib, Nasser Abdulatif, Sameh Hassan Mosilhey, and Fohad Mabood Husain. 2016. "Cross-Sectional Study on Food Safety Knowledge, Attitude and Practices of Male Food Handlers Employed in Restaurants of King Saud University, Saudi Arabia." *Food Control* 59 (January): 212–17.

APEC Business Advisory Council. 2016. *Non-Tariff Barriers in Agriculture and Food Trade in APEC: Business Perspectives on Impacts and Solutions.* Los Angeles: University of Southern California.

Asfaw, S., D. Mithöfer, and H. Waibel. 2009. "EU Food Safety Standards, Pesticide Use and Farm-Level Productivity: The Case of High-Value Crops in Kenya." *Journal of Agricultural Economics* 60 (3): 645–67.

Barrett, C. B., M. E. Bachke, M. F. Bellemare, H. C. Michelson, S. Narayanan, and T. F. Walker. 2012. "Smallholder Participation in Contract Farming: Comparative Evidence from Five Countries." *World Development* 40 (4): 715–30.

Baş, Murat, Azmi Şafak Ersun, and Gökhan Kıvanç. 2006. "The Evaluation of Food Hygiene Knowledge, Attitudes, and Practices of Food Handlers in Food Businesses in Turkey." *Food Control* 17 (4): 317–22.

Birol, Ekin, Bhushana Karandikar, Devesh Roy, and Maximo Torero. 2015. "Information, Certification and Demand for Food Safety: Evidence from an In-Store Experiment in Mumbai." *Journal of Agricultural Economics* 66 (2): 470–91.

Brannon, Laura, Valerie K. Pilling, Kevin Roberts, Carol Shanklin, and Amber Howells. 2009. "Appreciation of Food Safety Practices Based on Level of Experience." *Journal of Foodservice Business Research* 12 (2): 134–54.

Bruschi, Viola, Ksenia Shershneva, Irina Dolgopolova, Maurizio Canavari, and Ramona Teuber. 2015. "Consumer Perception of Organic Food in Emerging Markets: Evidence from Saint Petersburg, Russia." *Agribusiness* 31 (3): 14–32.

Campbell, P. 2011. "Assessing the Knowledge, Attitudes and Practices of Street Food Vendors in the City of Johannesburg Regarding Food Hygiene and Safety." University of the Western Cape. http://etd.uwc.ac.za/xmlui/bitstream/handle/11394/1827/Campbell_MPH_2011.pdf?sequence=1.

Choudhury, Manisha, Lipi Mahanta, Jayashree Goswami, Minakshi Mazumder, and Barnali Pegoo. 2011. "Socio-Economic Profile and Food Safety Knowledge and Practice of Street Food Vendors in the City of Guwahati, Assam, India." *Food Control* 22 (2): 196–203.

Cunha, Diogo Thimoteo da, Rose Magda Fiorotti, Juliana Garcia Baldasso, Maricy de Sousa, Nathália Moretti Fontanezi, Simone Caivano, Elke Stedefeldt, et al. 2013. "Improvement of

Food Safety in School Meal Service during a Long-Term Intervention Period: A Strategy Based on the Knowledge, Attitude and Practice Triad." *Food Control* 34 (2): 662–67.

Cunha, Diogo Thimoteo da, Elke Stedefeldt, and Veridiana Vera de Rosso. 2014. "The Role of Theoretical Food Safety Training on Brazilian Food Handlers' Knowledge, Attitude and Practice." *Food Control* 43 (Supplement C): 167–74.

El Derea, H., E. Salem, M. Fawzi, and M. Abdel Azeem. 2008. "Safety of Patient Meals in 2 Hospitals in Alexandria, Egypt Before and After Training of Food Handlers." *Eastern Mediterranean Health Journal* 14 (4): 941–52.

FAO (Food and Agriculture Organization). 2015a. *Assessment and Recommendations for Enhancements to Vietnam's Legislative Framework, Structural and Institutional Arrangements, National Management Arrangements and Related Implementation Strategies*. Hanoi: FAO.

———. 2015b. *Assessment and Recommendations for Strengthening Inter-Ministerial Coordination in Myanmar*. Yangon, Myanmar: FAO.

———. 2016. *Review of Food Safety Control Systems in Sri Lanka*. Colombo: FAO.

FiBL. 2018 "Data on Organic Agriculture 2016." The Statistics.FiBL.org website maintained by the Research Institute of Organic Agriculture (FiBL), Frick, Switzerland. Data are available at http://statistics.fibl.org/world.html.

Grace, D., S. Alonso, M. Lulietto, A. Kebede, J. Lindahl, R. Mader, V. Madukeh, et al. 2018. *Food Safey Systems Performance Assessment Tool: Results for Sub-Saharan Africa*. Nairobi: International Livestock Research Institute.

Grace, D., J. Olowoye, M. Dipeolu, S. Odebode, and T. Randolph. 2012. "The Influence of Gender and Group Membership on Food Safety: The Case of Meat Sellers in Bodija Market, Ibadan, Nigeria." *Tropical Animal Health and Production* 44 (Supplement 1): 53–59.

Handford, C. E., K. Campbell, and C. T. Elliott. 2016. "Impacts of Milk Fraud on Food Safety and Nutrition with Special Emphasis on Developing Countries." *Comprehensive Reviews in Food Science and Food Safety* 15 (1): 130–42.

Handschuch, C., M. Wollni, and P. Villalobos. 2013. "Adoption of Food Safety and Quality Standards among Chilean Raspberry Producers: Do Smallholders Benefit?" *Food Policy* 40 (June): 64–73.

Henson, S., and S. Jaffee. 2008. "Understanding Developing Country Strategic Responses to the Enhancement of Food Safety Standards." *World Economy* 31 (4): 548–68.

Henson, S., O. Masakure, and D. Boselie. 2005. "Private Food Safety and Quality Standards for Fresh Produce Exporters: The Case of Hortico Agrisystems, Zimbabwe." *Food Policy* 30 (4): 371–84.

Henson, S., O. Masakure, J. Cranfield. 2011. "Do Fresh Produce Exporters in Sub-Saharan Africa Benefit from GlobalGAP Certification?" *World Development* 39 (3): 375–86.

Henson, S., and W. Mitullah. 2004. "Kenyan Exports of Nile Perch: Impact of Food Safety Standards on an Export-Oriented Supply Chain." Policy Research Working Paper 3349, World Bank, Washington, DC.

Hoffmann, V., and K. Jones. 2018. "Improving Food Safety on the Farm: Experimental Evidence from Kenya on Agricultural Incentives and Subsidies as Public Health Interventions." IFPRI Discussion Paper, International Food Policy Research Institute, Washington, DC.

Hoffmann, V., C. Moser, and T. Herrman. 2017. "Demand for Aflatoxin-tested Maize in Kenya." Paper presented at the International Association of Agricultural Economists' Triennial Conference, Milan.

Humphrey, J. 2017. *Food Safety, Trade, Standards and the Integration of Smallholders into Value Chains*. Research Series 11. Rome: International Fund for Agricultural Development.

IFC (International Finance Corporation). 2011. *Implementing Food Safety Management Systems in Ukrainian Food Processing Enterprises*. Washington, DC: World Bank Group.

———. 2016. *Investing Wisely in Food Safety: How to Maximize the Benefits and Reduce the Costs*. Washington, DC: World Bank Group.

IITA (International Institute for Tropical Agriculture). 2013. AgResults Aflasafe Pull Mechanism Pilot Project to Incentivize Adoption of Aflasafe. Project brief.

Jaffee, S., S. Henson, and L. Diaz Rios. 2011. *Making the Grade: Smallholder Farmers, Emerging Standards, and Development Assistance Programs in Africa*. Washington, DC: World Bank.

Jin, M., and C. Zhao. 2008. "Consumers' Behaviour Intention and Purchasing Behaviour of Green Agricultural Products." *Chinese Rural Economy* 5: 44–55.

Kaitibie, S., A. O. Omore, K. Rich, and P. Kristjanson. 2010. "Kenyan Dairy Policy Change: Influence Pathways and Economic Impacts." *World Development* 38 (10): 1494–1505.

Kersting, S., and M. Wollni. 2012. "New Institutional Arrangements and Standard Adoption: Evidence from Small-Scale Fruit and Vegetable Farmers in Thailand." *Food Policy* 37 (4): 452–62.

Lapar, L., R. Deka, J. Lindahl, and D. Grace. 2014. "Quality and Safety Improvements in Informal Milk Markets and Implications for Food Safety Policy." Paper presented at the 8th International Conference of the Asian Society of Agricultural Economists, Savar, Bangladesh, February 14–17.

Le Vallée, J.-C., and S. Charlebois. 2014. *2014 World Ranking: Food Safety Performance*. Ottawa: Conference Board of Canada.

Leimeilleur, S. 2013. "Smallholder Compliance with Private Standard Certification: The Case of GlobalGAP Adoption by Mango Producers in Peru." *International Food and Agribusiness Management Review* 16 (4): 159–80.

Li, X. 2007. "Purchasing Behaviour of Urban Consumers to Green Food: A Survey on Green Milk in Nanjing City." Master's thesis, Nanjing Agricultural University, Nanjing.

Lindahl, J., M. Kakkar, P. Mehta, R. Deka, and D. Grace. 2014. "Risks with Urban and Peri-Urban Milk Production in India." Paper presented at the EcoHealth Conference, Montreal, August 11–15.

Liu, R., Z. Pieniak, and W. Verbeke. 2013. "Consumers' Attitudes and Behaviour towards Safe Food in China: A Review." *Food Control* 33 (September): 93–104.

Maertens, M., and J. Swinnen. 2009. "Trade, Standards, and Poverty: Evidence from Senegal." *World Development* 37(1): 161–78.

Maghraby, W., H. Toiba, W. Umberger, and N. Minot. 2013. "Exploring Indonesian Consumer Willingness to Pay for High-Value Agricultural Products." *Acta Horticulturae* 1006 (September): 397–404.

Marteau, Theresa M., David Ogilvie, Martin Roland, Marc Suhrcke, and Michael P. Kelly. 2011. "Judging Nudging: Can Nudging Improve Population Health?" *British Medical Journal* 342.

Martinez, M. G., A. Fearne, J. A. Caswell, and S. Henson. 2007. "Co-regulation as a Possible Model for Food Safety Governance: Opportunities for Public–Private Partnerships." *Food Policy* 32 (3): 299–314.

McIntyre, L., L. Vallaster, L. Wilcott, S. Henderson, and T. Kosatsky. 2013. "Evaluation of Food Safety Knowledge, Attitudes and Self-Reported Hand Washing Practices in FOODSAFE Trained and Untrained Food Handlers in British Columbia, Canada." *Food Control* 30 (1): 150–56.

Minten, B., L. Randrianarison, and J. F. M. Swinnen. 2009. "Global Retail Chains and Poor Farmers: Evidence from Madagascar." *World Development* 37 (11): 1728–41.

Narrod, C., D. Roy, J. Okello, B. Avendaño, R. Rich, and A. Thorat. 2009. "Public–Private Partnerships and Collective Action in High Value Fruit and Vegetable Supply Chains." *Food Policy* 34 (1): 8–15.

Nguyen, H. D., T. Tuyet-Hanh, F. Unger, S. Dang-Xuan, and D. Grace. 2017. "Food Safety in Vietnam: Where Are We and What Can We Learn from International Experiences?" *Infectious Diseases of Poverty* 6: 39.

Okello, J. J., and S. M. Swinton. 2009. "From Circle of Poison to Circle of Virtue: Pesticides, Export Standards and Kenya's Green Bean Farmers." *Journal of Agricultural Economics* 61 (2): 209–24.

Omore, A. O., and D. Baker. 2011. "Integrating Informal Actors into the Formal Dairy Industry in Kenya through Training and Certification. In *Towards Priority Actions for Market Development for African Farmers: Proceedings of an International Conference, Nairobi, Kenya, May 13–15*. Nairobi: Alliance for a Green Revolution in Africa and International Livestock Research Institute. http://cgspace.cgiar.org/handle/10568/16492.

Park, S., T. Kwak, and H. Chang. 2010. "Evaluation of the Food Safety Training for Food Handlers in Restaurant Operations." *Nutrition Research and Practice* 4 (1): 58. https://doi.org/10.4162/nrp.2010.4.1.58.

Reardon, T., C. B. Barrett, A. Berdegué, and J. F. M. Swinnen. 2009. "Agrifood Industry Transformation and Small Farmers in Developing Countries." *World Development* 37 (11): 1717–27.

Roy, D., and A. Thorat. 2008. "Success in High Value Horticultural Export Markets for the Small Farmers: The Case of Mahagrapes in India." *World Development* 36 (10): 1874–90.

Qing, P., F. X. Yan, and M. D. Wang. 2006. "Consumer Behaviour on Green Vegetable." *Issues in Agricultural Economy* 6: 73–78.

Samapundo, S., R. Climat, R. Xhaferi, and F. Devlieghere. 2015. "Food Safety Knowledge, Attitudes and Practices of Street Food Vendors and Consumers in Port-Au-Prince, Haiti." *Food Control* 50 (April): 457–66.

Schipmann, C., and M. Qaim. 2011. "Modern Food Retailers and Traditional Markets in Developing Countries: Comparing Quality, Prices, and Competition Strategies in Thailand." *Applied Economic Perspectives and Policy* 33 (3): 345–62.

Seaman, P., and A. Eves. 2010 "Perceptions of Hygiene Training amongst Food Handlers, Managers and Training Providers: A Qualitative Study." *Food Control* 21 (7): 1037–41.

Singh, A., P. Kumar, N. Dudeja, and S. Mukherji. 2016. "Impact of Health Education Intervention on Food Safety and Hygiene of Street Vendors: A Pilot Study." *Medical Journal Armed Forces India* 72 (3): 265–69.

Soon, J., and R. Baines. 2012. "Food Safety Training and Evaluation of Handwashing Intention among Fresh Produce Farm Workers." *Food Control* 23 (2): 437–48.

Soon, J., R. Baines, and P. Seaman. 2012. "Meta-Analysis of Food Safety Training on Hand Hygiene Knowledge and Attitudes among Food Handlers." *Journal of Food Protection* 75 (4): 793–804.

Subervie, J., and I. Vagneron. 2013. "A Drop of Water in the Indian Ocean? The Impact of GlobalGap Certification on Lychee Farmers in Madagascar." *World Development* 50: 57–73.

Tang, X. Y., S. P. Li, and Z. D. Jiang. 2010. "Motivation, Intention and Behaviour of Safe Agricultural Products: A Survey in Nanjing City." *Soft Science* 24 (11): 53–59.

Tetyora, V., E. Osmochescu, and K. Onul. 2017. "Learning from the Journey to New Markets: One Product at a Time." IFC SmartLessons, International Finance Corporation, Washington, DC.

UNIDO (United Nations Industrial Development Organization). 2015. *Meeting Standards, Winning Markets: Trade Standards Compliance*. Vienna: UNIDO.

Unnevehr, L., and L. Ronchi. 2014. "Food Safety Standards: Economic and Market Impacts in Developing Countries." Viewpoint Note Number 341, World Bank, Washington, DC.

Wansink, B., and K. van Ittersum. 2007. "Portion Size Me: Downsizing Our Consumption Norms." *Journal of the Academy of Nutrition and Dietetics* 107 (7): 1103–06.

Wongprawmas, R., and M. Canavari. 2017. "Consumers' Willingness-to-Pay for Food Safety Labels in an Emerging Market: The Case of Fresh Produce in Thailand." *Food Policy* 69 (Supplement C): 25–34.

Wu, Linhai, Shijiu Yin, Yingjun Xu, and Dian Zhu. 2014. "Effectiveness of China's Organic Food Certification Policy: Consumer Preferences for Infant Milk Formula with Different Organic Certification Labels." *Canadian Journal of Agricultural Economics* 62 (4): 545–68.

Yin, Shijiu, Linhai Wu, Lili Du, and Mo Chen. 2010. "Consumers' Purchase Intention of Organic Food in China." *Journal of the Science of Food and Agriculture* 90 (8): 1361–67.

Zanin, Laís Mariano, Diogo Thimoteo da Cunha, Veridiana Vera de Rosso, Vanessa Dias Capriles, and Elke Stedefeldt. 2017. "Knowledge, Attitudes and Practices of Food Handlers in Food Safety: An Integrative Review." *Food Research International* 100 (Part 1): 53–62.

Zhang, Lei, Yunan Xu, Peter Oosterveer, and Arthur P. J. Mol. 2016. "Consumer Trust in Different Food Provisioning Schemes: Evidence from Beijing, China." *Journal of Cleaner Production* 134 (Part A): 269–79.

Zhou, Y. H., L. Y. Huo, and X. J. Peng. 2004. "Food Safety: Consumers' Attitude, Behaviour Intention and the Influence of Information: A Survey on Supermarket Consumers in Nanjing City." *Chinese Rural Economy* 11: 53–59.

CHAPTER FOUR

Strengthening Food Safety Management Systems

INTRODUCTION

The foregoing analysis highlighted the considerable economic and social burden imposed on low- and middle-income countries (LMIC) by foodborne disease (FBD), and the importance of improving food safety management capacity in these countries for achieving the Sustainable Development Goals. A considerable gap clearly exists between the needed capability of LMICs to manage food safety and the actual level of capacity across the public and private sectors. This is especially true for those LMICs experiencing rapid economic and social change. Many upper-middle-income countries have, in contrast, invested in robust food safety management systems, which are beginning to pay dividends in terms of the safety of food for domestic populations and the competitiveness of agri-food exports.

For LMICs, the challenges posed by food safety hazards and the opportunities to leverage food safety management initiatives as part of efforts to achieve the Sustainable Development Goals are significant. This requires establishing and implementing a coherent policy framework for food safety governance that is both strategic and forward looking. In many LMICs, this framework is missing, making it difficult to make the case for more investment in food safety and to ensure that the money that is made available is well spent. In most LMICs, only modest investments are made in preventive measures and capacities, and the attention that food safety hazards deserve tends to be given only in reaction to sizable disease outbreaks, food scares covered by the media, and trade interruptions caused by food safety issues. The actions related to this response also tend to be more demonstrative than effective in achieving standards compliance or safer food. Enhanced inspections, testing, and fines may signal to stakeholders that "something is being done," yet reactive measures such as these do not normally deal with the underlying causes of FBD and weaknesses in capacities and incentives.

These modes of intervention in managing food safety also tend to occur in a policy vacuum in which there is a lack of coherent and transparent prioritization of investments, the roles and responsibilities of different stakeholders are not clearly defined, and the contours of a food safety management system are, at best, vaguely understood. This is hampering efforts for structured, evidence-based decision making, and coordinated action within and between the public and private sectors. In sum, policy incoherence is very much the norm for food safety in LMICs.

Most of these countries, especially low- and lower-middle-income ones, clearly need substantial investment in their food safety management systems. But simply spending more is unlikely to be effective in significantly reducing FBD burdens in most LMICs. Governments need to invest more smartly in food safety management capacity, and to do this using coherent, prioritized, and forward-looking policies on food safety governance. This means that increasing investments in these systems must be made, alongside policy reforms for how governments engage private sector stakeholders in food safety management.

This chapter offers broad-based guidance to LMIC policy makers on the needed directions and modalities for enhancing food safety management capacity. This report clearly cannot provide road maps or set specific investment priorities for individual countries. These priorities need to be determined nationally (or subnationally, in large and diverse countries). These priorities also need to reflect the status and trajectory of a country's agri-food system, the current and expected burden of FBD and how it relates to food safety management capacity, and the perspectives of stakeholders on immediate priorities and those in the short and longer terms.

The chapter offers guidance for establishing a more effective policy framework to govern food safety. It makes the following recommendations, which are then discussed in detail:

- Adopt a food safety system perspective and an inclusive concept of food safety management
- Shift the focus from hazards to risks and address risks at every stage of the agri-food chain
- Shift from a reactive to a preventive orientation that anticipates risks and opportunities
- Adopt a more structured and consistent approach to prioritized decision making

This chapter also offers guidance for improving the implementation of this policy framework, and makes the following recommendations:

- Reform food safety regulatory practice, shifting from policing to facilitating compliance
- Invest smartly in essential public goods for effective food safety management
- Institutionalize a structured approach to food safety risk management
- Leverage consumer concerns on food safety to incentivize better food business practices

STEPS TOWARD A MORE EFFECTIVE FOOD SAFETY POLICY FRAMEWORK

Nearly all LMICs have laws for different elements of food safety and for defining the responsibilities of specific public institutions for enforcing these laws. But far fewer LMICs have clearly defined policy frameworks governing food safety that lay out (1) how the system for food safety operates; (2) the mechanisms for coordinating activities and functions among concerned agencies; (3) the modes of engagement with food business operators and consumers, and the responsibilities of both; and (4) how food safety regulations and other related actions are prioritized.

Without a policy framework, strategic decisions on investments to build and maintain food safety management capacity tend to be lacking. And efforts to ensure food safety become fragmented, thereby missing an opportunity to take advantage of synergies or complementarities that could have helped fill important capacity gaps. Because of this, scarce resources are not used optimally, and capacity falls well short of needs. The following subsections delineate the priorities for LMICs to put in place an effective policy framework for food safety.

Adopt a Food Safety System Perspective and an Inclusive Concept of Food Safety Management

In many countries, official responsibilities for food safety are divided among multiple ministries, departments, and agencies—depending on the product, type of hazard, stage of the agri-food value chain, and, sometimes, the destination market. Ministries with responsibility for agriculture are often the lead agencies for the oversight of farm practices and inputs and intermediate stage operations; for example, abattoirs. Ministries of health are concerned with water, sanitation, and public health, including monitoring disease outbreaks. Ministries of trade are concerned with standards, border inspections and certification, negotiating trade equivalence, and promoting exports. Other agencies may also be involved; for example, environment ministries (for soil contaminants and chemical use) and ministries charged with consumer protection for food labeling and product fraud. Often, authorities operate at central and decentralized levels. For example, national agencies are responsible for monitoring food imports and municipalities are responsible for the oversight of local markets and street food vending.

Most LMICs do not have a lead designated agency with overarching responsibility for food safety regulation, or at least for coordinating functions across the food safety area (though, as box 4.1 shows, there are some notable exceptions). The lack of a lead agency makes it difficult to set strategic priorities and to engage effectively with stakeholders. Administrative procedures and hierarchies can also stand in the way of the effective management of food safety, especially where controlling FBD requires the aligned actions of multiple agencies. As an example of this, consider where the management of foodborne hazards requires action along the entire value chain. The overarching vision, therefore, should be of an integrated system of food safety management with closely coordinated actions and responsibilities, both vertically and horizontally.

A pitfall would be adopting institutional solutions ahead of a comprehensive food safety policy framework. Some LMICs have set up U.S. Food and Drug Administration–type entities, driven primarily, it seems, by regulatory concerns about drugs rather than food. While similarities exist between drug and food controls, there are significant differences. For example, regulatory measures for drugs tend to be focused on a few, large companies, which provide for full cost recovery, and generally involve company licensing and product preauthorization. Food controls need to address a broad range of hazards and dispersed value chain actors, and they often use different types of regulatory tools. Food and Drug Administration–type agencies in LMICs also often lack the mandate and capacity to tackle the risks associated with fresh or raw produce.

BOX 4.1 Food Safety Lead Agencies in Chile and India

Only a few low- and middle-income countries have lead designated agencies coordinating domestic food safety functions. Chile and India are among the few.

The Chilean Agency for Food Quality and Safety's structure, tools, and work methodology are geared toward generating and implementing collaborative interventions with different actors in food production. The agency's main tools include (1) national integrated programs (for example, on standards harmonization and validation of methods); (2) a food safety alert network; (3) an integrated food laboratories system; (4) a network of food safety scientists; and (5) chairing regional advisory commissions for food safety and quality.

The Food Safety and Standards Authority of India has comprehensive national and subnational programs. These include (1) coordinating scientific committees to create and revise standards, (2) oversight of food establishment licensing and inspections, (3) fostering an effective system for testing foods in accredited laboratories, (4) coordinating programs on food safety training and certification, and (5) coordinating a multitargeted platform for inducing behavioral changes to ensure safer food.

The concept of an integrated food safety management system needs to go well beyond the centralization of functions and improved coordination within government. The safety of food is the result of action—and inaction—by multiple stakeholders, including those directly involved with the production, processing, and distribution of food, and those that affect the wider physical and enabling environment in which food operations take place. The World Health Organization promotes the concept of a *shared responsibility* for food safety, which emphasizes the interdependent roles of government, business, and consumers (figure 4.1), but with important additional actors, including scientists, educators, and the media. The World Health Organization's framework usefully draws attention to the importance of leadership, partnerships, resources, and a range of core functions that a food safety management system needs to competently perform.

Applying the principle of shared responsibility diverges from the traditional model of official food safety controls, which are centered on government regulation enforced through the inspection of food facilities, product testing, and legal penalties for infractions. Although more nuanced in practice, this model is typified by (1) a strict application of rules, regardless of the relative importance of particular violations in terms of the risks to human health; (2) a focus on the process of regulation, regardless of the impact on food safety outcomes; and (3) a reliance on deterrence as the main driver of compliance, with a consequent emphasis on sanctions and punishment.

FIGURE 4.1 Framework for Action on Food Safety

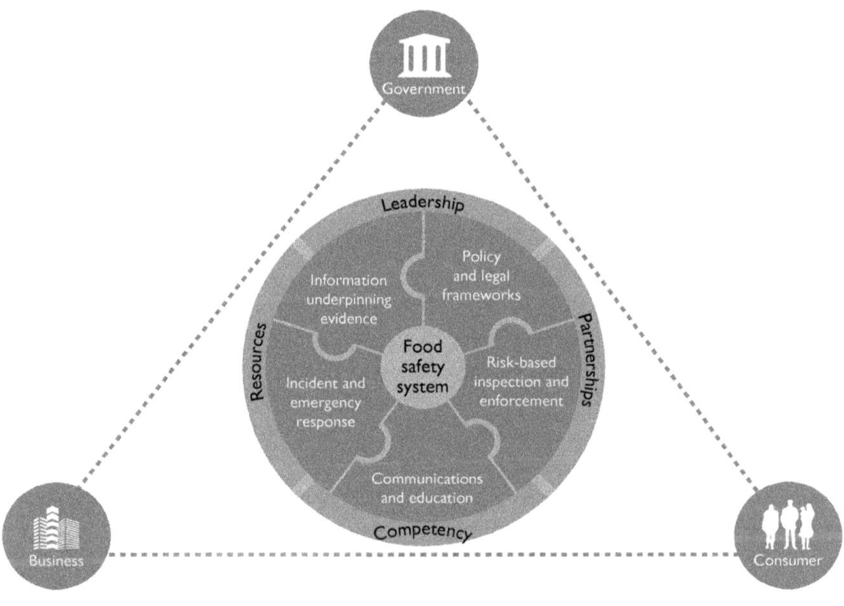

Source: World Health Organization.

This authoritative model goes together with performance indicators that are focused on output—notably, the number of infringements, value of fines collected, and number of businesses closed down—rather than outcomes for the magnitude of food safety risks or the prevalence of FBD. In practice, this system is susceptible to corruption, either opportunistically by individual businesses or systemically by enforcement agencies. This strict, authoritative approach is very appealing to the public, media, and therefore policy makers. When extreme cases of noncompliance or widespread outbreaks of FBD occur, even stricter enforcement and harsher penalties are demanded. In this way, the system becomes self-sustaining and difficult to reform.

Conversely, a system of food safety management based on the notion of shared responsibility tends to move from a regulator-regulated relationship toward government efforts to incentivize and facilitate the delivery of safe food production, processing, and distribution. The role of regulation in this context is to lay down an absolute minimum food safety standard that leaves businesses with some flexibility for how this standard is reached in terms of the processes and procedures that they use. This approach requires government to play a substantial, facilitative role by providing information and other resources, and support to motivate and help leverage investments and actions by actors along agri-food value chains and those providing supporting functions. The regulatory and facilitative actions of government are also risk-based, in that they are purposively directed at investments that can deliver the most significant food safety outcomes.

There is compelling evidence that more participatory systems of food safety management, in which governments play a facilitative and incentivizing role, use resources more efficiently, and have better food safety outcomes. That said, implementing these systems can be challenging. Moving away from the longstanding and predominantly authoritative approach to food safety regulation typically requires significant institutional change and a cultural shift among actors along the entire agri-food system. In this process, governments must avoid accusations of being compromised by agri-food business interests. Opportunities also exist for shifting toward a shared-responsibility approach, even where the traditional regulatory approach is firmly entrenched.

Shift the Focus from Hazards to Risks and Consider Risks at Every Stage of the Agri-Food Chain

The focus of food safety policies should shift from detecting foodborne hazards to prioritizing and addressing risks in the context of the foods eaten by the domestic population. Risk-based approaches consider the potential hazards of eating food and the probability that adverse health effects will occur. Because of this, risk-based approaches have proven to be the best way to reduce FBD within the population. These approaches also make better use of resources by focusing attention on foods with the greatest health risk and away from foods which, while hazardous in principle, present little risk to public health. These approaches are becoming standard in high-income countries. But while interest is growing in risk-based approaches to tackle FBD in LMICs, there are few examples of them being applied (box 4.2).

BOX 4.2 Uruguay's Risk-Based Approach to Strengthening Food Safety Controls

Since 2015, Uruguay's Ministry of Husbandry, Agriculture, and Fisheries has based the inspection and surveillance of firms in the dairy industry on risk-based principles. This involves identifying microbiological and chemical hazards, risk mapping products and production plants, and organizing inspections on the basis of these factors.

Table B4.2.1 summarizes the changes from adopting this approach, which is planned for expansion for other food chains under the Ministry of Husbandry, Agriculture, and Fisheries' authority.

TABLE B4.2.1 Comparison of Uruguay's Traditional and Risk-Based Inspection Approaches

Component	Traditional approach	Risk-based approach
Purpose of inspection	Designed to find problems if they occur	Designed to anticipate problems, thereby minimizing risk Noncompliance is ranked based on risk
Deployment of resources	Based on reaching administrative targets, such as coverage	More flexible resource allocation with level of product- and process-specific risks, and ongoing assessment of the food safety performance of plants
Work to do	Perform assigned procedures	Varies based on risk Basic procedures, based on inspection findings and decision criteria Results provide feedback to the system
Activities of inspection personnel	Procedures designed to find noncompliance	Focused on where loss of control is more likely to occur or have serious public health consequences Intensify inspection if plant is losing control In small businesses, risk-based inspection raises awareness of the importance of controlling risk
Response to inspection findings	Evidence of compliance or noncompliance has no effect on intensity of inspection Evidence of noncompliance could lead to enforcement action	Evidence of noncompliance could lead to enforcement action Intensity of inspection based on findings Good controls mean less intense inspection; poor controls mean intensified inspection
Response to emerging issues	Not designed to have inspectors make a judgment about risk of noncompliance	Inspection personnel have flexibility, data, responsibility, and training to be able to focus on emerging problems

Sources: Based on Masters and Derfler 2015, and interviews conducted by Jairo Romero.

Frameworks have been developed for analyzing the risks associated with hazards in food. The approach to risk analysis in the principles and guidelines adopted by the Codex Alimentarius Commission is accepted as a baseline worldwide. In this framework, the process of risk analysis consists of three interdependent components:

- *Risk assessment.* This quantifies risks so that their burden can be better understood, and progress in risk reduction can be measured. Risk assessment is perhaps the most methodologically developed aspect of the framework, which has four steps: hazard identification, exposure assessment, hazard characterization, and risk characterization.
- *Risk management.* This is the process of weighing alternatives and implementing strategies to reduce risk. Risk management involves considering what is feasible, the costs and benefits of risk reduction, and the opinions of stakeholders about appropriate levels of risk.
- *Risk communication.* This is the exchange of information on risk-related factors among risk assessors, risk managers, consumers, and other stakeholders. Risk communication ensures transparency in policy making, leads to informed actions by the public, and supports shared responsibility.

Parallel to adopting the risk paradigm should be the application of a system approach to food safety that focuses on the entire value chain and the wider environment in which the chain operates. This farm-to-fork approach recognizes that food can become contaminated at various stages of the value chain and, likewise, that corrective actions can be taken at multiple stages of the chain (table 1.1 in chapter 1 shows the food safety hazards on the farm-to-fork pathway). As part of enhancing food safety management capacity, it is therefore necessary to locate and deal with the weak stages of agri-food value chains, and to build in controls—often at multiple levels of the chain—to ensure food safety at the point of consumption. The primary emphasis, however, should be on avoiding hazards from entering the agri-food chain in the first place (for example, from soil, water, animals, production inputs, and food handlers), and building in ways to detect, remove, and otherwise neutralize hazards that occur.

Some food safety risks can best be managed—or in some cases, only managed—at the preharvest stage; for example, antimicrobial residues in animal source foods or pesticide residues in fresh fruit and vegetables. For other food safety risks, actions may be needed at multiple stages of the value chain. A lot of progress is being in high-income countries to reduce the risk of FBD that results largely from improving post-slaughter or post-harvest practices. In LMICs, most efforts to reduce food safety risks have focused on controls at aggregation stages of the value chain (slaughterhouses, wholesale markets, dairy cooperatives, for example), and by changing consumer behavior.

Shift from a Reactive to a Proactive Orientation That Anticipates Future Risks and Opportunities

Given the lack of reliable data in many LMICs on the nature and extent of foodborne hazards, and the prevalence of FBD and its economic impacts, it may not be an exaggeration to say that, in this respect, we know the future better than we understand the past or even the present. For LMICs, the circumstances faced by upper-middle-income countries—which have already experienced advanced rates of dietary transformation and urbanization, and have had to play catchup to reverse escalating food safety problems—can be observed. It is therefore reasonable to predict that, everything else being equal, countries at earlier stages of the food safety life cycle can expect a similar trajectory. This will be characterized by a rapidly escalating burden of FBD if these countries pursue a business-as-usual scenario and only take serious action when major food safety problems happen.

This is well illustrated by a study of FBD in India that predicts the prevalence of FBD will rise from 100 million cases in 2011 to 150 million–177 million cases by 2030 in a business-as-usual scenario (Kristkova, Grace, and Kuiper 2017). The predominant drivers of this trend are urbanization and dietary change, in particular increased meat consumption. Those predicted to be especially affected are higher-income population groups in urban and rural areas where more significant dietary change is expected. The study cautions that a rising FBD burden could compromise India's nutritional goals if a significant proportion of the population chooses to avoid or reduce the consumption of nutrient-dense foods that are bigger food safety risks, such as meat and fresh fruit and vegetables.

The notion of a food safety life cycle with levels of economic development, as discussed in chapter 1, has considerable support. But the typical trajectory of rapidly rising public health costs and trade disruptions from FBD is not inevitable. A significant share of food safety problems can be managed, and their heavy costs avoided. These costs can be lessened by recognizing the ways in which food safety challenges evolve with the level of economic development, and by taking measures to ensure that food safety management capacity is commensurate with that level. A proactive strategy such as this, accompanied by properly prioritizing food safety issues, will enable countries to avoid prospective economic losses and the burden these impose on the domestic population and businesses. The size of these avoided losses can amount to hundreds of millions of dollars a year—and run to several billion dollars for larger countries.

In adopting a prevention strategy, it is essential to approach capacity development as a continuous process of improvement that is guided by anticipated needs. Here, it is important to calibrate investments in food safety management capacity with current and anticipated needs, and to apply an incremental approach to upgrading. Aspirations for food safety capacity building that are overly ambitious and out of sync with current and foreseeable short-term needs will result in critical capabilities being unused or becoming obsolete, and heavy costs being imposed on the public and/or private sectors. Regulatory requirements can also be set at levels that are unachievable for key market actors, either rendering them meaningless or leading to conflict and inequitable outcomes.

A preventive approach is an essential feature of effective food-risk communication, but this not the norm. The communication of food risks in LMICs tends to be largely reactive; in other words, after there has been a significant risk incident. This primarily takes the form of crisis communication and rarely goes beyond attributing blame. This one-directional form of communication is basically a monologue. A more effective way of risk communication entails a long-term, interactive process, involving a dialogue among different stakeholders and conducted through multiple formats.

Adopt a More Structured and Consistent Approach to Prioritized Decision Making

LMICs typically face a broad array of food safety challenges. These are expected to become more difficult for low- and lower-middle-income countries as they move along the food safety life cycle because of very limited public and private sector resources. Because of this, it is essential to set clear and evidence-based priorities for investments in enhancing food safety management capacity, and to review these priorities as needs change. Inevitably, LMICs will have to do this using incomplete information, including a lack of reliable data on the prevalence of FBD and how it spreads across society.

Establishing priorities for enhanced food safety management capacity often takes place between multiple potential investments and vocal demands from competing and powerful interest groups. Against this backdrop, it is vital that priorities are set in a structured and transparent manner, not an ad hoc and opaque one. Fortunately, a framework for establishing investment priorities for LMICs has been developed by the Standards and Trade Development Facility—the Prioritizing Sanitary and Phytosanitary Investments for Market Access Framework. Although developed for enhancing sanitary and phytosanitary capacity in the context of trade, it can also be applied to food safety management capacity (box 4.3).

It is also worth highlighting that the Food and Agriculture Organization has developed a multifactor decision-making framework that is shared through a guidance document (FAO 2017). This approach is primarily designed to guide decisions on how to implement food safety decisions; that is, identifying which specific measures to take to manage a food

BOX 4.3 Prioritizing Sanitary and Phytosanitary Investments for Market Access

The Standards and Trade Development Facility launched the Prioritizing Sanitary and Phytosanitary Investments for Market Access Framework to improve trade-related sanitary and phytosanitary (SPS) capacity in low- and middle-income countries. The framework helps to prioritize SPS capacity building by using multiple decision criteria. It is designed to be used where there are many trade-related SPS issues requiring investments in capacity, but where resources are insufficient to address them all, and where the data needed to establish priorities are limited or of poor quality.

The framework process makes use of the best data available and clearly documents all the criteria and sources of information used, so that findings are open to scrutiny. Typically, the criteria used include the cost of upgrading SPS capacity; the costs of operating and maintaining this capacity; and the impacts on trade, agricultural productivity, public health, and the environment, as well as the implications on poverty and vulnerable groups. The framework uses a multicriteria decision analysis approach and computer software (D-Sight) to derive SPS investment priorities on the basis of these competing criteria.

A number of low- and middle-income countries have used this framework. They include Belize, Ethiopia, Malawi, Mozambique, Namibia, Rwanda, the Seychelles, Uganda, Vietnam, and Zambia. Their experience highlights the benefits of this structured and transparent approach for setting priorities. The benefits of using the framework also include facilitating public-private dialogue on SPS investments, increasing political awareness on the benefits of strengthening SPS capacity, informing and improving national SPS planning and decision-making processes, supporting project design, and leveraging additional funding to build SPS capacity.

A new Standards and Trade Development Facility project with the Common Market for Eastern and Southern Africa (COMESA) plans to use the framework to mainstream SPS investment priorities into the Comprehensive Africa Agriculture Development Programme and other policy and planning frameworks—for example, those focused on trade, the environment, and climate change—in selected COMESA member states. Standards and Trade Development Facility project preparation grants for Madagascar and Tajikistan are also making use of the framework.

safety risk. The framework's elements for prioritizing food safety investments for market access can also be useful for guiding structured processes to prioritize food safety capacity management investments. Five potential decision factors are identified: (1) public health impacts caused by foodborne hazards, (2) economic losses related to food products being removed from domestic or export markets, (3) food security concerns, (4) consumer perceptions and acceptance of food safety risks, and (5) sociocultural concerns related to protecting vulnerable groups. The relative weight which countries might give to these decision factors will likely vary. The framework is discussed later in the chapter.

BETTER IMPLEMENTATION: MOVING FROM POLICY TO ACTION

Operationalizing the principles discussed in the previous section will not be straightforward for most LMICs. Adopting a facilitated approach based on the principle of shared responsibility that is risk-focused, proactive, and with clearly articulated priorities represents a formidable cultural shift for most LMICs that will likely require significant institutional change and the realignment of responsibilities and resources. Operationalizing this new approach will be especially challenging for the agri-food sector because it is predominantly informal, and a large proportion of food produced is for household consumption. Another challenge is that the structure and modus operandi of value chains in LMICs are transforming rapidly.

So, what can public sectors in LMICs do to operationalize this fundamental paradigm shift? How can they make shared responsibility a reality? For instance, they can make businesses allies in tackling food safety, move away from an adversarial approach to enforcing food safety laws, and encourage the private sector to adopt best practices. And how can consumers and marginalized stakeholders—such as smallholder farmers and micro, small, and medium enterprises in food processing or distribution—become more engaged in establishing food safety policies and accept the notion of shared responsibility? How can these efforts move beyond a one-way street, with government communicating information about food safety risks, and what is it doing to protect consumers in a situation when they become more responsible for their food safety? They can do this, for example, through their demands on food sellers, their food choices and shopping behavior, and their food preparation and storage practices in the home.

A way forward is to leverage the public sector's convening power to motivate and coordinate actions within agri-food value chains. Governments potentially have a wide range of tools at their disposal to incentivize and empower businesses to enhance their food safety management systems, both individually and for the value chains and sectors in which these systems operate. The public sector can use a stick-and-carrot approach to motivate the desired actions by actors along agri-food value chains, and can make strategic public investments where there are substantive public good elements and a lack of private incentives to invest. In doing this, governments should ideally be informed by behavioral insights to optimize the use of scarce resources and to maximize the impacts of their engagement with business (box 4.4).

It is worth noting that some countries have been pursuing these transitions. There is also a growing body of experience and learning on how to make regulatory systems work better. Much of this is happening in high-income countries, including Australia, New Zealand, the United Kingdom, and the United States. But there are also nascent and more advanced efforts in some countries in Latin America, Eastern Europe, and Asia.

BOX 4.4 Professionalizing Food Inspectors and Food Service Industry Workers

Professionalization—which is generally achieved through a combination of training and complementary interventions—works through the "induction" of trainees into a professional group and identity. This approach builds on the recognition that individuals can be motivated to act in ways that they see as conforming to an identity to maintain a sense of belonging to a group, whether in their own eyes or in the eyes of others.

By creating a sense of professional identity among participants, training and complementary programs can contribute to the adherence of trainees to the practices they learned to conform to or reassert that identity.

Professionalizing food inspectors is particularly important. In low- and middle-income countries (LMICs), food inspectors have the potential to take on roles similar to extension workers in agriculture. Food inspectors are a government workforce interacting with key actors in the food safety world if the risk-based approach is properly applied, and their supportive approach to enforcement gives them an advisory role. Experienced inspectors are aware of how food businesses in their locality work, know what works and what does not to gain compliance, and are well aware of those businesses that are trying to improve and those cutting corners.

In high-income countries, the private sector can provide compliance advice, but in LMICs that service is rarely available, especially to small and medium enterprises. Food inspectors can, however, fill that gap by their remit being extended beyond sanctioning to include advising. In both LMICs and high-income countries, using "assured advice" has been a breakthrough in regulatory delivery methods.

There is scope to professionalize food service industry workers. They, too, can be given the opportunity to see themselves as professionals, and be motivated to assert this identity if it becomes a source of increased self-worth and social recognition. If keeping food safe is central to that identity, one way of asserting it would be to demonstrate "responsibility" by using safe food handling techniques and keeping food safe at different points in the supply chain.

The power of professionalization is that it can bring about self-policing behavior. To professionalize food service industry workers and reap its self-policing benefits, programs must not stop at teaching safe food handling protocols or even the importance of food safety. Programs need to cultivate this knowledge in tandem with a professional identity—preferably one that is demanding in terms of food safety and barred to the undeserving—through a combination of training and complementary interventions.

Reform Food Safety Regulatory Practice with a Shift from Policing to Facilitating Compliance

Many LMICs need to reform food safety regulatory thinking and practice. The implementation of regulatory systems is seeing a growing trend in the move from an authoritative model to a more extensive mixture of tools, predominantly related to supporting regulated businesses.

The traditional assumption behind deterrence and sanctioning is that regulated entities will try harder to be compliant under these conditions. But this ignores extraneous factors and the consequences of these actions. For example, a fined business can lose money and market share to such an extent that it is less able to upgrade its food safety management capacity. Where lack of capacity rather than explicit intention is the reason for noncompliance, a fine does not deliver an improved outcome. Food businesses that do not understand basic hygiene will not become more hygienic simply by being fined. Instead, they need to be informed about better hygiene and provided with the knowledge to be able to implement good hygiene practices. Punishment or the threat of punishment may well influence the decisions of some businesses. But this form of sanction needs to be credible, and the financial consequences substantive. In many LMICs, not enough resources are available for inspection and other forms of conformity assessment procedures. Because of this, the chances of being caught for breaking food safety regulations are generally slim outside of city centers. To combat this, enforcement agencies need to adopt innovative approaches.

Feeding an urban population of millions safely can be achieved only by raising the food safety management capacity of the food businesses that handle a large proportion of the food consumed. For LMICs, and especially low- and lower-middle-income countries, this includes many micro and small enterprises operating in the informal sector. Because the resources to enforce food safety standards are limited, public agencies charged with managing food safety must find ways to encourage and support businesses to enhance the food safety management practices of these enterprises so that they are able to comply with minimum regulatory requirements. In practice, the number of businesses that knowingly break food safety regulations in a criminal sense tends to be small. Most businesses, when aware of the standards, try to comply within the context of the financial and other constraints they face.

The experience in many LMICs is that food businesses are generally trying to get it right and respond to advice on how to improve safety levels. Because of this, the food safety challenge in this context is about supporting compliance, rather than going after what are probably a small number of violators that are knowingly—and therefore criminally—breaking food safety regulations (figure 4.2).

Regulators must understand the constraints faced by food businesses that impede their ability to comply with food safety requirements and find ways of facilitating compliance in a way that imposes the least burden on businesses. In some cases, the most effective way of removing barriers to compliance is to make it easier for businesses to know what constitutes compliance in the first place. This can involve simplifying regulations and, as has proved effective, sharing with businesses the checklists used by inspectors. Even better is explaining to businesses the reasons behind

FIGURE 4.2 Reducing Noncompliance versus Raising Compliance

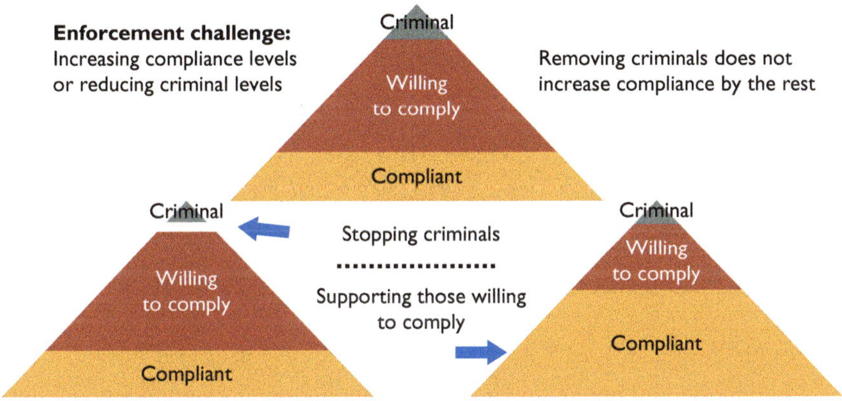

Source: Donald Macrae.

the regulatory requirements. The willingness to comply is generally stronger if businesses know that the authorities are genuinely trying to work with them.

While incidents of criminal noncompliance may be statistically insignificant, they can nevertheless be politically sensitive, especially when highlighted by the media or associated with notable FBD outbreaks. Even the internationally publicized scandal of melamine contamination of infant formula in China led to few fatalities relative to the population as a whole and the routine burden of FBD. It is not surprising that public regulators devote considerable resources to identify and prosecute those that are criminally noncompliant, and typically these are large businesses. But it could be argued that these resources would be better spent promoting enhanced food safety management practices by the multitude of micro and small enterprises that supply food to a large proportion of the urban populations in LMICs.

Once most food businesses are compliant with minimum food safety requirements, regulators should concentrate their resources on the smaller businesses that need to upgrade their standards and otherwise divert attention away from supporting compliance. In Australia and the United Kingdom, for example, regulatory compliance is increasingly being left to the private sector itself.[1] Governments should also look to a wide set of tools to incentivize not

[1] Australia's red meat industry has the Livestock Production Assurance program, the National Feedlot Accreditation Scheme, and the National Vendor Declaration, all overseen by Meat and Livestock Australia, a producer-owned, not-for-profit organization. In the United Kingdom, the Red Tractor Scheme has an on-farm assurance program for a range of commodities; the Soil Association, a registered charity, certifies food products as organic; and the British Retail Consortium oversees a meta-standard for food manufacturers and distributors.

only compliance with regulatory requirements but also the continuous upgrading of food safety management capacity. These tools include tax exemptions, concessional credit, and matching grants for advisory and auditing services. These actions can also be "tiered" toward priority businesses on the basis of size and market orientation, for example. One promising area is the direct or indirect support that governments could provide small and medium enterprises for industry benchmarking schemes, such as the Global Food Safety Initiative's Global Markets Programme.[2]

For the informal sector, regulatory sticks are not particularly effective in bringing about enhanced food safety management capacity, and they tend to have more symbolic value, in the sense of government being seen to be "doing something about" food safety. But there is scope for broad interventions to bring about behavior change. For example, many interventions have been undertaken to address the safety of street-vended food. Programs to induce behavior change tend to involve some combination of the following:

- Education and awareness-raising for vendors, consumers, and government inspectors.
- Providing basic food preparation equipment, which is sometimes accompanied by training and support for self-help groups.
- Registering, licensing, and rating vendors and their premises for food safety risks.[3]
- Surveillance, involving routine and seasonal checks by inspection teams; this can involve using mobile test kits and checklists for raw materials, food handling, personal hygiene, and environmental surroundings.
- Infrastructure upgrades that improve access to potable water supply, access to electricity, and waste disposal systems; these sometimes involve relocating vendors, as Singapore did.

Indeed, Singapore's experience in promoting incremental upgrades in street vendor food safety and environmental management, and the formalization of street food businesses in hawker centers, is instructive for how a combination of regulatory and facilitative tools was used in this process (box 4.5).

[2] The program was launched in 2010 to provide an unaccredited entry point for companies with a step-by-step approach designed to build capacity within production and manufacturing operations, and improve market access through certification to one of the schemes recognized by the Global Food Safety Initiative (GFSI). The program includes a toolkit for self-assessments based on a checklist of GFSI requirements, a training and competency framework, and a protocol to guide the user. Toolkits are available for primary production and manufacturing in many languages. Collaborative GFSI programs for training small and medium enterprises have been implemented in China, Georgia, Kazakhstan, and Ukraine, among other countries.

[3] In some countries, it will be important to address the legal ambiguity of street food vendors to reduce their vulnerability to punitive actions by local authorities.

BOX 4.5 How Singapore Formalized Its Street Food Businesses

Some 40,000 hawkers plied Singapore's streets and riversides selling food and other low-cost goods and services in the 1960s, raising serious food safety and environmental concerns. To tackle this, a licensing and inspection scheme was introduced, but the main strategy to formalize Singapore's street food business was to relocate these vendors to hawker centers. Fifty-four of these were built in the late 1970s, and another 59 in the early 1980s.

During the 1980s and 1990s, a "regulate and educate" policy was used to improve hygiene practices, with hawker centers being increasingly recognized as playing important social roles in communities. In 2001, the government allocated S$420 million for infrastructure improvements to the sector under the Hawker Centre Upgrading Programme. Some hawker centers were completely rebuilt, and most acquired central freezers and cleaning areas. By 2014, 109 centers had been upgraded, accommodating 6,000 vendors. In 2016, two hawker stalls were awarded a Michelin star. Hawker centers have loyal local customers and are a tourist attraction.

The National Environment Authority manages and oversees Singapore's hawker centers. Its mission for these centers is for them to be "vibrant, communal spaces, offering a wide variety of affordable food, in a clean and hygienic environment." Here, the authority's role covers overseeing stakeholders, developing and implementing policies for the hawker sector, and maintaining the infrastructure of centers and developing new centers. The authority also manages the assignment and rents for tenancies, licenses, and public relations.

Invest Smartly in Essential Public Goods for Effective Food Safety Management

Governments of LMICs not only need to invest more in food safety but also to invest more smartly. The chances of making more effective and efficient investments in food safety management capacity are greater if the following principles are adhered to:

- *Invest for the right reasons.* This means being specific about the food safety goals being pursued and how proposed investments relate to these goals.
- *Invest in the right things.* Investments in food safety should be driven both by considerations of food safety risks and by seeking to achieve an appropriate and synergistic balance between the "hard" and "soft" aspects of food safety management capacity. Laboratory infrastructure is an example of a hard aspect; managing systems and procedures are examples of soft aspects.
- *Use public investment to leverage private investment.* But avoid measures that might crowd out private investment for food safety management capacity.
- *Track the impacts of investments.* This needs to be done for food system stakeholder behavior, the safety of food, and FBD incidents. A rigorous approach to

monitoring and evaluation will contribute to the cost-effectiveness of interventions and show where adjustments are needed to realize desired outcomes.

- *Ensure the sustainability of investments and capacity outcomes.* This can be done by ensuring that sufficient operating resources for food safety management will be available on a continuous basis, and by maintaining physical and human assets. This principle, however, is often ignored. Box 4.6 looks at investments in laboratory testing capacity.

BOX 4.6 Investing More Smartly and Sustainably in Laboratory Testing Capacity

Many low- and middle-income countries (LMICs) plan to expand or upgrade their public food safety laboratory testing capacity to help boost food exports and for domestic surveillance and regulation. Improved testing capacity is often an essential component of efforts to strengthen broader food safety governance. Even so, experience shows that many investments in public food safety laboratories are financially or technically unsustainable (or both). A World Bank (2009) review of multiple investments highlighted the following contributing factors:

- Lack of a clear mission statement, either for individual laboratories or the laboratory system
- Failure to realize economies of scale, either because of insufficient demand for sophisticated services or the failure of surveillance and inspection agencies to deliver samples or invest in the testing facilities capacities of other laboratories, including in the private sector
- A disconnect between investment and operational decisions, with recurrent operational resources often being insufficient to maintain purchased equipment or professional laboratory staff
- Low incentives to improve quality management in the delivery of regulatory or other services
- The absence of enabling rules and management capabilities to run laboratories as a business

On the last point, many laboratories in LMICs do not have administrative or financial autonomy, are not permitted to charge fees which cover their full costs, and are often not required to implement clear business plans. The contributing factors in the list point to the need for a careful assessment of public laboratory investment needs, not in isolation but as part of the capacity needs for overall food safety governance.

Larger LMICs need to consider the appropriate geographic distribution of testing capabilities and the relationship between central and state/provincial laboratories in their overall network. For all LMICs, and especially the smaller ones, the scope for outsourcing laboratory services to certified private laboratories needs to be considered, especially for specialized services. Argentina does this. Its public food safety agency has authorized two private laboratories to test aflatoxin in groundnuts intended for export.

Where investments are made, strict attention should be given to quality control, through proficiency testing, staff training, and accreditation.

It is important to point out that not all investments that can reduce the burden of FBD are specifically "food safety" ones. For example, critical investments that do not fall in this category can be those that tackle environmental health issues, such as increasing access to potable water and improved sanitation, and reducing or mitigating environmental contaminants in soil, water, and air. Such measures reduce the propensity for cross contaminating the food supply at various stages of agri-food value chains. Another important area is investment in public health systems, including increasing access to and the quality of hospitals and clinics; training and funding more doctors, nurses, and other health workers; and increasing access to immunization programs and pharmaceuticals. These initiatives reduce the morbidity and mortality outcomes of FBD, and thus the ultimate socioeconomic burden on LMICs.

Other potential investments are more dedicated to food safety. These can include system-wide surveillance and testing for food safety hazards; addressing hazards and risks in specific value chains (infrastructure upgrades, promoting better practices); and import controls (quarantine and preborder, border, and postborder inspections). The relative emphasis that can and should be given to these dimensions will vary among countries at different points in the food safety life cycle, a topic discussed in chapter 5. Regardless of country circumstances, LMICs can make forward-looking investments for which they will almost always have "no regrets," because these investments are foundational aspects of food safety capacity. The foundational aspects include:

- *Sound science and evidence.* This pertains to risk assessment and FBD surveillance, the economics of unsafe food, and the effectiveness of measures to enhance food safety management capacity.
- *Human capital.* This is the cadre of food safety professionals needed to populate new technical and managerial positions in government and the private food sector, and various technical service industries.
- *Producer and consumer food safety awareness and knowledge.* These should be thought of as essential platforms for bringing about behavior changes along agri-food value chains.

Strong scientific capability is a prerequisite for introducing effective preventive measures as part of measures for food safety management capacity, and for effective risk surveillance and risk management functions. Some LMICs have begun to invest heavily in food safety science, enabling them to adopt a more risk-based approach to food safety management. China is one of these countries. Under a World Bank–supported project in Jilin Province, 65 basic and applied research projects were implemented over six years. These covered a broad range of risk-based themes, including using alternative green and safe techniques for pest and disease management, animal health and nutrition, rapid detection methods for harmful substances, gauging links between environmental hazards and food safety, risk analysis of food contact materials, and using information platforms for product and hazard tracking.

Advances are being made globally in chemical and microbiological risk assessment and analytical testing using hazard detection technologies that are both advanced and low-cost, and in processing and packaging technologies. Whole genome sequencing has great potential for rapidly identifying foodborne pathogens (box 4.7). While these advances can play a potentially significant role in managing FBD in LMICs, their effective use depends on competencies being substantially increased. Legal, administrative, and other barriers to sharing data must be overcome. Nevertheless, multiple applications of information technology—including mobile phones, internet, satellite imagery and "big data"—are enabling new approaches to the detection and surveillance of FBD. LMICs should monitor the experiences of first movers and how these can be adapted to local conditions (Santillana et al. 2015; Wiedmann 2015).

It is important to emphasize that the private sector can play a major if not a leading role in advancing food safety science and applying emerging biological, information, and other so-called disruptive technologies. Food manufacturers are investing heavily to reformulate products in response to multiple consumer food safety concerns. They are developing new food products—for example, "clean" meat—which may have profound impacts on the risk profile of changing diets. Food manufacturers are also exploring alternative food processing

BOX 4.7 Whole Genome Sequencing and Food Safety

Whole genome sequencing is an emerging tool with the potential to greatly assist foodborne hazard surveillance, and to improve outbreak detection and response (Allard et al. 2016). Whole genome sequencing involves identifying the entire DNA sequence of an organism's genome.

Knowing the complete nucleotide content of pathogen genomes enables public health professionals to use the most specific form of molecular subtyping to more accurately identify foodborne pathogens that are genetically related. For foodborne disease outbreaks, this increased specificity can help to link the sequences of isolates derived from clinical cases back to isolates derived from contaminated food or environmental sources.

Information on subtyping, virulence, and antimicrobial resistance profiling are a few examples of the power of whole genome sequencing and its immediate benefit for public health and food safety. Whole genome sequencing can be used as part of preventive controls to improve good agricultural and manufacturing practices. For example, knowing the genomic sequence of multiple pathogens collected within a facility over a given length of time can help distinguish between resident or transient pathogens, thereby providing greater insight into the source of contamination events.

WHO (2018) summarizes the state of whole genome sequencing for food safety. The World Health Organization will soon issue a guidance document on the prerequisites for using this technology successfully. The will include multiple technical capabilities and institutional issues, especially those related to data sharing.

The costs of setting up whole genome sequencing capabilities and the ability to sustain them are likely to be linked to broader national risk assessment skills and infrastructure. Because of this, adopting whole genome sequencing may be difficult for many low- and lower-middle-income countries. This is discussed in FAO (2016).

and packaging methods. And blockchain technologies are being used or evaluated by large food manufacturers to strengthen food product and ingredient traceability, and to reduce their vulnerability to food fraud.

The significant contributions that the food industry is making in food science and advancing supply chain traceability mean that LMIC governments should be trying to leverage private sector initiatives and investments in food safety management capacity wherever possible. This goes well beyond reenforcing the "business case" for the better management of food safety by private companies. The private sector can make many contributions that extend well beyond the specific context or operations of individual companies. Table 4.1 gives examples of investments that businesses can make to reduce food safety risks and the constraints that sometimes inhibit such investments in LMICs. Some of these constraints arise from government policy actions or inactions. Regulatory and other reforms can be effective remedies for this.

A review of the practitioner literature shows there are promising, cost-effective investments that governments can make or facilitate others to make. Investments

TABLE 4.1 Private Sector Food Safety Investments and Possible Constraints

Private investment or service	Possible constraints
Apply industry standards and codes of practice at enterprise or value chain levels	Lack of consumer awareness, nonrecognition by government or inconsistency with laws, lack of adequate human capital
Promote safer production practices and technologies among farmers and intermediate suppliers.	Weak regulations and enforcement on production inputs, restrictions on technology imports, restrictions on private advisory services or direct sourcing from farmers
Invest in and/or manage improved rural or urban food market infrastructure (i.e., collection stations, wholesale and community markets)	Public monopoly or other restrictions on private market facility operations, land use restrictions, absence of long-term financing, absence of public utility services
Conduct food science, epidemiological, or other primary or applied research	Restrictions on nonpublic research or access to public or international research funding
Provide laboratory testing services	Competition from subsidized public laboratories, mandatory testing by public laboratories, nonaccreditation, inadequate human capital
Provide professional food safety training and education services	Nonaccreditation and recognition by public agencies, and competition from subsidized public and donor programs
Implement programs for consumer awareness and education	Conflicts or inconsistencies with public risk communication and other consumer outreach
Assume responsibility for monitoring industry compliance with regulatory requirements	Government does not adopt, or a trade partner does not recognize, comanagement arrangements

Source: World Bank.

in technologies, training, information, and new processes have often been successful. At the farm and community levels, promising investments include those involving organizing producers in cooperatives or self-help groups that make food safety capacity building easier. These include, for example, community-based or group certification to meet food safety standards, out-grower or contract schemes that include farmer training and support, farmer field schools and training in good agricultural practices and integrated pest management, and technologies to reduce risk on farms, such as vaccines for pig tapeworms. These interventions can also improve smallholder farmer incomes, introduce other practices for better business and environmental protection, and improve the safety of food produced and consumed by farmers. Along the marketing segments of agri-food value chains, supportive public measures could include providing and upgrading infrastructure, such as roads and electricity; improving community markets; supporting the adoption of technical innovation, such as cooling devices and water disinfection; and supporting enterprises to use good manufacturing processes and approaches, such as hazard analysis and critical control points.

Institutionalize a Structured and Risk-Based Approach to Food Safety Management

A wide range of instruments can be used to tackle long-standing or emerging food safety risks in LMICs. These include traditional regulatory approaches, investments in public food safety; markets, sanitation, and other infrastructure; and information, technical support, and other measures that can augment incentives to investments in enhanced food safety management capacity within agri-food value chains. The feasibility of these alternative measures and their effectiveness in managing FBD depend on the soundness of administrative structures and technical competencies. The challenge for LMICs is to make investments that are appropriate to their stage of the food safety life cycle, and that form part of a staged plan for the sustained enhancement of food safety management capacity.

In high-income countries, proposed food safety regulatory and other measures tend to be subjected to an extended process of public and intra-industry consultation. For example, when regulations were proposed, the Food Safety Modernization Act in the United States received tens of thousands of registered comments from industry and consumers. A similar process occurred when the European Union's General Food Law was proposed. In Chile, a multistakeholder advisory committee is permanently involved in reviewing and updating the country's food code. In many LMICs, processes for getting stakeholder feedback on proposed food safety legislation and other initiatives tend to be less formalized, and often lack transparency. Because of this, investments tend to be driven more by established interests that have the loudest "voice."

Economic analysis, in the form of cost-benefit and cost-effectiveness analyses, is frequently incorporated into decisions about proposed food safety measures in high-income countries (box 4.8). Examples include the studies, ex ante and ex post, quantifying the costs and benefits of implementing enhanced food safety controls, such as hazard analysis and critical control points (Unnevehr 2000) and food safety

BOX 4.8 Cost-Benefit and Cost-Effectiveness Analyses in Food Safety

A cost-effectiveness analysis for food safety compares the costs of alternative capacity-building options with the benefits, with the latter measured in physical numbers. The ratio of dollar costs to physical benefits is expressed as the cost per physical benefit, and the program with the lowest cost is ranked as the most cost-effective (Kuchler and Golan 1999).

The benefits can be expressed in absolute numbers (for example, numbers of cases of animal disease) or as a percentage change (for example, a 10 percent increase in the value of exports). When comparisons are made between interventions that have identical benefits, cost-effectiveness analysis results in a cardinal ranking of the options. The option with the lowest cost-effectiveness can then act as a baseline against which all other options can be considered and a measure of the sacrifice in terms of efficiency, should the most cost-effective not be chosen.

Cost-effectiveness analysis is generally used where it is difficult to assign a monetary value to the stream of benefits associated with an investment (Mushkin 1979). It is also an obvious choice when a decision has been made to enhance a particular aspect of sanitary and phytosanitary capacity; for example, access to a market that is subject to quarantine restrictions, but where various options are nevertheless available to achieve access.

In all these contexts, cost-effectiveness analysis can be used as a guide to minimize costs. In general, cost-effectiveness analysis is a less costly and burdensome technique than cost benefit analysis, making it attractive to decision makers faced with time or resource constraints. It cannot be used, however, where the range of options for capacity building has varying qualitative and quantitative impacts.

It is important to recognize that cost-effectiveness analysis does not show whether a particular option yields a net benefit, since no attempt is made to value the benefit side of the equation.

improvements more generally, predominantly in the United States. There are also examples of economic analysis being applied to regulatory options, again mostly in the United States (FDA 1995; FSIS 1996).[4]

Applying cost-benefit and cost-effective analyses to food safety measures in LMICs is rare. The instances of these have been mainly for upgrading

[4] Most of these studies focus on estimating the economic value of improvements in human health. Thus, estimates tend to be highly variable and sensitive to the choice of key parameter values. To assess net benefits, industry costs from regulatory requirements can be compared to the reduction in disease burden in a cost-benefit analysis. Several studies of regulatory impact focus on the effect of the U.S. Pathogen Reduction Hazard Analysis Critical Control Program on regulations for the meat and poultry industry that began in the 1990s and were strengthened by subsequent regulation. For example, Crutchfield et al. (1997) showed that U.S. industry costs of controlling microbial pathogens in meat were much smaller than the value of improved human health resulting from these mandated controls, based on ex ante estimates. Ollinger (2011), Ollinger and Moore (2008, 2009), and Muth, Wohlgenant, Karns (2007) provide survey-based ex post evidence on Pathogen Reduction Hazard Analysis Critical Control Program rule impacts. These studies found that (1) compliance costs were larger than ex ante estimates when the rule was implemented, but still smaller than the public health benefits; (2) regulation tended to favor large, more specialized plants over small, diversified ones, which have higher per-unit costs from using hazard analysis and critical control points; (3) regulatory and private incentives fostered the adoption of new technologies to control microbial pathogens; and (4) regulation was not the only reason why plants invested in technology or in third-party audits—market incentives from buyers were equally or more important.

controls to overcome restrictions in export markets because of noncompliance with food safety regulations. Henson, Saqib, and Rajasenan (2004) estimated the costs and benefits of hygiene improvements in Kerala's shrimp sector to comply with European Union food safety regulations, including government controls and upgrading of processing facilities. The nonrecurring costs of compliance for processing facilities averaged US$265,492, though this varied as a proportion of production value, from 2.5 percent to 22.5 percent. Many firms that bore the heaviest of these costs did not survive. In 2001, Kerala had 51 shrimp-producing facilities approved by the European Union, suggesting sector-wide nonrecurring costs of US$13.5 million, representing 1.7 percent of the value of Kerala's total shrimp exports over the three years before the initial implementation of these investments.

Unnevehr and Ronchi (2014) review studies of high-value horticultural exports in 10 countries that estimated the costs and benefits of compliance with both regulatory requirements and private sector standards. The World Bank (2005) gives other examples of estimates of compliance costs and benefits associated with LMIC trade in high-value food. Box 4.9 summarizes the results of a more recent study, using a cost-benefit analysis of food safety compliance among CARIFORUM countries.

Cost-effectiveness analysis is being used to tackle aflatoxin risks in Africa. In Kenya, comparisons have been made between the costs and effectiveness of farmers or farm groups adopting various technologies and introducing product testing, product labeling, and other measures. Training in aflatoxin management, accompanied by providing plastic sheets for sun-drying crops, has been shown to reduce aflatoxin contamination in maize and groundnuts by about 50 percent at a material cost of US$2.50 per farmer a year in Kenya and Ghana (Pretari, Hoffmann, and Tian 2018; Hoffmann, Moser, and Herrman 2017). By comparison, achieving the same level of reduced contamination was estimated to cost US$5.24 through Aflasafe, and US$10.79 by using tarpaulins and a fully subsidized drying service. Table 4.2 summarizes the broader evidence on the strengths and weaknesses of the various approaches piloted in Kenya to tackle aflatoxin risks (box 3.5 in chapter 3 looks at the limitations of market-based incentives for aflatoxin controls for maize in Kenya).

A Food and Agriculture Organization guidance document on evidence-based decision making provides a possible framework for LMICs to apply when addressing risks that have already been prioritized (FAO 2017). In this framework, the key decision factors to be considered for implementing a prospective policy or risk management option are the expected

- benefits, including reduced health care costs
- costs (and who bears them)
- technical and institutional feasibility
- practicality in relation to the structure of production or the value chain; and
- political considerations, including coherence with other government policies.

BOX 4.9 Investing in Food Safety for Small Importing Countries: The Case of CARIFORUM

An Inter-American Institute for Cooperation on Agriculture (IICA) study of the costs of compliance with international standards in 15 small Caribbean countries that belong to the CARIFORUM shows the value of food safety investments for meeting many economic goals, including export promotion, import substitution, public health, and tourism promotion (Goulding 2017). The CARIFORUM countries are net importers of most foods, but they export fish and horticultural products. For fish, these countries have few companies which have approved access to European Union markets. Yet, if they could better comply with international standards, this would lead to reduced transactions costs, better access, fewer rejections, higher prices, and more scope for import substitution. The benefits for the CARIFORUM countries would also be improved human and animal health, and improved productivity. Compliance costs include public costs for investments in regulatory control and related infrastructure; operating costs for inspections and risk assessments; private investment costs for upgrading facilities; costs for developing hazard analysis and critical control points and training; and operating costs for monitoring, control, and certification.

The IICA study explored three cases on the costs and benefits of compliance in detail: fishery sector exports from Suriname to the European Union, processed ackee from Jamaica to the United States, and poultry production for import substitution in the Dominican Republic and Trinidad and Tobago. The findings are summarized in table B4.9.1. For fishery and horticultural products, the benefits were added export value; the benefits for poultry production were lower imports. All of these investments showed positive cost-benefit ratios.

TABLE B4.9.1 Case Study Costs and Benefits of Compliance

Industry	Benefits (US$, millions)	Public costs (US$, millions)	Private costs (US$, millions)	Benefit/cost
Fishery	30.0	5.5	0.9	4.7
Horticultural products	18.0	5.4	2.6	3.3
Poultry	16.1	3.0	3.6	2.4

Source: Goulding 2017.
Note: IICA = Inter-American Institute for Cooperation on Agriculture.

These cases were extrapolated for the entire agri-food sector to illustrate the costs and benefits. Goulding (2017) finds that increasing investments in sanitary and phytosanitary compliance of 2.4 percent of agri-food export trade value (US$97 million a year) would deliver trade benefits of US$306 million a year for the 15 CARIFORUM countries as a group. The costs of investment are about equally shared between the public and private sectors. Benefits that are not included because they are difficult to estimate include reduced foodborne illness, greater stability of income for smallholder agriculture, and lower risk of tourism losses.

The cost-benefit ratios are found to decline with country size, while still remaining positive. There are economies of scale in making sanitary and phytosanitary investments, with higher costs and lower benefits for the smallest countries. Regional inspection and laboratory services for the smallest countries might overcome these scale problems.

TABLE 4.2 Evidence on Strategies for Aflatoxin Control in Kenya's Maize Market

Strategy	Adoption	Strengths	Weaknesses
Test for aflatoxins and reject	Followed by most large- and medium-sized millers	Relatively cheap	Testing capacity weak, incentives to accept failures, unsafe maize goes to informal markets
Label for tested safe maize	Attempted but discontinued by one miller	Potential market advantage with sufficient private or social marketing effort	Draws regulatory attention, difficult to maintain compliance, no lasting market impact on sales shown in studies
Premium for tested safe maize	Exists in higher-priced brands despite lack of explicit labeling	Could be passed on to farmers	Achieved through testing, lower-priced brands are consumed by the poor
Premium for farmers	Experimental or donor-driven	Encourages adoption of aflatoxin control technologies	Costly to implement
Contractually linking farmers to millers	None to date	Reduces aflatoxin at source	Aflatoxin-prone areas are far from premium markets, inclusion of smaller farmers likely to require public subsidy due to cost

Source: Background paper prepared by Vivian Hoffmann.

The guidance document contains several case study examples for using the framework. To tackle risks associated with street foods, for example, the options are (1) introducing a central government training, licensing, and inspection program; (2) introducing similar programs involving local governments; (3) establishing community training and certification programs; and (4) focusing on consumer education, leading to more informed choices. The analysis weighs the likely effectiveness in reduced FBD, the social acceptability of the interventions, the likely implementation costs, and the likelihood of sustained changes in behavior.[5]

An alternative approach is the Standards and Trade Development Facility's framework for prioritizing sanitary and phytosanitary investments for trade-related market access in both these areas. This framework can easily be adapted

[5] Another example is tackling the presence of heavy metals in seafood. The options considered included (1) an outright ban on the harvesting, catching, and sale of fish with potentially high mercury levels; (2) putting limits on the harvest and sale of different species in different locations; and (3) pursuing the second option in tandem with a consumer information and education campaign. The analysis looked at the likely effectiveness, acceptability, and implementation feasibility of the different options. Potential trade-offs are found among cost and compliance considerations. This structured approach to policy and program decision making allows for the explicit consideration of these and other types of trade-offs.

to examine food safety management capacity specifically, but it can also be used in domestic markets. For this purpose, the framework has been used in Belize. A key strength of the framework is its participatory nature and the fact that all its elements are highly transparent. This promotes accountability and more active debates on priority investments and the basis on which priorities are established. The framework can also be applied even where data are of poor quality or missing.

An important insight from using these frameworks is that there are often significant and potentially complex interdependencies and complementarities across investments in food safety management capacity, and in the risks associated with food, such that it is often important to adopt multiple approaches simultaneously. This is because of their potential to reinforce one another and to help realize synergies. This concept appears to be especially relevant for food safety because of the multiple pathways through which people can become ill from exposure to food-related hazards (box 4.10). And there may be co-benefits from interventions to reduce food safety hazards (box 4.11).

BOX 4.10 Gains from Multisector Coordination: The One Health Approach

Most human infectious diseases have their origin through cross-species transmission of pathogens from animals to humans, and many of the diseases in humans evolved from diseases in animals. Among zoonotic diseases, foodborne diseases are an important cause of morbidity and mortality in humans. Animals can be direct sources of pathogens in animal source foods and also indirect sources through fecal contamination of water and plant-derived foods. Having control measures on farms and at subsequent stages of the food chain has proven to be most effective for reducing risks related to foodborne disease.

The welfare of animals is also important because their condition has implications for food safety. For example, tail biting in pigs is a welfare issue and a well-known risk factor for abscesses and infections in carcasses. The health and welfare of animal populations contributes to the economic benefits that are derived from them, and is connected to public health and the health of the environment. The One Health concept recognizes these connections and promotes coordination across sectors to better understand and manage health risks.

In applying One Health, the European Union (EU) has coordinated control programs for *salmonellosis* that have reduced the number of cases in humans from more than 200,000 reported cases each year before 2004 in 15 member states to less than 90,000 cases in 2014 in 28 member states.

The EU's integrated approach to food safety—from primary production to food consumption—involves all major actors for zoonotic diseases in the EU: member states, the European Commission, the European Parliament, the European Food Safety Authority, and the European Centre for Disease Prevention and Control. Several elements of the EU's One Health approach have been key to its success, including targets for the reduction of Salmonella in poultry flocks and pigs, and trade restrictions imposed on the products from infected flocks.

Overall, the One Health concept formulates the need for and the benefits from cross-sector collaboration.

BOX 4.11 Realizing Co-Benefits for Tackling Farm Food Safety Hazards

Many food safety hazards originate on the farm, and it is important to understand the practices that exacerbate them. Interventions targeting the farm sector can help prevent some food safety hazards from entering the food supply in the first place. Moreover, certain interventions targeting the farm sector offer multiple win-win opportunities, with benefits extending beyond food safety.

Measures can be taken to mitigate foodborne disease risks that can also benefit pollution prevention and control—and hence for public health, wildlife protection, climate stability, and even farm profitability. This potential for co-benefits is significant from a cost-benefit perspective, considering that changing farming practices can be both challenging and costly, especially where farming involves large numbers of small farms with a limited capacity. Table B4.11.1 shows how responses to food safety challenges that originate on the farm can sometimes address farm-related pollution, although some responses present trade-offs and others are neutral.

TABLE B4.11.1 Win-Win Responses to Farm Food Safety Challenges

Farm food safety challenges	Possible responses	Pollution and public health co-benefits associated with the response
Presence of pesticide residues on food crops	Measures to minimize pesticide use, and favoring the use of less toxic and less persistent chemicals	(+) Less localized air pollution and exposure of farm workers and rural communities to ambient pesticides (+) Less pesticide contamination of surface water and groundwater, and hence of drinking water and habitat
Uptake by food crops of toxic heavy metals present in soil, exacerbated by soil acidification	Measures to increase fertilizer use efficiency and to reduce fertilizer waste Switch to alternative crops less affected by heavy metals	(+) Less nutrient pollution of soil, water, and air—and hence less soil acidification, fewer harmful algal blooms, less eutrophication of surface waters, fewer fish kills and dead zones, less nitrate contamination of drinking water, less urban air pollution, and less climate destabilization
Presence of pathogenic mycotoxins in soil or crops	Measures to reduce or eradicate pathogenic strains of fungi in soil or to slow fungal growth during plant growth, harvest, and storage (via temperature and moisture control)	( ) No pollution co-benefits

(Continued)

(Continued)

BOX 4.11 Realizing Co-Benefits for Tackling Farm Food Safety Hazards *(Continued)*

TABLE B4.11.1 Win-Win Responses to Farm Food Safety Challenges *(Continued)*

Farm food safety challenges	Possible responses	Pollution and public health co-benefits associated with the response
Presence of pathogens in the guts of animals (which can go on to contaminate foods downstream if exposed to manure)	Improved sanitation, using probiotics, and judicious use of antimicrobials and pesticides	(+) Less contamination of freshwater (drinking and habitat) with pathogens via the release of manure—and hence less contamination of food from using contaminated water in its preparation (–) Depending on the treatment chosen, potential contamination of freshwater with chemicals that could affect the health of humans and wildlife
Storage and management of manure or feces-laden water that create the potential for cross contamination (for instance, by wildlife or by contaminated irrigation waters)	Measures to improve the storage and management of manure and feces-laden water	(+) Some forms of storage can decrease nutrient runoff and pollution of water, improving drinking water quality and reducing eutrophication (+/–) Storage can either increase or decrease the volatilization of nitrogen from manure in the form of ammonia and nitrous oxides, which contributes to urban air pollution and, when it deposits, to biodiversity and soil fertility losses

Leverage Consumer Concerns on Food Safety to Incentivize Better Food Business Practices

Empowering consumers to influence the food safety management capacity and practices of actors along agri-food value chains is a major avenue for public sector action, especially because governments have little direct influence on the actions of food products, processors, and distributors. Frequently, public regulators face difficulties in monitoring actors at different stages of the supply chain, limiting the potential to use a range of "top down" interventions to change the behavior of food suppliers. And perhaps even more important, many of the most promising interventions for influencing the everyday behavior of agri-food value chain actors are the ones over which the public sector has little control or leverage (for example, behavior engendering a food safety culture). This is especially the case for the agri-food value chains that are dominated by a multitude of micro and small enterprises operating predominantly in the informal sector, as in many LMICs.

Governments can indirectly incentivize safer practices along agri-food value chains by raising awareness of both FBD actions needed to minimize the risks associated with food among consumers. In so doing, consumers will not only be more motivated to look for and demand foods they perceive to be safer, but the inherent asymmetry in food markets on food safety information will be reduced. For example, the public sector can play an active role in developing, implementing, and supporting schemes that give consumers the tools to make more informed decisions about food safety, including the food they buy and how it is prepared, stored, and handled by vendors. The public sector, for its part, can do this through voluntary certification and mandatory disclosure.

Voluntary certification involves writing or otherwise supporting certification standards that inform consumers about food safety and aligning these standards with known food safety risks. Consumers often rely on labels for food safety information, using them as a guide for safe food or at least what they perceive to be safer food. Consumers sometimes use labels as sources of information about the safety of food products, whether the labels are intended to be used in this way or not.[6] In LMICs, voluntary food safety certification and labeling schemes are growing, and these often have the strong backing of governments. For example, China's Ministry of Agriculture supports three voluntary food standards: for safe (or hazard-free) food, green food, and organic food.[7] In Thailand, the government has backed the consumer-facing Q-Mark label, which shows that good voluntary agricultural practices have been used, and private actors have introduced other labels and brands linked to food safety.[8] In Vietnam, a "safe vegetable" program and label has been backed by the Ministry of Agriculture and Rural Development for many years. It is too soon, however, to know how effective these efforts are in fostering food safety management in agri-food value chains. But, arguably, public sector support for credible, science-based information in certification schemes can foster the right kind of incentives as markets develop.

Through mandatory disclosure, some foods and food services are required to disclose certain information about their production processes, food safety precautions and performance, and other related areas. Food safety inspection reports offer the public a means of evaluating food safety practices at restaurants and other food establishments. This information can be disclosed in different forms, including numerical scores (for example, 1–100); category grades (A, B, C, or pass/conditional pass); pictures or nonalphanumeric symbols; and as written narratives that describe inspection findings. This information can also be made public in different places, including storefronts and websites.

[6] For example, a review of studies of certified food in China found that food safety was the main motivation for buying, followed by health, nutrition, taste, and environmental concerns (Liu, Pieniak, and Verbeke 2013).

[7] As of 2012, green food certification covered over 11 percent of China's farmed area (Yu, Gao, and Zeng 2014).

[8] These include Safe Produce, which does not depend on independent certification, and the Royal Project and Doctor's Vegetables brands, which display the Q-Mark label and are certified as good manufacturing practice and for using hazard analysis and critical control points (Wongprawmas and Canavari 2017).

Canada, China, and the United States are among the countries that are using these kinds of disclosures. Posting inspection results on food establishments sometimes has an effect on consumers' perceptions of food safety and their intentions to eat in these establishments. A report by the National Research Council (2011) on the public disclosure of establishment-specific inspection results in the United States across a range of food-safety areas found that they not only helped consumers to make more informed choices but also heightened their sensitivity to a range of concerns, including impact on the environment and nutrition.

Engaging consumers constructively in the processes that drive enhanced food safety management capacity in agri-food value chains can be challenging. Doing this requires changing more or less well-founded consumer fears about food safety risks that sometimes lead to perverse behaviors, such as avoiding healthy foods, into beliefs and attitudes that motivate them to play an active and constructive role in food safety management. Because consumers have only a limited knowledge of food safety, they often find it difficult to interpret the "signals" on food labels, even where these are available. Consumers are often reluctant to act on their concerns about food safety; for example, by rejecting some foods or voicing their concerns, especially in the context of local food markets that are a social setting and where often long-standing relations exist between consumers and food vendors. Informing and empowering consumers is very challenging in the absence of consumer organizations that are trusted for the information they provide and that command "voice" on the national policy stage. In most LMICs, such organizations are weak or just not there. One measure governments can take to help remedy this is to support the creation or strengthening of organizations that represent consumer interests and are active in building awareness of food safety issues.

Governments can and should draw on behavioral insights to design smarter food safety information programs and consumer campaigns to increase their effectiveness, and to make best use of limited public resources. For example, visual and sensory-rich formats can be used, including role models; "edutainment," including TV and radio shows and stars; and street theater. The Government of India is using a range of behavioral-change communication principles in its expanding food safety information programs (box 4.12).

Crowdsourcing is another instrument that can be used more to extensively engage consumers, both in surveillance and in communications (Soon and Saguy 2017). Crowdsourcing is already being used to engage consumers in identifying and tracing FBD, and reporting the unhygienic practices or conditions of food businesses, including restaurants. Crowdsourcing platforms can also function as a two-way street, offering a means of alerting businesses and the public to food safety risks. But the rapidity with which information can flow on social media platforms has a good and bad side; while it may help to save lives when risks are real, it can do unnecessary economic harm when they are not.

Crowdsourcing certainly has untapped potential, but exploiting it will require tackling its challenges, especially in LMICs. Systems are needed to verify the validity and accuracy of the data that crowdsourcing efforts generate.

BOX 4.12 India's Behavioral Change Communication Principles for Food Safety

A broad range of initiatives are being carried out in India to strengthen the contributions that consumers can make to better food safety outcomes. In 2017, the Food Safety and Standards Authority of India launched an interactive educational on-line portal to convert "all food purchasers into smart, alert and aware consumers." The portal uses food safety display boards showing practices that food business operators must follow, and provides contacts for consumers to provide feedback, queries, and complaints.

The authority's Food Safety Connect initiative provides consumers with several modalities to channel two-way information between regulator and itself. Partnership programs are being pursued to promote improved food safety in schools, workplaces, workshop, hospitals, and the railway system. Colorful mascots are being used to raise food safety awareness among school-age children.

These programs are not unique, but their breadth of coverage is impressive. Chile, for example, has also been using a broad-based program for consumer food safety awareness and education, such as the food safety and quality agency's food safety theater.

Users sometimes make unintentional errors; for example, when they mistake an allergic reaction for food poisoning or trace the source of an illness to the wrong place. Consumers without technical food safety assessment tools or expertise may also conflate an unpleasant sensory experience with food safety risk, even if these are not objectively aligned; for instance, for microbiological risk. Crowdsourcing is vulnerable to malevolent efforts to intentionally spread false information.

REFERENCES

Allard, M., E. Strain, D. Melka, K. Bunning, S. Musser, E. Brown, and R. Timme. 2016. "Practical Value of Food Pathogen Traceability through Building a Whole-Genome Sequencing Network and Database." *Journal of Clinical Microbiology* 54: 1975–83.

Crutchfield, S. R., J. C. Buzby, T. Roberts, M. Ollinger, and C. J. Lin. 1997. *An Economic Assessment of Food Safety Regulations: The New Approach to Meat and Poultry Inspection.* Agricultural Economic Report No. 755. Washington, DC: U.S. Department of Agriculture.

FAO (Food and Agriculture Organization). 2016. *Review of Food Safety Control Systems in Sri Lanka.* Colombo: FAO.

———.2017. *Food Safety and Risk Management: Evidence-Informed Policies and Decisions, Considering Multiple Factors.* Rome: FAO.

FDA (U.S. Food and Drug Adminstration). 1995. *Final Regulatory Impact Analysis of the Regulations to Establish Procedures for the Safe and Sanitary Processing and Importing of Fish and Fishery Products.* Washington, DC: FDA.

FSIS (U.S. Food Safety and Inspection Service). 1996. "Pathogen Reduction; Hazard Analysis and Critical Control Points (HACCP) Systems; Final Rule." *Federal Register* 61 (144).

Goulding, Ian. 2017. "Cost/Benefit Analysis and Impact of Compliance and Non-compliance with Sanitary and Phytosanitary Requirement for CARIFORUM Countries." Paper presented at Inter-American Institute for Cooperation in Agriculture, February.

Henson, S., M. Saqib, and R. Rajasenan. 2004. "Impact of Sanitary Measures on Exports of Fishery Products in India: The Case of Kerela." Agriculture and Rural Development Discussion Paper 17, World Bank, Washington, DC.

Hoffmann, V., C. Moser, and T. Herrman. 2017. "Demand for Aflatoxin-Tested Maize in Kenya." Paper presented at the International Association of Agricultural Economists Triennial Conference, Milan.

Kristkova, Z., D. Grace, and M. Kuiper. 2017. *The Economics of Food Safety in India—A Rapid Assessment*. Amsterdam: Wageningen University and Research Centre and International Livestock Research Institute.

Kuchler, F., and E. Golan. 1999. *Assigning Values to Life: Comparing Methods for Valuing Health Risks*. Washington DC: U.S. Department of Agriculture.

Liu, R., Z. Pieniak, and W. Verbeke. 2013. "Consumers' Attitudes and Behaviour towards Safe Food in China: A Review." *Food Control* 33 (September): 93–104.

Masters, B., and P. Derfler. 2005. "Risk-Based Inspection." Presentation at the National Advisory Committee on Meat and Poultry Inspection Conference, U.S. Department of Agriculture, Washington, DC, November 15–16.

Mushkin, S. J. 1979. *Biomedical Research: Costs and Benefits*. Cambridge, MA: Ballinger Publishing.

Muth, M. K., M. K. Wohlgenant, and S. A. Karns. 2007. "Did the Pathogen Reduction and Hazard Analysis and Critical Control Points Regulation Cause Slaughter Plants to Exit?" *Review of Agricultural Economics* 29 (3): 596–611.

National Research Council. 2011. The Potential Consequences of Public Release of Food Safety and Inspection Service Establishment-Specific Data. Washington, DC: The National Academies Press. https://doi.org/10.17226/13304.

Ollinger, M. 2011. "Structural Change in the Meat and Poultry Industry and Food Safety Regulations. Agribusiness." 27 (2): 244–57.

Ollinger, M., and D. Moore. 2008. "The Economic Forces Driving Food Safety and Quality in Meat and Poultry." *Applied Economics Perspectives and Policy* 30 (2): 289–310. doi:10.1111/j.1467-9353.2008.00405.

———. 2009. "The Direct and Indirect Costs of Food-Safety Regulation." *Applied Economics Perspectives and Policy* 31 (2): 247–65. doi:10.1111/j.1467-9353.2009.01436.

Pretari, A., V. Hoffmann, and L. Tian. 2018. "Post-Harvest Practices for Aflatoxin Control: Evidence from Kenya." IFPRI Discussion Paper, International Food Policy Research Institute, Washington, DC.

Santillana, M., A. T. Nguyen, M. Dredze, M. J. Paul, E. O. Nsoesie, and J. S. Brownstein. 2015. "Combining Search, Social Media, and Traditional Data Sources to Improve Influenza Surveillance." *PLOS Computational Biology*. October 29. https://journals.plos.org/ploscompbiol/article%20?id=10.1371/journal.pcbi.1004513.

Soon, J., and I. Saguy, S. 2017. "Crowdsourcing: A New Conceptual View for Food Safety and Quality." *Trends in Food Science & Technology* 66: 63–72.

Unnevehr, L. J. 2000. "Food Safety Issues for Fresh Food Product Exports from LDCs." *Agricultural Economics* 23: 231–40.

Unnevehr, L. J., and L. Ronchi. 2014. "Food Safety Standards: Economic and Market Impacts in Developing Countries." Viewpoint Note 341, World Bank, Washington, DC.

WHO (World Health Organization). 2018. *Whole Genome Sequencing for Foodborne Disease Surveillance: Landscape Paper*. Geneva: WHO.

Wiedmann, M. 2015. "Can Big Data Revolutionize Food Safety?" *Food Quality and Safety* October/November.

Wongprawmas, R., and M. Canavari. 2017. "Consumers' Willingness-to-Pay for Food Safety Labels in an Emerging Market: The Case of Fresh Produce in Thailand." *Food Policy* 69 (Supplement C): 25–34.

World Bank. 2005. *Food Safety and Agricultural Health Standards: Challenges and Opportunities for Developing Country Exports*. Washington, DC: World Bank.

———. 2009. "Guide for Assessing Investment Needs in Laboratory Capacities for Managing Food Safety, Plant Health, and Animal Health." Working Paper 55006, World Bank, Washington, DC.

Yu, Xiaohua, Zhifeng Gao, and Yinchu Zeng. 2014. "Willingness to Pay for the 'Green Food' in China." *Food Policy* 45: 80–87.

CHAPTER FIVE

The Way Forward

CONCLUSIONS

The data and analyses presented in this report make a compelling case for greater and smarter investments in food safety management capacity in low- and middle-income countries (LMICs). These investments should be driven by rigorous and transparent prioritization of capacity-building needs that is risk-focused and proactive, rather than seeking to offset food safety problems when they happen. That said, effective surveillance and rapid response are key aspects of the performance of food safety systems. Enhancing food safety management capacity should be seen as an effort that cuts across the public and private sectors, rather than as following an outdated notion of who does what.

The demands for public and private sector investment to tackle development challenges in LMICs are often overwhelming, especially in lower-middle-income countries, where processes of economic and social change are accelerating the fastest. Thus, ministries of finance face a constant stream of stakeholders demanding action to address critical needs. It is only in countries where the political commitment is sufficiently strong to deal with food safety problems that the necessary investments are forthcoming. A critical first step to get to this stage is to engage political decision makers at the highest level and promulgate broad-based strategies for enhancing food safety management capacity.

Some countries are working on addressing food safety risks, but they do not refer to them as such and are not organized institutionally to tackle food safety as a discrete problem. Instead, they tackle, say, diarrheal disease as a public health problem with interventions centered on water and sanitation, or they bundle food safety with other trade and market access issues. This approach also relegates food safety to the level of being the poor stepchild, so to speak, in the regulatory oversight of food and drug agencies. These agencies have little or no contact with the main actors in LMIC food systems, including smallholder farmers, micro and small enterprises, and informal sector food distributors. The challenge therefore goes beyond simply understanding the importance of food safety or allocating adequate resources. In many cases, the most effective and forward-looking way to engage governments on food safety management may require restructuring the mandates of various government institutions.

Because this call to action may seem daunting or even overwhelming to some, this final chapter synthesizes guidance based on a review of evidence presented in the previous chapters. The recommendations are organized in two ways to make them accessible to various audiences. First, specific recommendations are provided for first steps and best practices for various food system actors and stakeholders in the following section. These recommendations follow an outline of the important roles and responsibilities for building and applying food safety management capacity, and will be especially useful for those who perhaps view their actions as peripheral by defining how best to be engaged. Second, suggested actions by country level of development are offered for the stages of the food safety life cycle. These may not fit all countries within each stage, but the aim is to show that actions can be taken at all stages to get ahead of food safety challenges and to avoid significant economic losses.

A CALL TO ACTION FOR VARIOUS STAKEHOLDERS

Many different actors are involved in efforts to strengthen food safety systems in LMICs. This section lays out a call to action to a subset of important actors. Local institutional settings vary, especially in the degree of formality of the main food distribution channels and in how governments are organized to provide food safety coordination and oversight. So, there will be some variance among countries in who and how leadership functions are vested and where critical competencies are needed. A flavor of this variation is reflected later in the chapter in the different priorities proposed for countries at different points in the food safety life cycle. The following are the calls to action for specific actors involved in enhancing food safety systems in LMICs.

LMIC Ministries of Finance and Other Coordinating Economic Ministries

- *Make public spending proportionate to the challenges and opportunities.* Calibrate the level of spending on food safety to the economic costs of foodborne disease (FBD) and to the benefits of investing in its prevention and management. This calculation should factor in both near- and longer-term impacts. Consider the economic costs of lives lost and disability, public health spending, trade interruptions, reputational damage to the food system in the eyes of trade partners and consumers, longer-term impacts on the productivity of people, and forgone economic growth related to these impacts.

- *Implement preventive forward-looking investments.* In multiyear national strategies, draw on expert advice to factor in anticipated food safety risks given expected changes in demographics, diets, and trade-related developments. Support investments that may prevent or minimize future costs (avoidable losses) in relation to public health and market development. Forward-looking, preventive investments in food safety are likely to be far less costly than measures undertaken only in reaction to serious adverse events.
- *Balance hard and soft public spending.* Important food safety investments relate to both hardware (laboratories and market places) and software (management systems and human capital). The effectiveness of investments and the sustainability of enhanced capacities depends on the simultaneous development and maintenance of both types. Sufficient spending on staff and operations is critical for realizing the full return on larger, lumpy public investments for improved food safety.
- *Economically justify spending.* Ensure that technical agency or other proposals for significant public investments or programs for food safety are justified on the basis of cost-benefit or cost-effectiveness analyses, and that alternative approaches, including regulatory measures and facilitating private investment, have been considered.
- *Leverage public spending.* Use public investment and public programs to leverage and incentivize private investment and other nonpublic activities to build food safety capacity and improve outcomes. The private sector can play a major role in advancing food safety science, applying emerging technologies, developing human capital, and promoting safer practices in primary production and food value chains.
- *Strategically focus resource allocations.* Demand and, if necessary, facilitate the development of a unified strategy for food safety investment and management to ensure that food safety resources are expended judiciously on a coherent set of policies and interventions across all parts of the food system. In the absence of a food safety agency, facilitate or arrange for an institutional mechanism for coordinating the action of technical ministries and other stakeholders.

LMIC Lead Food Safety Agency or Other Coordinating Body

- *Unify strategy and coordinate action.* Develop a unified food safety strategy that defines priorities and responsibilities, and establishes funding needs. In developing a strategy and setting priorities, weigh trade-offs both analytically and by convening all relevant agencies and stakeholders to assist in this. Coordinate actions by ministries, agencies, and private sector partners to ensure that interventions are developed to address food safety at every stage of the food value chain. In particular, coordinate with ministries of agriculture, health, and commerce to ensure the prevention of FBD as far upstream as possible.

- *Apply a structured approach to prioritization.* Define and regularly update evidence-based priorities, using risk analysis to make more strategic use of resources. Specifically, align resources with the risks in the domestic food system, taking into account the hazards posed by actual consumption patterns, as well as exposure and vulnerability to these hazards. Prioritize interventions that are feasible and cost effective.[1]
- *Punish less and facilitate more.* Redefine institutional roles to be less about finding and penalizing noncompliance and more about facilitating compliance. This can be done by providing information, advice, incentives, and interventions to motivate and leverage investments and actions by value chain actors. Reorient food safety inspection services to give more prominence to awareness raising and capacity building. Focus the attention of food safety inspection services on the parts of the food system where food safety violations are likely to have the most serious public health consequences. Foster a culture of proactivity by giving agents more autonomy and responsibility to identify and focus on emerging problems, while providing them with adequate data access, training, and agency support.
- *Engage consumers more fully.* Provide consumers with the tools to become partners in food safety through their own actions, and through incentivizing and motivating food suppliers. To this end, develop education materials, standards, certification infrastructure, and other signaling mechanisms—or work with other ministries and technical partners to do this. For example, support the development of voluntary food certification programs and the quality infrastructure they rely on. Institute food business rating systems and public disclosure systems. Educate consumers on food safety risks, risk avoidance actions, and how to demand safer food.
- *Use the science of behavior change.* This should be incorporated in the design and redesign of training programs, information campaigns, and other interventions. For example, develop training programs and information campaigns for farmers and downstream food handlers that are more easily retained and put into action. Share food safety checklists with enterprises. Develop certification programs that professionalize food inspectors, food handlers, and managers of all kinds, and redesign administrative requirements to feature measures that improve participation and compliance. Develop campaigns that inform consumers and food handlers about food safety, and socially legitimize and normalize behaviors that are consistent with the prevention of FBD.

---

[1] For a structured approach to setting priorities, consider using tools such as multifactor decision making, the Prioritizing Sanitary and Phytosanitary Investments for Market Access Framework developed by Standards and Trade Development, and the Food and Agriculture Organization's guidance on evaluating trade-offs.

LMIC Technical Ministries (Agriculture, Health, Trade, Environment)

Where a lead food safety agency is not designated, then technical ministries or coordination bodies linking these ministries will need to undertake the strategy, coordination, and prioritization roles outlined in the previous subsection. The other principles covered in that subsection also apply to programs developed by technical ministries. The following are more specific recommendations for these ministries:

- *Shift objectives and measure outcomes better.* Change key performance indicators to be less about policing outcomes (value of fines collected, number of infringements and businesses closed) and more about food safety outcomes (magnitude of food safety risks, incidence of FBD, standards-compliant trade). Invest in surveillance and reporting systems that enable effective monitoring of risks and performance.
- *Take measures to minimize hazard entry into the food supply on farms.* Focus particularly on measures that offer co-benefits for public health and environmental protection. Examples include measures that improve the efficiency of fertilizer and pesticide use, minimize the presence and spread of pathogens in farmed animals, and improve manure management in ways that reduce opportunities for cross contamination.
- *Pay attention to small and informal actors in the food system.* Facilitate food safety compliance by businesses, especially micro, small, and medium enterprises and ones operating in the informal sector, by helping them understand what compliance consists of and the reasons for compliance requirements. Simplify regulatory texts, share the checklists used by inspectors, and offer these enterprises opportunities to learn about safe food-handling practices. Recognize the contributions that informal sector actors such as street vendors and venues such as wet markets make to vibrant and inclusive food systems. But also recognize the risks they pose, and invest in their upgrading, professionalization, and formalization.[2]
- *Develop technical standards to help correct asymmetry of information.* This divides buyers and sellers of food, including ones engaged in farming, processing, and marketing. When appropriate, consider enhancing standards that consumers use as proxies for food safety—notably organic standards—to help them better fulfill their actual use.
- *Remove policy, regulatory, and other barriers to private investment and services.* The private sector can make major contributions to food safety science, laboratory testing, human capital development, and standards

[2] Successful interventions have tended to combine multiple supportive instruments, including education and awareness raising, surveillance, business licensing, and investments in electricity, access to clean water, and waste management infrastructure.

compliance. However, its initiatives may be hindered by nonaccreditation and recognition by public agencies, public monopolies for certain services, or restrictions on private activity (advisory services and direct purchasing from farmers). These constraints should be reviewed to facilitate increased private investment in capacities and services that contribute to national or value-chain-specific food safety systems.

- *Apply risk-based approaches to govern food trade.* Develop basic trade facilitation capabilities to reduce barriers at borders, ensure the safety of food imports, and promote exports. These capabilities include providing clear information on standards and requirements, and implementing consistent preborder and border controls that focus on the most important hazards. They also include equivalence agreements with major trading partners, participating in regional agreements to harmonize standards, and ensuring that recognized sanitary and phytosanitary certifications can be obtained by exporters.

LMIC Chambers of Commerce and Food Industry Associations

- *Engage in national strategy and prioritization processes.* Work with the public sector to identify opportunities for public action. These include strategic infrastructure investments, applied research and technology demonstration projects, developing a cadre of food safety professionals, setting up food safety advisory and auditing services, and negotiating with trading partners for standards or capacity recognition. Also, participate in structured processes to identify priority hazards and to evaluate the feasibility and cost-effectiveness of alternative solutions.
- *Play active advocacy roles.* This is to ensure that small-actor interests and constraints are factored into policy making. Advocate for the least-burdensome means and realistic time frames for achieving regulatory compliance. Educate members in food safety regulations and new developments in food safety that are likely to affect their businesses.
- *Take collective action.* This is needed to build food operator awareness; facilitate the adoption of good agriculture and management practices, and industry codes of practice; and strengthen food quality and the safety management of industry leaders, small and medium enterprises, and organized primary producers. Engage with the Global Food Safety Initiative and other international and regional schemes to mainstream the adoption of benchmarked standards.
- *Support programs to improve food and pathogen traceability and transparency.* This can be done by establishing industry-wide norms and standards for record-keeping and sharing information along the value chain. Establish industry standards for handling food safety failures, including voluntary product recalls. To the extent feasible, provide consumers with information on production methods and product origins.

Research Institutes and Academia

- *Build capacity in the basic disciplines to deal with food hazards.* These disciplines include microbiology, parasitology, food chemistry, risk analysis, food science, health economics, and consumer behavioral science. Use this capacity to do research on the epidemiology of FBD, to carry out risk assessments, and to evaluate feasible alternatives for risk management. Work with the public sector to develop surveillance systems, and to use food safety data to inform public priorities and public information campaigns.
- *Develop, adapt, and pilot food safety technologies and approaches.* This should be done in partnership with private industry or civil society. Identify whether available technologies can be adapted to local conditions and practices. Test the viability of these technologies with partners, such as food processors or handlers. Consider potential consumer risk-mitigating practices and whether these will be acceptable, taking into account gender-specific constraints if they are adopted.
- *Develop training and certification programs for food safety professionals.* The aim is to create a cadre of trained personnel for the food industry and the public sector. These programs could train individuals at the postsecondary level or be offered through extension and outreach to raise the skills of food industry personnel.

Bilateral Development and Trade Partners

- *Strengthen the incentives for preventive actions by LMIC trading partners.* This can be done by instituting more streamlined trade consignment inspection protocols for countries and approved suppliers that have demonstrated certain capacities, and through memoranda of understanding, twinning arrangements, and other programs to achieve mutual recognition of sanitary and phytosanitary management systems. Increase efforts to inform policy makers, technical counterparts, and industry representatives in LMICs on proposed regulatory changes that may affect their exports.
- *Improve the quality of bilateral food safety capacity support programs.* This can be done by using cost-benefit analyses; doing more rigorous monitoring and evaluation; putting greater emphasis on capacity sustainability; balancing support for public and private sector capacity building; taking advantage of potential synergies (One Health initiatives, for example); and investing in networks of collaboration with universities, nongovernment organizations, and consumer organizations, which can be maintained beyond periods of specific project funding.
- *Put a higher priority on food safety interventions to promote domestic public health.* A disproportionate amount of bilateral support for food safety has focused on trade-related capacities that have often had few or no spillovers for managing domestic food safety risks. Various factors contribute to this, not least the self-interest of countries to protect their own consumers from hazards from traded food products. Although less visible, the socioeconomic

burden of unsafe food is far larger in the domestic setting of LMICs than is the impact on trade. To best contribute to the Sustainable Development Goals, bilateral development assistance should be focused on domestic settings. Even for trade-related capacity, increased attention is needed to support the adoption of risk-based food import controls as LMIC imports of high-value food grow in importance.

- *Promote low-cost, high-impact investments in food safety management capacity.* The aim of these investments is not only to make the most effective and efficient use of scarce public and private sector resources but also to enable these resources to be mobilized quickly. Another aim is to show the substantial economic and social benefits that can flow from efforts to enhance food safety management capacity. Importantly, these investments will likely revolve around insights into behavioral aspects of food safety management by actors along agri-food value chains and by consumers, and this will be combined with modest changes to support infrastructure. The challenge is to determine what relatively small changes can be made to bring about substantial changes in food-safety-related behavior at a low cost and that do not require premature regulatory action.

Multilateral Organizations and Partnerships

- *Develop and apply a food safety commitment index.* The index should be a global or regional benchmarking tool to monitor the level of commitment that LMIC governments are making to food safety, and to motivate them to take action to improve underlying capacities and performance. The index could be based on other "commitment type" models for indexes being used for nutrition that cover legal frameworks, policies, and public spending. This could be combined with capacity measures along the lines of the World Organisation for Animal Health and the Inter-American Institute for Cooperation on Agriculture's performance of veterinary services assessment tools. It is important that ratings should be made public, periodically updated, and based on objective data and expert assessment rather than self-reporting.
- *Promote experience sharing among LMICs.* While LMICs can continue to learn from the experiences and applied institutional models of high-income countries, there is a need for more systematic sharing of experiences among LMICs on the measures they are taking to enhance food safety management capacity in the public and private sectors. This needs to be done in the context of rapid economic and social change, weak regulatory systems, and the predominantly informal agri-food value chains that characterize LMICs. Sharing mechanisms could involve establishing direct relations between LMICs for the specific purpose of building food safety management capacity, most probably within particular geographical regions and through, for example, personnel exchanges. Multilateral agencies—such as the World Bank, Food and Agriculture Organization, World Health Organization, United Nations

Industrial Development Organization, the Standards and Trade Development Facility, the Inter-American Institute for Cooperation on Agriculture, Asian Development Bank, and the African Development Bank—and international foundations can play a role in monitoring and assessing the experiences of LMICs in enhancing this capacity. They could also identify and promote best practices for different levels of development.

- *Promote the use of formal processes for prioritization.* This should be done as part of the development of national strategies for enhancing food safety management capacity. Two potential approaches to the prioritization of investments have been developed by the Standards and Trade Development Facility and the Food and Agriculture Organization, which are both discussed in this report. Cost-benefit and cost-effectiveness analyses can be combined with these frameworks. The objective of this approach is not only to ensure that scarce resources are used effectively but also to engage stakeholders across the public and private sectors to promulgate, promote, and apply national food safety strategies.
- *Promote multidisciplinary, development-oriented research.* The dearth of strong, empirically based evidence on the public health burden of FBD, its interlinks with LMIC nutritional issues, and its economic consequences persists, despite recent improvements in gathering this evidence. Even less empirical evidence exists on the socioeconomics of alternative technologies, institutional approaches, and incentive-based schemes for improving the management of food safety risks in a context dominated by smallholder farmers and small food businesses operators. Resources to support global and regional research in these areas that can inform strategies, policies, and programs need to be mobilized.

PRIORITIES AMONG COUNTRIES AT DIFFERENT STAGES OF THE FOOD SAFETY LIFE CYCLE

Building food safety capacity needs to be seen as a continuous process of development, upgrading, learning, adjustment, and refinement. The World Health Organization's Regional Framework for Action on Food Safety in the Western Pacific appropriately calls for a stepwise approach, associated with a country's level of economic development (WHO 2018). This begins by establishing basic minimum rules and capabilities; moving on to preventive, risk-based approaches; and, ultimately, developing a fully documented and coordinated system. The World Health Organization's advocacy for a stepwise approach is consistent with the findings of this report and its understanding of the challenges and opportunities facing countries at different stages of the processes of dietary transformation, economic structural change, and food system modernization. In other words, advocacy for a stepwise approach is consistent with this report's concept of a food safety life cycle with different stages. This approximates the World Bank's classification of low-income, lower-middle-income, upper-middle-income, and high-income countries.

As countries pass through this life cycle, they encounter a somewhat different mix of food safety hazards and risks, and have different institutional circumstances and capabilities for managing these risks.

Table 5.1 shows the different sets of priorities proposed for countries in the traditional, transitioning, and modernizing stages of the food safety life cycle. These are clustered under four headings: (1) policy, strategy, and regulation; (2) risk assessment; (3) risk management; and (4) information, education, and communication.

At the strategic level, food safety is likely to be aligned with somewhat different development goals over time. For example, countries at the traditional stage will more typically link food safety concerns with matters of food and nutritional security, while countries at the transitioning stage may more closely link the food safety agenda with efforts to promote agricultural transformation and food trade competitiveness. The degree of sophistication in food safety policy development and prioritization is expected to grow, sequentially, over time, with increased access to scientific information, more use of economic analysis, and more comprehensive approaches to policy and regulatory consultation. Approaches to risk assessment and risk management will also become more sophisticated. This will involve a more systematic use of data, analytical tools, and information technology, and more systematic approaches to documentation for hazard and illness surveillance, and product traceability and recall, among other purposes. The professionalization of food safety actors in government and the private sector is expected to occur continuously and sequentially.

In traditional food systems, governments and other actors will need to give considerable attention to mitigating risks in informal food channels. In the progressive transitioning and modernizing stages, meanwhile, attention will largely center on incentivizing and supporting better farm and enterprise practices in the formal sector and influencing consumer awareness and behavior. The expectation for countries at the modernizing stage is that the private sector will make most dedicated food safety investments, although supportive public investments in science, human capital, and physical infrastructure will continue.

As noted in chapter 4, it is critically important to recognize the interfaces between dedicated food safety measures and those addressing broader public health or environmental health matters. Although to different degrees, these measures also play a vital role in lowering the burden of FBD for countries across the entire food safety life cycle. For example, improved access to basic public health services can reduce the high levels of mortality associated with FBD in traditional food systems, while reducing the exposure to food from industrial pollutants becomes a significant challenge in many food systems in the transitioning and modernizing stages.

Table 5.1 shows the priorities proposed for strategic, policy, and program initiatives to address the evolving challenges for building food safety management capacity and the stepwise approach for doing this for stakeholders along food value chains. Greater specificity on this would come through country-level structured discussions on priorities and needed short- and longer-term actions.

TABLE 5.1 Priorities for Countries at Different Stages of the Food Safety Life Cycle

Priority area	Traditional	Transitioning	Modernizing
Policy, strategy, and regulation	Integrate food safety concerns in national food and nutritional security strategies to mobilize attention. Establish a basic legislative framework for food safety (roles and responsibilities, legal authority). Update regulations for the use and marketing of agricultural chemicals and veterinary drugs.	Integrate food safety concerns into national strategies for agricultural transformation and trade diversification to mobilize attention. Align sanitary and phytosanitary standards with the potential for trade in relevant commodities. Develop a national multisector food safety strategy that sets priorities, addresses institutional strengthening and coordination, and lays out approaches for private sector collaboration and consumer engagement. In line with available enforcement and compliance capacity, strengthen the legal framework and align it with the Codex Alimentarius. Participate in regional harmonization efforts.	Integrate food safety concerns in national strategies for managing public health costs. Strengthen regulatory convergence with trading partners and international standards. Negotiate equivalence agreements to facilitate trade with important partners. Conduct cost-benefit analyses of proposed regulatory measures and incorporate regulatory impact assessments into policy making.
Risk assessment	Undertake qualitative assessments and quantitative risk ranking, where feasible, to identify the most significant risks to public health. Incorporate information from other health-reporting systems. Pay particular attention to issues associated with neglected zoonoses and staple foods. Undertake value chain assessments to determine the locus and nature of risks in relation to food-safety-sensitive exports. Develop basic laboratory testing capacities while using regional and international labs for specialized or low-volume testing.	Set up programs for monitoring food consumption and purchasing patterns, and for estimating total dietary exposure to hazards. Develop an FBD surveillance and reporting system. Pay particular attention to microbial hazards, and hazards-related adulteration and use of agricultural inputs. Establish programs to monitor food safety hazards of public health concern and supplement them with studies to generate additional surveillance data to prioritize risks. Invest and facilitate investment in more extensive and professional quality assurance laboratory testing capacities.	Draw up a national research plan to address food safety, with input from industry. Set goals of continuous reduction in FBD (as reported by surveillance systems). Pay particular attention to emerging FBD and novel technologies. Apply mechanisms for the systematic collection, evaluation, and use of FBD surveillance data. Ensure that laboratory systems are internationally accredited, effectively networked, and financially sustainable.
Risk management	Ensure synergies between water and sanitation upgrade initiatives and community-level food hygiene programs. Improve basic hygiene conditions in markets by investing in infrastructure, especially targeting markets where poor populations buy high-nutrient and perishable foods.	Develop a registry of food businesses in the formal sector and undertake risk profiling. Implement programs for the hygiene grading of food premises. Professionalize food inspectors and implement risk-based inspection plans. Introduce local good agricultural and animal husbandry practice programs targeting specific commodities in emerging formal sectors.	Build attitudes and incentives to mix robust enforcement and constructive compliance support for businesses. Incentivize the adoption of food safety management systems by small and medium enterprises (SMEs) and internationally benchmarked standards by larger enterprises.

(Continued)

TABLE 5.1 Priorities for Countries at Different Stages of the Food Safety Life Cycle *(Continued)*

Priority area	Traditional	Transitioning	Modernizing
	Improve access to basic health services to minimize serious complications from untreated FBD. Support community-based and peer-to-peer mechanisms for improving food safety in smallholder agriculture and the informal food sector linked with development initiatives. Establish border controls with a focus on likely high-risk products. Target important single-source hazards for feasible control measures. Undertake public-private initiatives to develop compliance with external requirements for sectors with significant export growth potential.	Leverage consumer awareness and demand for safer food. Invest in (through public-private partnerships, if possible) improved food market infrastructure for perishable foods. Mainstream the adoption of good agricultural and animal husbandry practices through technical and market support programs, and ensure multisector synergies (through One Health, for example). Introduce procedures for investigating and responding to food safety incidents and emergencies, and for early warning systems. Strengthen border controls on a risk basis, and ensure that controls follow good trade facilitation practices. Develop an early warning system and contingency plan for food emergencies.	Remediate important environmental hazards. Strengthen fully documented national food recall and traceability systems. Strengthen decentralized capacities for regulatory oversight and advice. Use emerging information, biological, and other technologies in regulatory delivery and supply chain management. Ensure that border controls for food imports are consistent and effective. Ensure that procedures for recalls and food emergencies are well established.
Information, education, and communication	Educate consumers on basic food hygiene and avoidance of specific hazards. Develop targeted training for SMEs and informal food retailers, and street food vendors. Raise awareness of synergies and trade-offs between food safety, nutrition, and equity; and food safety and Sustainable Development Goals.	Implement national food safety awareness programs, targeting all stakeholders and age groups. Work with industry and universities to develop training and advanced education programs in food safety management. Develop and implement various elements of a risk communications program, including guidelines for different stakeholders and use of electronic platforms.	Establish a mechanism to systematically monitor public perceptions to inform food safety communications and education programs. Develop communication strategies to correct public misperceptions. Use behavioral science principles and empirical testing methodologies to design programs that influence consumer and food handler behavior. Support private efforts to label and certify products to promote consumer trust and reduce information asymmetry.

Source: World Bank.

REFERENCE

WHO (World Health Organization). 2018. *Regional Framework for Action on Food Safety in the Western Pacific*. Manila: WHO.

Environmental Benefits Statement

The World Bank Group is committed to reducing its environmental footprint. In support of this commitment, we leverage electronic publishing options and print-on-demand technology, which is located in regional hubs worldwide. Together, these initiatives enable print runs to be lowered and shipping distances decreased, resulting in reduced paper consumption, chemical use, greenhouse gas emissions, and waste.

We follow the recommended standards for paper use set by the Green Press Initiative. The majority of our books are printed on Forest Stewardship Council (FSC)–certified paper, with nearly all containing 50–100 percent recycled content. The recycled fiber in our book paper is either unbleached or bleached using totally chlorine-free (TCF), processed chlorine–free (PCF), or enhanced elemental chlorine–free (EECF) processes.

More information about the Bank's environmental philosophy can be found at http://www.worldbank.org/corporateresponsibility.

green press INITIATIVE